A Concise History of Revolution

Presenting a new framework for the study of revolutions, this innovative exploration of French, Russian, Chinese, Vietnamese, Cuban, Iranian, South African, and more recent Arab revolutions provides a theoretically grounded and empirically comprehensive demonstration of how revolutions mean more than mere state collapse and rebuilding. Through the examination of multiple historical case studies and the use of extensive historical examples to explore a range of revolutions, Mehran Kamrava reveals the range and depth of human emotion and motivations that are so prevalent and consequential in revolutions, from personal commitment to sacrifice, determination, leadership ability, charisma, opportunism, and avarice.

Mehran Kamrava is Professor and Director of the Center for International and Regional Studies at Georgetown University, Qatar. He is the author of numerous journal articles and books, including *The Modern Middle East: A Political History since the First World War*, 3rd edition (2013), *Qatar: Small State, Big Politics* (2013), *The Impossibility of Palestine: History, Geography, and the Road Ahead* (2016), *Troubled Waters: Insecurity in the Persian Gulf* (2018), and *Inside the Arab State* (2018).

A Concise History of Revolution

Mehran Kamrava
Georgetown University, Qatar

CAMBRIDGE
UNIVERSITY PRESS

University Printing House, Cambridge CB2 8BS, United Kingdom

One Liberty Plaza, 20th Floor, New York, NY 10006, USA

477 Williamstown Road, Port Melbourne, VIC 3207, Australia

314–321, 3rd Floor, Plot 3, Splendor Forum, Jasola District Centre, New Delhi – 110025, India

79 Anson Road, #06–04/06, Singapore 079906

Cambridge University Press is part of the University of Cambridge.

It furthers the University's mission by disseminating knowledge in the pursuit of education, learning, and research at the highest international levels of excellence.

www.cambridge.org

Information on this title: www.cambridge.org/9781108485951

DOI: 10.1017/9781108662581

First published 2020

Printed in the United Kingdom by TJ International Ltd. Padstow, Cornwall

A catalogue record for this publication is available from the British Library.

ISBN 978-1-108-48595-1 Hardback
ISBN 978-1-108-72538-5 Paperback

CONTENTS

Acknowledgments vi

1 Introduction 1

2 From Rebellion to Revolution 11

3 From Social Movement to Revolution 42

4 Revolutionary States 74

5 Revolutionary Polities 104

6 Conclusion 125

Chronology of Revolutions 132
Notes 160
Bibliography 176
Index 185

ACKNOWLEDGMENTS

All books are products of collective efforts, and this one is no exception. I wrote this book while serving as the director of the Center for International and Regional Studies of Georgetown University, Qatar. It is no exaggeration to say that I could not have written the book had it not been for the support of CIRS's truly remarkable staff. Colleagues Zahra Babar, Islam Hassan, and Suzi Mirgani, along with James Reardon-Anderson, read the manuscript and offered invaluable advice and suggestions. I am grateful to research assistants Amie Hewka, Aiza Khan, and Mehaira Mahgoub for their help with the chronology of revolutions that appears near the end of the book. The manuscript also benefited greatly from perceptive comments and helpful suggestions by John Foran and Eric Selbin, two of today's most astute scholars of revolutions. Grateful acknowledgment also goes to Qatar Foundation, of which Georgetown University, Qatar is a member, for its support of research and various other scholarly endeavors.

1 INTRODUCTION

This is a book about revolutions, whose study is as old as despotic political rule. How states fall, how rebels mobilize into insurgents and fight, how leaders organize their rule and put down rebellions – all have long been studied and analyzed by generations of scholars. This book travels down some well-trodden paths. Many of the topics the book discusses have been covered by well-known political scientists and sociologists for some time. My goal here is not to challenge our assumptions about why revolutions come about or why they are waged. Rather, I present here a framework for placing revolutions into broadly different categories based on their causes and processes. The book's originality, I believe, lies in its classification of revolutions into three ideal types. These ideal types are *planned, spontaneous*, and *negotiated* revolutions.

Before examining each of these categories in some detail, it is important to present a definition of revolution. Zoltan Barany offers a useful, minimalist definition of revolution, "simply as *a bottom-up mass popular challenge to the established political regime and/or its ruler(s)*."[1] Along similar lines, I see revolutions as entailing fundamental changes to three key aspects of politics: changes to the state, its leaders, its institutions, and their functions; changes to the nature and quality of state–society relations and the ways the two interact; and changes to the prevailing political culture, in the overall ways in which society conceives of politics, political institutions and leaders, and political principles.

By and large, revolutions are mass-based affairs of great magnitude, brought on and carried forward through the mobilization of masses of people in order to achieve specific political goals. Frequently, though not always, they are accompanied by tremendous violence, either in the lead-up to the capture of power or once power is captured, or, as is often the case, both before and after state power changes hands. Contrary to popular assumption, however, revolutions do not always necessarily come through or are followed by considerable violence. The late 1980s, for example, bore witness to the eruption of revolutions in Eastern Europe that entailed comparatively little violence.

In the lexicon of political rule, few words appear to have been abused by politicians and political aspirants more than *revolution.* Few politicians, in fact, and even fewer political contenders do not consider their mandate or their exercise of power to be revolutionary. In reality, however, revolutions are rather rare historical occurrences. They turn the world of politics upside down, change the basic premises on which political culture is based, and transform the principles according to which political conduct is governed. In this respect, revolutions are distinctively political episodes, although their precise occurrence is brought on by a coalescence of not only political but also social and cultural factors.[2]

Despite the frequent abuse of the word, actual revolutions are a historical rarity. There are several reasons for this. As we shall see shortly, all revolutions require the simultaneous appearance of at least three developments: the weakness and vulnerability of state institutions; the appearance of mobilized groups who could take advantage of these state vulnerabilities; and a receptive mass of people who are willing to be mobilized for the purpose of overthrowing the present rulers. But on their own, each of these conditions is unlikely to emerge, and their concurrent appearance is even rarer.

To start, dictators seldom give up power without a fight, and all too often in fact they are careful not to create conditions that make political opposition possible. Seldom do dictators rule by the stick only. More often than not, they collect around themselves elites and oligarchs who become deeply vested in the status quo by occupying strategic positions in the state machinery and in the economy's commanding heights. More importantly, dictators devise a variety of means to maintain a praetorian guard and to keep a vigilant eye on the armed forces. Even when the civilian institutions of the state lose much of their efficacy and cease largely to function properly, the security services tend to continue as usual and can effectively stifle dissent. Securing the support of powerful international patrons is equally significant.

In addition to the state's continued ability to repress potential dissenters, there are difficulties inherent in mounting a coordinated uprising. In any rebellion, there are different levels of involvement, with some groups and individuals being the constituents (target community or social base), and others serving as sympathizers, actual members, activists, or militants. The rebels have a dilemma in that as far as potential participants in the cause are concerned, inaction is the most rational option: The costs of rebellion can be very high, or at best unknown, whereas the benefits of not participating in the rebellion, if it succeeds, are still the same. Thus "extensive collective dissent is improbable," and "most rebels do not actually rebel."[3] According to Mark Lichbach, "Active dissidents are a small minority in *all* types of collective dissent." He argues that there is overwhelming evidence that

> the five percent rule holds for neighborhood organizations, community conflicts, urban rebellions, student revolts, trade unions, guerrilla wars, and rural populist movements. Rebels, moreover, are a small minority in *all* major instances of collective dissent. The rule holds for the American, Russian, Algerian, and Cuban revolutions, and several fascist movements.[4]

Rebels can mitigate the dilemma of low participation through several means, most notably increasing the benefits of participation and lowering the costs of doing so; increasing resources; improving the productivity of their tactics; increasing the probability of winning and making a difference; and restricting the exit of those who have joined.[5] None of these options, however, are necessarily easy and without some cost.

Despite the many difficulties that undermine the possibility of their occurrence, revolutions do on occasion take place. What I have set out to do in this book is to present an analysis of their causes, their consequences, and, just as importantly, the different categories to which they belong.

The Central Argument

I argue here that of the three key ingredients that all revolutions require – i.e., state breakdown, revolutionary leaders, and mass mobilization – each appears in a different order depending on the broad category to which a revolution belongs. There are some revolutions that are largely *spontaneous*, as in the one in France in 1789, in Russia in February 1917, in Iran in 1978, and in Tunisia and Egypt in 2010–2011. In these spontaneous revolutions, usually the first development that occurs is cracks in the authoritarianism of the state. The political opening thus created provides the space for the emergence of a social movement. This social movement then grows into mass mobilization and is directed by leaders emerging from within those mobilized. The resulting force eventually pushes the crumbling state to collapse. These revolutions do not have an obvious endgame other than the collapse of the Old Order, with their leaders, ideologies, and visions of the post-revolutionary era slowly emerging only as the revolutionary process unfolds. Even after the revolution succeeds, the first crop of leading figures seldom ends up being the revolution's eventual victors. Only those with access to institutions can wrest the spontaneity of the revolution and direct it for their own purposes.

Not all revolutions enable the masses to overwhelm and overthrow the state. There are instances, in fact, when the empowered forces of society and the actors in charge of the state reach a negative equilibrium of sorts. This occurs when social actors are empowered just enough to be able to defy the state but not overthrow it, and when state actors are weakened but not enough to lose their grip completely. In such circumstances, often the only option is for actors from both sides to negotiate and to agree on certain broad parameters based on which a new political system can be constructed. This kind of a revolution, in which mass mobilization results in a significant weakening but not collapse of the state, may be classified as a negotiated revolution.

What turns a revolution into a negotiated one is the way in which power is transferred from incumbents to victorious revolutionaries. If in the aftermath of mass mobilization the state begins to crumble – through, for example, mass desertions from the army or the defections of its key figures – then the revolutionary wave sweeps increasingly confident, assertive victors into office. This is what occurred in the spontaneous revolutions of France in 1789 and Iran in 1979. But when state institutions remain relatively intact and defections are sufficiently limited so as to erode but not completely deplete the powers of the incumbents, the two sides often see compromise and negotiation as the most viable, and often the safest, option before them. These negotiated transitions can have equally revolutionary outcomes, as they did in Eastern and Central Europe in the late 1980s and in South Africa in the early 1990s.[6]

There are some other revolutions that are planned. In these revolutions the first development is the appearance of revolutionary leaders, whose goal it is to garner mass support in order to topple the dictatorship. These revolutions have a clear plan for capturing power, a tool-kit of ideological implements for getting the people to follow them, and a clear vision of what the post-revolutionary era looks like. Part of the plan, a big part actually, is to militarily defeat the incumbent regime. Doing so requires launching an armed campaign from the countryside, where the state's reach is often already precarious. Only if and when the state collapses does mass mobilization occur in any meaningful way, directed now by leaders of the new state and put to use for purposes of consolidating the gains of the revolution.

Spontaneous, planned, and negotiated revolutions are ideal types. What matters in each revolution is the extent to which planning and deliberate actions, spontaneity and situational developments, and negotiated exits versus flights from power become preponderant. Most revolutions involve elements of all. The key distinguishing factor between the different types of revolutions has to do with the *timing* of the appearance of state weakness, organized opposition groups, and individuals who perceive of themselves – and are generally seen by the public – as leaders of the revolution. In spontaneous revolutions, state weakness occurs first, opening up space for political opposition, from within which one of the many groups jockeying for the leadership of the brewing movement emerges on top and leads the revolution. In planned revolutions, groups seeking to defeat the state and to capture political power appear first, and if they succeed in their goal of leading a revolution, then they use state power to mobilize the broader population. In both instances, the pre-revolutionary state's military defeat, or the defection of its armed forces, are key to the revolution's success. But if the state's weakness is not to the point of total defeat, but it cannot effectively reverse society's empowerment either, then most often the next step involves negotiations and a negotiated transfer of power.

In most instances, we see the concurrent occurrence of multiple developments. In Russia, for example, anti-state activists had been plotting the Tsarist state's overthrow long before the February and October Revolutions of 1917 took place. But it was largely the state's self-inflicted wounds, beginning especially with the humiliating loss to Japan in the Russo-Japanese War of 1905, that paved the way for the largely spontaneous revolution of February 1917. The fragile state that subsequently came to power was too saddled with economic and institutional dysfunctions, and its own ineptitude, to withstand the highly organized Bolsheviks' plans for capturing political power. Essentially what transpired in Russia was a spontaneous revolution in February 1917 followed in October by a planned one.

In examining the key aspects of planned revolutions, I draw heavily from the examples of the Russian, Chinese, Vietnamese, and Cuban revolutions, as well as Che Guevara's failed Bolivian adventure. Nicaragua's 1979 revolution was also largely planned and carried out by the Sandinista National Liberation Front, FSLN, though in addition to guerrilla warfare and urban insurrection it also included a number of general strikes; political work among workers and peasants; and support from important sectors such as the bourgeoisie, intellectuals, and the church.[7] Another planned revolution was attempted in South Africa, led by the African National Congress and its imprisoned leader Nelson Mandela. The resulting political impasse between the ANC and the ruling National Party, all in the international glare, prompted the two to negotiate their way into a new era for the country.

Similar to South Africa, the revolutions that brought down communist regimes in Eastern Europe between 1989 and 1991 culminated in and were largely made possible through negotiated power transitions. Some scholars have called these revolutions "anti-revolutionary" because of their commitment to nonviolence and their concern not so much with the capture of power but with reclaiming public space for thought and self-organization.[8] But what transpired in countries such as Poland, Hungary, Czechoslovakia, Bulgaria, Romania, and East Germany does indeed meet all the criteria of revolutions laid out earlier; not all revolutions must entail violence in order to succeed.

Indeed, the question of when or whether at all revolutions "succeed" is most elusive in the case of spontaneous revolutions. In these revolutions, the goals of the revolution are seldom clearly articulated in the early periods of the uprising, and the many competing groups that take part in the effort to overthrow the state each have their own goals and their own interpretations of what the post-revolutionary era should look like. At least at the very beginning, there are no clear leaders. There is in fact no "revolution" to speak of at first, and therefore there are no clear ideological blueprints for an ideal tomorrow. Differences within the increasingly "revolutionary" coalition are only settled when one group manages to maneuver its way to the top and to emerge as the revolution's leading force. Spontaneous revolutions by nature have competing visions, and seldom is there room in the post-revolutionary era for more than one vision.

This inherently hazy nature of spontaneous revolutions has prompted the sociologist Asef Bayat to question whether the Arab Spring uprisings of 2011 were revolutions at all. Bayat's argument is premised on the assertion that the 2011 uprisings "lacked any associated intellectual production," and had no "set of ideas, concepts, and philosophies" that informed "the ideational subconscious of the rebels, affecting their vision or choice of strategies and type of leadership." Moreover, he argues, the Arab uprisings lacked similar levels of radicalism in political and economic outlook as compared to similar, earlier rebellions.[9] Therefore, what transpired in Tunisia, Egypt, and Yemen was neither a revolution nor a reform but what Bayat calls a "refolution," a "revolutionary movement that emerged to compel the incumbent states to change themselves, to carry out meaning reforms on behalf of the revolution."[10] These uprisings, he maintains, "looked like revolution in terms of mobilization but like reform in terms of change."[11]

Bayat is not necessarily incorrect in questioning whether what transpired in the Arab world was indeed revolution or something else – mere chaos and instability, civil wars fueled by regional rivalries, machinations by outside powers, etc. Admittedly, in terms of the sheer time they took to unfold, the Arab uprisings of 2011 lacked the scale and length of the French and Iranian revolutions. But the absence of "concepts and philosophies" is a characteristic of all spontaneous revolutions, and the revolution's supposed hijacking is a corollary of who succeeds in getting power and who does not. In the same way that Iran's secular opponents of the Shah felt their revolution was hijacked by Ayatollah Khomeini and his religious collaborators, Egypt's Muslim Brotherhood activists and the armed forces both accused each other of hijacking the country's January 25 Revolution. That fateful day in 2011 in Egypt did indeed mark the highlight of what was quickly becoming a revolution of historic importance. But the July 2013 coup by General Abdel Fatah el-Sisi restored old patterns of state–society relations and reversed whatever changes were beginning to be initiated in the interim. Elsewhere, in Libya, Syria, and Yemen, elite divisions and outside intervention combined to plunge the countries into civil war, and talk of any revolution in these places in the sense discussed here would be meaningless. Only in Tunisia did a revolution take place, with a power transition that involved comparatively little violence but was instead anchored in talks and negotiations. The outcome, for the time being at least, has been no less revolutionary.

In constructing the book's argument, I have relied on insights offered by all four generations of revolutionary theorists as delineated by George Lawson. Lawson points out that the study of revolutions so far can be divided into four principal, if not necessarily distinct, generations.[12] The first generation, appearing prior to the Second World War and of whom Crane Brinton's writings were the most representative, approached revolutions from a "natural history" perspective, focusing on the symptoms of political decay and social disequilibrium in the lead-up to and after revolutions. A second generation of studies, appearing mostly after WWII, examined the causal links between modernization and uprisings, alternately focusing on social dissynchronization (Chalmers Johnson), unfulfilled expectations (James Davies), or relative depravation (Ted Robert Gurr). Structuralist analyses of revolutions, popular from the 1960s to the 1980s, constituted a third generation. These studies pointed to the formative roles played by domestic and international structures – e.g., more powerful patron states, domestic classes such as the peasantry and the bourgeoisie, wars, etc. – and were represented by the pioneering works of Barrington Moore, Theda Skocpol, and Jack Goldstone. A fourth generation, to which I presume this book belongs, looks at the complex interactions between international relations, political crises, and social developments that lead to the eruption of revolutions and in turn shape their outcomes and their consequences.

More specifically, in the chapters to come, I draw the reader's attention to the continued reoccurrence of four factors in all revolutions, be they planned, spontaneous, or negotiated. In theorizing about revolutions, these four factors constitute the central pillars of any analytical framework. They include institutional factors, the international context, leadership and agency, and the economy. Any analysis of revolutions must take these factors into account, all of which are interconnected and cannot be altogether disentangled from one another. Institutions determine or influence power relationships, within the state, between the state and society, and among social actors and contenders for power. These institutional power relationships take place within a larger, international context, with direct bearing on their strength or weakness and the resources at their disposal.

Resources, and more broadly the economy, are also important, as they all too often influence not only the strength of institutions but also, as we will see in the case of Eastern Europe in the late 1980s, the priorities of social actors and how they steer the emerging post-revolutionary state. This touches on the importance of agency, conceptualized here as the ability of individuals to make their own decisions. Especially in planned revolutions, and at the historic critical junctures that emerge in the aftermath of all revolutionary captures of power, the decisions that are made by leaders can have lasting and monumental consequences.[13] In simple terms, Nelson Mandela had democratic convictions, but Lenin, Mao, Ho Chi Minh, Castro, and Khomeini did not. While not the sole determinants in the revolutions these individuals led, their personal convictions were not unimportant in shaping the institutional outcomes and arrangements that emerged following their ascent to power.

Plan of the Book

The following chapters lay out a theoretical framework for the study of the causes, processes, and outcomes of planned, spontaneous, and negotiated revolutions. Chapters 2 and 3 examine planned and spontaneous revolutions respectively. Chapter 2 analyzes the means and methods employed by would-be revolutionaries in their deliberate, planned efforts to capture political power. The chapter argues that regardless of their specific ideological coloring, all such efforts are essentially motivated by deep-seated nationalist sentiments, feature important roles for the group's leadership and the vanguard party, and are accomplished through armed struggle and the mobilization of guerrilla fighters and other revolutionary foot soldiers.

Chapter 3 examines spontaneous revolutions, focusing on how state vulnerability and collapse provide opportunities for the emergence of scattered acts of protest and opposition, which in turn grow into social movements, and from there snowball into revolutionary mass mobilization. In the process, and only with time and emerging opportunities, do the revolution's leaders and their ultimate vision for the post-revolutionary order become clear.

Once a revolution succeeds, the state that emerges is not only constituted differently from the one it replaces, but it also assumes a different profile and posture in relation to its domestic and international environments. Chapter 4 analyzes the institutional makeup and priorities of post-revolutionary states. The chapter focuses specifically on how new state leaders set out to craft the institutional arrangements through which they govern, and the challenges, both political and economic, they are likely to face in the process.

Society also assumes certain specific features following revolutions, a product not just of the experience of having gone through the revolutionary movement but of the efforts and priorities of the new, emerging post-revolutionary state. Chapter 5 examines state–society relations in the aftermath of revolutions. Revolutions blow the lid off of societies that have long suffered the pressures of dictatorship and despotism. The natural impulse is to hold on to the gains and freedoms thus acquired, not all of which sit well with the new heirs of the state. What ensues may not necessarily be a state–society tug of war, though it often is, but efforts by the state to create a new conception of citizenship in line with a newly emerging political culture. Within this context, dissent and opposition to the new order assume specific features.

Throughout, in highlighting the importance of the various themes and factors under discussion here, I make references to and draw examples from various episodes involving different revolutions. I present a brief chronology of these revolutions at the end of the book. This chronology is preceded by the book's Conclusion, Chapter 6. In addition to summing up the book's main findings, the final chapter analyzes some of the more effective ways in which the states of the twenty-first century try to stave off revolutions. Such efforts have gone some ways toward strengthening authoritarian regimes and prolonging their longevity. So long as there are dictatorships, however, future revolutions remain very much a possibility.

2 FROM REBELLION TO REVOLUTION

What inspires revolutionaries? By now it should be amply evident that there is no simple answer to this question. Revolutionaries may be inspired by the promises and charisma of their comrades or by their own self-generated belief that a better political future, one free of injustice, is both possible and worth striving for. Unlike spontaneous revolutions, in which largely unwitting participants steadily find themselves in revolutionary circumstances, in planned revolutions willful revolutionaries set out to create conditions in which a revolution is made possible. In doing so, they need certain tools, templates and blueprints, and tactics and strategies. These tools and ingredients are examined in the present chapter.

If spontaneous revolutions grow out of haphazard, largely unorganized eruptions of mass anger and frustration, planned revolutions emerge from deliberately organized and orchestrated rebellions. This particular category of revolutions, the chapter argues, contains several key, interrelated elements. First, regardless of their declared ideological beliefs, all self-declared revolutionaries are essentially nationalist. They are invariably motivated by a deep desire to better the conditions of their country and its citizens. Even when revolutionaries adhere to ideologies that are inherently antinationalist, as in communism, their underlying motivation for launching a revolution is to capture power not necessarily for the sake of power itself but in order to improve conditions around them, at the level of the neighborhood, the city, and the country.

Two other, related elements characteristic of planned revolutions are those of leadership and the party. Planned revolutions will not appear unless several highly dedicated individuals commit themselves to planning, organizing, and leading a takeover of power. Out of necessity, this cabal is often initially organized into a secretive cell. Sooner or later, the cabal gives rise to a political party or a guerrilla organization whose chief, often only, mission is to lead a revolution. The party sees itself as the revolution's vanguard. Among the planners involved in this vanguard, usually an individual with greater ambitions, or better organizational skills and opportunities, or through sheer chance, emerges as its leader. While planned revolutions cannot succeed without the work of an organized revolutionary party, the party's leader becomes the face of the revolution, and, if the revolution succeeds, he then becomes the leader of the country.

Planned revolutions are initiated and carried forward by highly dedicated individuals who are often singularly driven by the goal of effecting wholesale and drastic changes to the body politic. Once they have decided on or embraced the cause of the revolution, they devote their lives to its victory, single-mindedly pursuing the objective of overthrowing the current order and ushering in a new one. In the meanwhile, many of the other facets of their lives suffer as they remain oblivious to most other endeavors not directly related to the revolutionary cause.

The revolution will not succeed unless the revolutionaries militarily defeat the forces of the government and bring the state to its knees. Doing so requires engagement in armed struggle, which is another key ingredient of planned revolutions. In their efforts to launch a revolution, much of the revolutionaries' attention is devoted to the ways and means of fighting and defeating the forces of the regime. If the strategic objective of the revolutionaries is to defeat the state and to capture political power, their tactics revolve around the employment of violence in general and armed struggle in particular.

Leaders need parties, and parties need strategies and tactics. But equally important are actual foot soldiers who would become members of the party or at least support its goals and ideals. Every vanguard party needs recruits who are sufficiently committed to the revolutionary cause to take up arms and to actively carry the revolution forward. Almost all revolutions are waged and fought in the name of the downtrodden and the destitute – the urban poor, the working class, the peasantry. But very few of the recruits are actually drawn from these classes, most being educated young idealists from wealthier urban areas.

Whatever classes they are drawn from, without such recruits, or at least a sufficiently robust number of them, the revolution is doomed to failure. This was a lesson, as we shall see soon, that Che Guevara learned the hard way.

In the following pages, I will examine each of the central elements of planned revolutions – nationalism, leadership, vanguard party, armed struggle, and foot soldiers – drawing on specific examples from the October 1917 Russian revolution as well as the Chinese, Vietnamese, and Cuban revolutions. For each of these elements, I will limit the examples to the revolutions or revolutionaries most representative of the phenomenon under discussion. When necessary or appropriate, I will highlight other pertinent examples as well.

Nationalism

Whatever ideological convictions revolutionary leaders may have, what animates them the most is the unshakable belief that their efforts and their cause will necessarily improve the lives of their compatriots and have overall benefit for the whole country. Someone with Lenin's ideological persuasion would likely object vehemently to being called a *nationalist*. But belief in the betterment of Russia, and a commitment to improving the lives of its citizenry and the country as a whole, is precisely what we find in Lenin in the lead-up to 1917. In the strictest sense of the word this may not be *nationalism*. But a commitment to improving Russian lives and Russia itself, it certainly is. Lenin's demagogic advocacy of *inter*nationalism did little to dampen his commitment to bettering Russian lives.

Perhaps in no other planned revolution is the compelling force of nationalism more evident than in the Vietnamese revolution. Throughout his life, in fact, Ho Chi Minh was dogged by questions about his nationalist versus communist leanings.[1] After the end of the First World War, French exploitation of Indochina kicked into high gear, and, commensurately, so did Ho's criticism of France on nationalist grounds. In fact, while he was still in France, in the 1920s Ho was becoming increasingly radicalized in his nationalist, anti-colonial sentiments. During this time, one of his central concerns was the seeming obliviousness of fellow French socialists to France's exploitative practices in its colonies. Somewhat reluctantly, he soon began realizing that European socialists cared little about the colonial question.[2] He also often complained bitterly that the proletariat of the metropole were ignorant of, and frequently deliberately ignored, the proletariat of the colonies.[3] In his speech to the Comintern meeting in Moscow in 1920, Ho could not hide his frustration with fellow socialists from the metropole:

> You must excuse my frankness, but I cannot help but observe that the speeches by comrades from the mother countries give me the impression that they wish to kill a snake by stepping on its tail. You all know that today the poison and the life energy of the capitalist snake is concentrated more in the colonies than in the mother country.[4]

As early as 1921, Ho was calling on French colonial authorities to grant a wide array of liberties to the Vietnamese, believing that national liberation was a necessary precondition for social emancipation.[5] His 1925 publication of the book *French Colonialism on Trial* (*Le Procès de la Colonisation Française*) was a searing indictment of France's colonial enterprise in general and in Indochina in particular.[6]

Ho soon adopted Lenin's two-stage formulation of revolutions – the February and October Revolutions – to advocate colonial liberation first and then a communist revolution.[7] The fact that Ho was trying to mobilize his fellow countrymen against foreign occupation required him to pay more attention to nationalist sentiments. He did, of course, call for simultaneous struggles against both feudalists and colonialists, seeing the two groups as equally exploitative and plundering.[8] Ho firmly believed that Vietnam's revolution would necessarily have to be communist and be carried forward by the proletariat.[9] However, in calling on the Vietnamese to rally against French colonialism and to take part in the resistance war, there are few traces of communist doctrine in his many declarations. Instead, his rhetoric was often couched more in nationalist terms than in anything resembling Marxist-Leninism.[10]

As the liberation war against France was intensifying, in 1944 Ho directly addressed the question of his leanings toward nationalism and communism:

> I am a communist but what is important to me now is the independence and the freedom of my country, not communism. I personally guarantee you that communism will not become a reality in Vietnam for another fifty years [if the French remain].[11]

Around this time, Ho wrote a number of tracts in which he exalted Vietnam's history and its glorious past.[12] In reality, Ho saw little contradiction between nationalism and communism, as evident in the Vietnamese Declaration of Independence, which he drafted in September 1945. Modeled closely after the American Declaration of Independence and read aloud amid much public euphoria and celebration, there is actually little trace of communism in the document itself.[13] Ho's resort to nationalist sentiments was for more than purely instrumentalist purposes. Even after Vietnam's independence, he repeatedly called for national unity and for greater attention to all elements of Vietnamese national identity, including, especially, respect for the country's ethnic and religious minorities.[14]

Similar nationalist tendencies can also be detected in many of the actions and maneuvers of Mao Zedong, and to a lesser extent in some of his writings. At the same time as ensuring that the ideological platform of the Chinese Communist Party (CCP) remained highly doctrinaire, Mao held up Marxism-Leninism as a blueprint for action, much more pragmatic in its application to China and the conditions that prevailed in the country in the lead-up to 1949.[15] For Mao, national unity and the defense of Chinese sovereignty, especially against Japanese occupation, was of paramount importance. The communist revolution, he argued, would only succeed once China was united and the Japanese had been ejected from the country.[16] Despite the persecution by the nationalist Kuomintang (KMT) that had set in motion the Long March in 1934, by 1937 Mao's pragmatism prompted the CCP to enter into an alliance with the KMT in order to fight Japanese occupation.

Nationalist sentiments were equally pervasive among Cuban revolutionaries in general and in the person of Fidel Castro in particular. In the lead up to the success of his movement, in fact, Castro was far less of a Marxist-Leninist and more of a "radical nationalist with strong beliefs about social justice."[17] In many ways, the genesis of Cuba's revolutionary movement was far more nationalist than anything else, and the revolution's ideology was essentially anti-imperialist and, at least initially, only vaguely Marxist. This nationalism was formulated largely in reaction to US presence and machinations in the Americas, especially in Cuba, and therefore had an anti-American tone and flavor from the beginning. The writings and poetry of José Martí (1853–1895), an icon of Cuban independence, were a source of inspiration for the country's young revolutionaries. For Castro, as with Ho Chi Minh and Mao Zedong, Cuban nationalism meant first and foremost improving the lives of his compatriots and the conditions of the country in general. And, as with his fellow revolutionaries, Castro saw the prevailing political system as the most fundamental obstacle to achieving Cuba's national aspirations. As one of his biographers has observed, similar to Martí, Castro "possessed an organicist, almost ahistorical picture of true Cuba, free from the aberration of dictatorship, whose essence was waiting to be discovered."[18] With his revolution, he assumed, historic wrongs would be righted and a road to a better future opened.

The Leader

In addition to nationalist aspirations, all planned revolutions have the common element of a highly committed leader whose life is devoted, often single-mindedly, to the pursuit of the revolution's cause. As discussed shortly, all revolutions, especially planned revolutions, require direction by a group dedicated to ensuring the state's collapse. Another equally pervasive common denominator that all planned revolutions have is a leader for whom the revolutionary movement is an all-consuming cause. Not surprisingly, planned revolutions invariably give rise to a larger-than-life figure whose name and life become synonymous with the revolution itself. Revolutionaries are romantics with the courage to act on their convictions, and *leaders* of planned revolutions are a special breed of romantics for whom life other than in the revolution has little meaning and value. What sets revolutionary leaders apart from others is their single-minded focus on and their near complete devotion to the revolutionary cause. Nelson Mandela's words – "the struggle is my life"[19] – capture what others like him must have felt. Reflecting on his distance and separation from his wife Winnie, Mandela recorded the following thought in his diary:

> It seems to be the destiny of freedom fighters to have unstable personal lives. When your life is struggle, as mine was, there is little room left for family. That has always been my greatest regret, and the most painful aspect of the choice I made.[20]

This single-mindedness was especially characteristic of Lenin and his pursuit of communist revolution in Russia. At times ruthlessly, Lenin was relentless in seeking the overthrow of the Romanovs and ensuring the success of Bolshevism. In his grand pursuit he literally ran himself aground, seldom resting, and often suffering from ill health as a result. In trying to ensure the ideological purity of the movement, he was often pedantic and unyielding, writing endless tracts to ensure that his interpretation of the party's correct path won the day.[21] As one of his biographers wrote, "In the small world of organized Russian Marxism, he became the figure whom everyone either loved or detested. He left hardly anyone neutral toward him."[22] Lenin often decried the elitism of intellectuals among fellow Bolsheviks, labeling it as "intellectualism," and dismissed it as opportunism.[23] At the same time, he combined doctrinal purity with a sense of pragmatism, as shown by his embrace of the soviets, which had developed independent of the Bolshevik party.[24] As fate would have it, it was the Bolshevik nexus with and utilization of the soviets that proved critical in the fateful months of February to October, 1917.

None of this, of course, is meant to reduce the depth and weight of the revolution to the efforts of just one person, no matter how deeply committed to the cause he or she may be. But there is an undeniable pattern in all planned revolutions of the emergence of at least one individual, prior and in the lead-up to the capture of power, as the key leader of the revolutionary effort. Perhaps nowhere was this more apparent than in China, where "Mao Zedong Thought" had already become the Chinese Communist Party's new orthodoxy as early as 1938.[25] At the Seventh Congress of the CCP in 1945, his peers certified Mao as the charismatic Supreme Leader, and from that point on he was known as Chairman Mao.[26]

Very few individuals, revolutionary or otherwise, have achieved the near complete deification that Mao Zedong commanded before and especially after the success of the Chinese revolution. In some ways, nevertheless, Castro, who inspired his band of *Fidelista* guerrillas into the jungles of Sierra Maestra, comes in at a distant second. At his trial following the disastrous attacks on the Moncada Barracks on July 26, 1953, Castro defiantly declared: "Condemn me, it does not matter, history will absolve me."[27] In many ways, from the very start Castro's whole revolutionary enterprise appeared reckless. Many Cubans at the time actually dismissed him as yet another rabble-rouser among a whole cast of political malcontents. But somehow he managed to succeed. Imprisoned following his trial, Castro appears to have only strengthened his resolve to launch a revolution.

For rebels and revolutionaries, prison is often said to be the best school. Perhaps for no one was this more the case than for Fidel Castro, who actually went so far as to say that "this prison is the best classroom."[28] Castro later talked of his fondness for French literature while in prison and how he enjoyed the works of Victor Hugo, Romain Rolland, Maxim Gorky, H. G. Wells, Cervantes, Dostoevsky, and Karl Marx.[29] Once he was released, however, he cast aside books and once again set out to lead a revolution in earnest. In a letter dated July 7, 1955, he wrote:

> All roads to a peaceful political struggle have been closed to me. [It is time to] seize our rights instead of asking for them, to grab instead of beg for them. Cuban patience has its limits.[30]

Declaring himself to be "a Cuban who has given and will go on giving everything to his country," Castro left Cuba, this time for Mexico. There he regrouped, formed the July 26 Movement, and devised a plan for the downfall of the Batista regime.

It was in Mexico where a young Argentine physician named Ernesto "Che" Guevara first met Fidel Castro, and he was immediately drawn in by Castro's personality, charisma, and revolutionary spirit.[31] Those who knew him as Che did credited Castro for his dogged persistence in the face of intolerable odds, and also for his courage, integrity, intuition, and his political flexibility in pursuit of strategic goals. Also, while Castro was not necessarily an original thinker, he could be an effective facilitator of ideas.[32] It was, in fact, Che who was more ideological and a more serious thinker, while Fidel reveled in being a man of action.

The Vanguard Party

Revolutions, of course, go beyond the activism and the commitments of individuals, no matter how deeply dedicated to the cause they may be. Planned revolutions are pushed forward by a group of conspirators who perceive themselves as its vanguard. In planned revolutions, the activities and operations of a vanguard party – whether highly regimented and discipline-oriented, such as the Russian Bolsheviks, or loosely sewn together like Fidel Castro's July 26 Movement – are essential to planning, organizing, and advancing the revolutionary movement.

This vanguard invariably takes the form of a political party whose primary task it is to plan for and strategize the revolutionary capture of power. Vanguard parties often pursue three interrelated objectives. First, they outline the broader ideological and theoretical framework through which they intend to capture power and, frequently, what they hope to do with that power once they have attained it. As we have seen so far, this ideological blueprint for action is frequently a composite of nationalist sentiments and ideals on the one hand and various interpretations of Marxism on the other. Second, vanguard parties devise specific tactics. They create plans of action, identify targets, coordinate attacks, allocate personnel and resources, and, as much as possible, try to direct the revolution on the ground. Third and finally, parties serve as important tools for attracting new recruits and broadening their pool of sympathizers. Together, these functions of theorizing the revolution, devising its strategies and tactics, and enhancing its recruitment efforts and its broader support base make some form of a vanguard organization indispensable to planned revolutions.

The critical necessity of a vanguard party was one of the main innovations that Lenin introduced to Marxist ideology. For Lenin, the party needs to have several essential characteristics:

- a program based on Marxism and its application to reality in a way that advances the struggle for socialism;
- professional activists who agree on its core programs and their application;
- open and democratic principles at all levels of organization; and,
- a disciplined and detailed internal hierarchy for organizational and decision-making processes.[33]

Lenin defined "democratic centralism" within the party as "freedom of discussion, unity in action."[34] And discussion the Bolsheviks, especially their leadership, often had plenty of, at times very bitterly. As far back as the 1880s and the 1890s in Munich, where many had ended up in voluntary exile, Russian revolutionary émigrés constantly quarreled over revolutionary tactics and strategy. Despite a strong streak of pragmatism, Lenin could be highly dogmatic at times and was fully committed to what he perceived to be Marxist orthodoxy. One of the central points of contention between Lenin and other Marxists was how to adapt and apply Marxism to a Russian society that in the late 1800s was comprised of some 90 percent peasants and only 7 percent wage-workers. Among the Russian revolutionaries, many of whom had gathered within the Social-Democratic Labour Party (RSDLP), two main groups soon emerged. The Bolsheviks (Majority), led by Lenin, advocated a more disciplined party, a worker–peasant alliance, and the subsequent establishment of a "dictatorship of the proletariat and the peasantry." The Mensheviks (Minority) favored a coalition between workers and industrialists, seeing such an alliance as the most effective means of overthrowing Tsarism.[35]

In 1912, Lenin and a few like-minded comrades made a clear break from the Mensheviks and established the splinter Bolshevik RSDLP. Soon, the Bolsheviks articulated a clear strategy of how they conceived of the revolution and devised a clear program of action, including calling for an eight-hour workday for workers, land reform for peasants, and democratic elections for a new parliament. Not surprisingly, their popularity soon soared. This popularity was to reemerge once the initial shock of Russia's devastating losses in the Great War wore off. As 1917 approached, workers councils – soviets – which had originally appeared in the aftermath of the 1905 Russo-Japanese War, began reappearing in Russian factories and towns, this time under socialist leadership. In April 1917, Lenin articulated what came to be known as the April Thesis: "All power to the soviets," and "peace, bread, and land."[36] As the summer months wore on and as the Provisional Government found itself more and more out of step with the radicalizing mood of the country, Lenin's stridency and his revolutionary message became increasingly resonant.

By September, Lenin was relentless in calling on fellow Bolsheviks to keep up the pressure on the Provisional Government and to push the revolution forward. If they failed to act, he decried, "the Bolsheviks will cover themselves in eternal shame" and "we shall ruin the revolution."[37] Lenin's moment was not long in coming. The insurrection began on October 24 in Petrograd, where by the next day, the Winter Palace, the new residence of Prime Minister Kerensky, was, in a rather calm and eerily quiet manner, stormed and captured.[38] The Bolsheviks then marched on to and captured other government buildings, declaring the end of Tsarism and the establishment of a new, soviet-run political system. Soon thereafter, the Bolsheviks renamed themselves as the Communist Party. To dampen expectations of communist revolutions elsewhere, at least in the near future, Lenin soon declared that the October Revolution was not the blaze that would set the rest of Europe on fire.[39] Russia, as it turned out, had its own civil war to contend with.

The Chinese Communist Party played a similarly critical role in bringing about and directing the Chinese revolution. Mao had discovered the importance of organization relatively early on, when in 1917 he started a student discussion group called the New People's Study Society. By the early 1920s, he was already organizing peasant associations. Throughout his career, Mao remained keenly aware of both the scale of his country's geographic and population size and the scope and historic significance of his movement. Both before and after the communist victory, therefore, organization and discipline remained among his central preoccupations. From the earliest days of joining the Communist Party, he paid close attention to the means and mechanisms through which revolutionary mobilization was achieved, discipline was instilled among the rank and file, and goals and objectives were articulated, understood, and accomplished. As early as 1938, Mao called on his comrades to be mindful of the importance of the theory and practice of revolution:

> No political party can lead a great revolutionary movement to victory unless it possesses revolutionary theory and a knowledge of history and a profound grasp of the practical movement.[40]

If Lenin saw the party as an indispensable component of the revolution, Mao saw it as inseparable from the revolutionary army. Mao's innovation to Marxism-Leninism, in fact, lies in the introduction of the notion of the party-army. In fact, Mao and other Chinese revolutionary leaders used the CCP far more for purposes of peasant mobilization and armed action, against both the Japanese and the Koumintang, than for ideological deliberations concerning the proper direction of the revolutionary struggle. Much more so than the strict application of Marxist doctrine, what the Chinese communists really advocated was more "rural egalitarianism," a proposition that found much appeal throughout the countryside and among the peasantry.[41] Throughout, Mao remained concerned with the pragmatic aspects of the revolution instead of abstract theorizing, so much so that his advocacy of pragmatism extending even into the arts.[42]

In broad terms, the Chinese communists believed that the successful fulfillment of Sun Yat Sen's "bourgeois-democratic" revolution was a necessary first step to the establishment of a socialist society.[43] Of course, Mao declared in 1945, "We Communists never conceal our political views. Definitely and beyond all doubt, our future or maximum programme is to carry China forward to socialism and communism."[44] But he also reminded fellow party members that "policy and tactics are the life of the Party; leading comrades at all levels must give full attention and must never on any account be negligent."[45]

Both during the peasant revolution, when the CCP acted as a party-army, and after the revolution's success, when the CCP turned into the state party, Mao used the institution in order to solidify his personal hold over the revolutionary movement and the Chinese body politic. In 1941 he launched the Rectification Movement, lasting until 1944, during which all CCP members were meant to engage in intensive study, reflection, criticism, and self-criticism. The Rectification Movement, ruthless iterations of which occurred with great frequency after the revolution's success, enabled Mao to strengthen his hold over the party. By the mid-1940s, Mao's cult of personality was already well established.

In January 1949, Mao's forces marched into Beijing, and, defying the wishes of Stalin, who had given the Chinese communists logistical support and advice, they pushed on until the Koumintang fled to Taiwan. Access to Mao, already remote shortly after the end of the Long March in 1935, became even rarer after victory, and his personality cult grew exponentially.[46] Once in power, Mao repeatedly used the party apparatus to launch massive political and economic campaigns – such as the 1958–1962 Great Leap Forward and the 1966–1976 Cultural Revolution – through which he sought also to eliminate rivals and to ensure the consolidation of his hold on power.[47]

The communist party was equally integral to the journey of the Vietnamese revolution as it evolved from clandestine meetings by loosely organized discussion groups into a full-fledged guerrilla uprising. Having spent time in Canton in the 1920s, Ho's first-hand observations of and experiences with the communist revolutionary movement in China led him to several key conclusions: Indochina needed its own communist party; the "national question" and the "social question" – independence and agrarian reform, respectively – would necessarily have to be linked; and the principles of Lenin and San Yat Sen could be fruitfully blended.[48] Upon settling in northern Vietnam in the early 1930s, Ho began holding regular discussion groups and meetings, while at the same time living extremely modestly and engaging in regular and often hard labor. In the process, he emerged as a role model to which many local peasants looked up. In the meanwhile, in order to foster grassroots mobilization, he set up a number of friendship associations. As one of his biographers recounts, "Like a good ethnologist, he always practiced 'participant observation,' as well as 'observant participation,' and never forgot that a good example is better than a hundred lectures."[49]

In February 1930, Ho established the Indochinese Communist Party. The party's platform called for the overthrow of French imperialism and an end to feudalism and to the reactionary bourgeoisie; the complete independence of Indochina from French rule; the establishment of a worker–peasant–soldier government; access to education for the masses; the implementation of an eight-hour workday; and democratic freedoms for the masses.[50] According to Ho, the Party "must assume a tactful, flexible attitude towards the national bourgeoisie ... urge them into action if possible, isolate them politically if necessary."[51] The Party, he argued, needs broad appeal among all different groups and social strata in order to achieve its most urgent priority, namely national liberation.[52]

In his 1927 book *The Revolutionary Path,* Ho had distinguished between three forms of revolution – bourgeois, national, and social – and outlined the essential ethical qualities of a revolutionary. He also blended Asian ethics with Europeans ideals, and Confucianism with socialism.[53] For Ho, it was important for party cadres to have a "revolutionary morality," which he saw as having three characteristics: absolute loyalty and devotion to the party in preference over personal and individual commitments; an in-depth understanding of the theory and practice of Marxism-Leninism; and "constantly [using] self-criticism and criticism to heighten one's ideological standard, improve one's work, and progress together with one's comrades."[54] At the same time, Ho believed that the party must necessarily be led by the working class, because workers constitute "the most advanced, conscious, resolute, disciplined and best-organized class."[55]

By the early 1940s, Ho had resolved to drive the French and Japanese colonizers out of Vietnam and to establish a "people's democracy" there.[56] In pursuing his objectives, the Communist Party played a key role in recruiting, indoctrinating, and directing the guerrillas fighting the French.[57] This centrality of the party carried over into the post-independence era, when Ho relied on the party apparatus, much like Mao was doing in China at about the same time, to create and operationalize the institutions of a new state. From the moment Ho announced Vietnam's independence in September 1945 until the end of 1946, he sought to establish a functioning state through issuing 181 decrees on everything from education to justice, the army, the police, taxes, agriculture, business and industry, and even forestry.[58] Unlike Mao, Ho did not see himself as larger than life and as the embodiment of the Vietnamese revolution. Like Mao, however, he was not above concentrating power in his own hands, at times ruthlessly. By the 1950s, some Vietnamese were likening Ho's centralization of power to the Jacobin's reign of terror in France.[59]

Similar to the roles that the Bolsheviks, the CCP, and the Indochinese Communist Party played in the Russian, Chinese, and Vietnamese revolutions, respectively, the July 26 Movement was decisive in guiding and directing the Cuban revolution. In the 1940s, Castro came to the growing realization that party politics in Cuba was futile and that armed struggle was the only viable option for changing the political system.[60] These feelings were confirmed when former President Fulgencio Batista (1940–1944) forcibly took over power in 1952. Castro's thoughts, recorded soon thereafter, are revealing:

> The present moment is revolutionary, not political. Politics is the consecration of the opportunism of those who have means and resources. The revolution opens the way for true merit, for those who bare their chest and take up the standard. A Revolutionary Party needs to be young and needs a revolutionary leadership drawn from the people in whose hands Cuba can be saved.[61]

Named after the ill-fated attack on the Moncada barracks in 1953, Castro's July 26 Movement (also known as the M26–7) was comprised of a broad cross section of aggrieved and anti-Batista groups that included fisherman, agricultural laborers, peasants, industrial workers, and students.[62] In many ways, the July 26 Movement was non-ideological, or at least its goals were formulated not around what should exist but rather what should not. Carlos Franqui, the movement's chief propagandist, later recounted the obstacles to the country that the revolutionaries had identified: "the army, caudillism, oligarchism, monoculture, and dependency of foreign nations."[63] According to Franqui, the group agreed that "propaganda, or public information, was the decisive weapon in our struggle," and that the revolutionaries would aim for "a minimum of physical destruction and a maximum of psychological penetration."[64]

The July 26 Movement was not the only group fighting for the overthrow of the Batista regime. It was, however, the most determined one.[65] In November 1956, eighty-two revolutionaries, including Che Guevara, set sail for Cuba from Mexico onboard the yacht *Granma*. On landing, most of the would-be attackers lost their way in the unfamiliar terrain and a number of them were captured. The surviving party, numbering twelve and including the brothers Fidel and Raul Castro and Che Guevara, sought shelter in the jungles of the Sierra Maestra region and decided to wage their peasant revolution from there. For the rebels, the region offered the right mixture of demographic and geographic features from where they could launch their revolution.[66] Atypical of most Cuban peasantry across the island, the peasants of the Sierra Maestra region were among Cuba's poorest, were often squatters, and led highly precarious lives. In reality, Castro initially did not intend to launch a peasant-based revolution. But once his small band started operating in the Sierras, a mythology of peasant revolution gradually took hold.[67] The Cuban revolution was thus born.

What followed in the Sierras was a test of resolve reminiscent of what the Chinese communists had experienced in the lead-up to and during the Long March. After the disastrous *Granma* landing, Che recorded the group's difficult journey: "We were an army of shadows, ghosts, walking as if to the beat of some dark, psychic mechanism."[68] The Cuban rebels faced a chronic cash crunch, and many of the weapons they bought or acquired through clandestine means were defective and did not operate properly. Food and other basic necessities, especially medicine and arms, were not always easy to come by, especially as new recruits joined and as the needs of the group grew.[69] It would be inaccurate, and wholly unfair, to call the July 26 Movement the gang that couldn't shoot straight. Nevertheless, the self-declared revolutionaries repeatedly suffered setbacks, often miscalculated their own strength and the enemy's vulnerability, and learned by trial and error, an example of which was the ill-fated attack on the presidential palace on March 1957.[70] By their own admission, the "climate of illusion" and especially the "illusion of victory" often resulted in rebels overestimating their strength and committing "tactical errors."[71]

Within the anti-Batista revolutionary movement, two broad tendencies developed – the Sierra and the Llano – with the former believing in peasant mobilization first and the latter advocating all-out strike in the cities and urban-based insurrection.[72] It is through sheer resolve and determination that the Sierra, to which the Castro brothers and Che belonged, emerged on top. "The myth of the Sierra," a valorized struggle in a region with significant symbolic meaning from the days of Cuba's independence wars, should not overshadow important contributions made to the revolution by various urban-based groups.[73] Ultimately, nevertheless, it was the Sierras who were victorious, and it was they who wrote the revolution's official history and shaped its myths.

Fidel was a man of action, and whereas those affiliated with the Llano spent much time debating the proper methods of the revolution, Castro busied himself with peasant recruitment, revolutionary mobilization, and armed action. What "manifesto" he did issue, on February 20, 1957, was essentially designed to dispel regime-sponsored rumors that he had been killed in action. His expositions often took the form of "guidelines to the country" on how to more effectively resist and undermine the economic livelihood and the political machinery of the state.[74] In March 1958, the July 26 Movement did issue a more robust manifesto, this time calling for "total war against tyranny" and declaring that "the struggle against Batista has entered its final stage."[75] The end of the Batista regime was indeed near. On January 1, 1959, Batista fled the country.

Throughout the two-year journey from the time the Cuban revolutionaries gathered in Mexico and planned their takeover of power in 1956 until Batista's flight in 1958, Fidel Castro played a critical role in planning and carrying out the revolution. Exactly how central this role was from the very start, and how Castro was viewed within the movement, is not fully clear. According to the researcher Julia Sweig, up until the last six to eight months before the success of the revolutionary movement, most of the decisions affecting the revolution were made by lesser-known individuals instead of by Fidel, his brother Raul, or Che.[76] Carlos Franqui, however, one of the July 26 Movement rebels who later had a falling out with Castro, accused him of ignoring procedures and instead making rash and arbitrary decisions, accepting no criticism, and treating "the Sierras as if it were his personal property."[77] Whatever the truth, by the time 1958 was drawing to a close, Castro's leadership of the July 26 Movement was unrivaled and complete. Soon he set up an office of Revolutionary Plans and Coordination, which amounted to a situation of dual power similar to what had developed in the heady days of Lenin's and Mao's revolutions. By the time Batista fled, no one else could command the level of respect, popularity, and revolutionary legitimacy that Castro enjoyed.

Armed Struggle

As important as vanguard parties are, they would be vacuous without actual revolutionary foot soldiers, who most often take the form of guerrilla fighters. The primary objective of the self-declared revolutionaries is to bring about the collapse of the state. To achieve this goal, insurgents and guerrillas resort to a variety of violent actions, ranging from acts of sabotage against regime-affiliated targets to all-out attacks against political personalities and institutions. Invariably, violence in general and armed struggle in particular become integral to planned revolutions. This resort to violence is part of an ethos of struggle that emerges in the process of contestation for power: Political power is held on to through resort to violence and repression, and therefore the only way it can be captured is also through violence.[78] Mao famously justified armed struggle in the following terms:

> A revolution is not a dinner party, or writing an essay, or painting a picture, or doing embroidery; it cannot be so refined, so leisurely and gentle, so temperate, kind, courteous, restrained, and magnanimous. A revolution is an insurrection, an act of violence by which one class overthrows the power of another.[79]

For Mao, violence was an inescapable facet of the revolutionary struggle. "*War,*" he wrote in 1936, "is the highest form of resolving contradictions, when they have developed to a certain stage, between classes, nations, states, or political groups, and it has existed ever since the existence of private property and of classes."[80] His call to arms was blunt and direct: "Every Communist must grasp the truth, 'Political power grows out of the barrel of a gun.'"[81]

Other revolutionary leaders have been equally adamant in their defense of the need for violence in general and armed struggle in particular. In his 1964 trial, for example, Nelson Mandela defended his leadership of the armed wing of the African National Congress, uMkhonto we Sizwe or MK, and its resort to armed struggle:

> Firstly, we believe that as a result of Government policy, violence by the African people had become inevitable, and that unless responsible leadership was given to canalize and control the feelings of our people, there would be outbreaks of terrorism and hostility between the various races of this country which is not produced even by war. Secondly, we felt that without violence there would be no way open to the African people to succeed in their struggle against the principle of white supremacy. All lawful means of expressing opposition to this principle had been closed by legislation, and we were placed in a position in which we had either to accept a permanent state of inferiority, or to defy the Government.[82]

Lenin, Che Guevara, and Mandela saw violence as the quickest means to attain power, a necessary evil needed for the overthrow of the pre-revolutionary state. Out of necessity, Ho Chi Minh saw the struggle for power, what he called a "protracted war of resistance," as a much longer process. "We use the strategy of a protracted war of resistance," he wrote, "in order to develop our forces and gather more experience. We use guerilla tactics to wear down the enemy forces until a general offensive wipes them out."[83] This guerilla war needs a vanguard party with a guiding military strategy, which must "cling to the people because they are the source of strength of the army."[84] According to Ho, "*military activity* is the keystone in the war of resistance."[85]

As subsequent history was to bear witness, Ho saw this war of resistance as a protracted one: "We must understand that protracted resistance is closely connected with preparations for a general counter-offensive. As the war of resistance is a long one, long preparations are also needed for a general counteroffensive."[86] For Ho, resistance at the local level was key to weakening and eventually defeating the colonizers. He exhorted his comrades to "effectively organize and train militiamen and guerrillas in *each village*" and to "*take the village militiamen and guerrillas as basis.*" The party must give combatants "a clear grasp of guerrilla tactics," while at the same time "realize self-supply and self-sufficiency by effectively increasing production."[87]

Mao, of course, agreed with such instrumentalist use of violence. But for him the value of armed struggle went beyond the mere capture of power. Mao, and to a lesser extent Che Guevara later on, saw an additional benefit to armed struggle, not simply as a means but as an integral part of the revolutionary process. The masses, they both believed, needed to be awakened, both to the need for a revolution and to their own potential to push a revolution forward. Mao believed that "all genuine knowledge originates in experience," reminding his comrades that one must "discover truth through practice and through practice again verify the truth."[88] As Mao was to himself admit in 1948, just a year before finally capturing the state,

> If we tried to go on the offensive when the masses are not yet awakened, that would be adventurism. If we insisted on leading the masses to do anything against their will, we would certainly fail. If we did not advance when the masses demand advance, that would be Right opportunism.[89]

More specifically, Mao utilized the concept of "people's war" not only as a means of organizing and mobilizing the peasantry, but also as a tool for ideological and practical indoctrination and education at the grassroots level. After the 1911 Republican Revolution, China had descended into civil war, foreign occupation, and warlordism, and chaos, war, and displacement were regular facts of life. This had inured the Chinese revolutionaries to violence. Even after the revolution's success and reaching the pinnacle of power, violence was never far from Mao's *modus operandi*. As state leader, resolving what he saw as "contradictions" among his peers and the people at large became the central means through which Mao sought to continually eradicate real or perceived enemies and to maintain his unchallenged consolidation of power.

For Mao and his comrades, the revolution essentially had to be fought simultaneously on three fronts, the first and the second involving battle against the Koumintang and the Japanese occupation, while the third revolved around the continued mobilization of the peasant army. The PCC was compelled to look for support in the countryside not so much because of ideological belief in the revolutionary potential of the peasantry but out of necessity. Comparatively, the peasantry was the less difficult of the social forces to mobilize. But once the CCP was pushed into the countryside, it discovered the potential of the peasantry as a powerful army of recruits capable of affecting meaningful, and often immediate, change on ground. Facing persecution by the

Kuomintang government, in 1927 Mao and a peasant army of 1,000 fellow communists moved to the mountainous Jinggangshan region in the Jiangxi province and established the Red Army.[90] By 1930, the Red Army had a force of no fewer than 60,000 to 70,000 troops.[91] To capitalize on its presence in the countryside and to channel the mobilizational potentials of the peasantry, in the early 1930s the CCP organized peasant soviets in most places where its members found themselves.[92]

By 1934, the KMT's military campaign against the Communists had become so effective that Mao and his comrades decided to evacuate the Jiangxi province. In what came to be known as the Long March, from 1934 to 1936 some 100,000 individuals left for the Communist base areas in the northern Shaangxi region, of whom approximately 85,000 were soldiers. "In concrete terms," Mao declared in 1936, "and especially with regard to military operations, when we talk of the people in the base area as a factor, we mean that we have an armed people."[93] But the Long March was a decidedly unhappy endeavor. Many of the marchers dropped out or died of exhaustion over the course of the perilous journey, with only one in ten reaching the north after a year on the march.[94] Nevertheless, despite the ordeal the group suffered, due to his bravery and leadership, Mao's political standing rose during the march. By the time the Long March came to an end in the northern city of Yan'an, Mao was seen as the undisputed political and military leader of the Chinese Communist Party.[95]

Mao's resolve to wage war on the KMT and the Japanese and to also bring about a communist revolution only hardened after the Long March ended. In 1937, for example, he made the following statement:

> Revolutions and revolutionary wars are inevitable in class society, and without them it is impossible to accomplish any leap in social development and to overthrow the reactionary ruling classes and therefore impossible for the people to win political power.[96]

A year later the theme of his speeches had changed little:

> The seizure of power by armed force, the settlement of the issue by war, is the central task and the highest form of revolution … We are advocates of the abolition of war, we do not want war; but war can only be abolished through war, and in order to get rid of the gun it is necessary to take up the gun.[97]

The Foot Soldiers

Revolutionary leaders inspire and lead. Revolutionary parties recruit and mobilize. And armed struggle fosters and hastens the collapse of the regime and the revolution's victory. But there is no revolution if it has no foot soldiers, those rank and file fighters who are willing to take up arms, face off against government soldiers, and risk the consequences. In the planned revolutions under study here – the Russian, Chinese, Vietnamese, and Cuban revolutions – the revolution's rank and file was invariably made up of the peasantry, or at least it sought to portray itself as having come from the peasantry. Often times, the leaders are urbanites and frequently from the comfortable if not affluent classes. Historically, in fact, some of the most prominent roles in guerrilla movements, both successful and unsuccessful ones, have been played by university students and professors.[98] But they lead the revolution in the name of the downtrodden and the dispossessed, and it is to this strata of society that they direct their message and whom they seek to mobilize. In each of the societies where revolutions occurred, there are vast armies of urban poor and marginalized. But the paucity of regime control over and reach into the countryside pushed the revolutionaries into rural areas, where the fighters available to them were peasants. Not surprisingly, the revolution's ideology is bent and contorted in order to address "the peasant question." The peasantry is valorized and romanticized in the process, its "heroic sacrifices" quickly added to the revolution's mythology.

The efforts of revolutionary leaders in mobilizing and directing peasant activism require, more than anything else, a solid and viable organizational apparatus. In addition to an agitated and mobilizable peasantry, guerrilla revolutions require a disciplined army and a party organization, one that can provide the coordination and tactical vision necessary for peasant unity and ultimately for capture of state power.[99] Peasant-based revolutions depend directly upon the mobilization of the peasantry by revolutionary organizations, making the sheer availability and effectiveness of such groups a necessary precondition of revolutionary situations.[100] Often times, spontaneous political acts by peasants have forced a scramble for the mobilization and formation of their would-be leadership.[101] The degree of interaction between peasants and the leadership, and the extent to which leaders can absorb the peasantry into their organization and to expand their power base, determine the viability and success of the revolutionary movement. Adversely, an absence of solid bonds between revolutionary leaders and followers, especially in guerrilla revolutions where planned revolutionary initiatives play an extremely important role, can substantially reduce a movement's chances of success.[102] Moreover, for guerrilla organizations to succeed in achieving their revolutionary goals, they need to have a sustained ability to recruit new members, structurally and organizationally evolve and develop, and to endure the adverse consequences of military confrontation with the regime.

The social composition of the leadership of peasant-based revolutionary movements is often decidedly non-rural. It is, in fact, frequently the disaffected members of the middle classes, most notably urban-educated students and intellectuals, who occupy most of the leadership positions of guerrilla organizations. Disjointed processes of social, political, and economic development turn the middle classes into potential revolutionary groups, groups whose oppositional inclinations are likely to rise along with their levels of education and social awareness. Given their greater sensitivity to their surrounding environment, the most revolutionary of groups are often middle-class intellectuals, and the most revolutionary of intellectuals are students.[103] Historically, there have been many dissatisfied literati elites who have turned into professional revolutionaries. They have entrusted themselves with the task of establishing solid revolutionary coalitions and alliances that can overcome social, ethnic, and economic divides and are also capable of eventually replacing the current regime.[104] In search of an audience willing to follow and to obey them, they most frequently find the peasantry.

The preponderant role of the peasantry in guerrilla organizations arises out of a combination of rural conditions that are conducive to oppositional mobilization, as well as the political and ideological inclinations of revolutionary leaders themselves. To begin with, urban-based political activists are drawn to the peasantry because of a number of practical political considerations. Frequently, a lack of political penetration by the government machinery into distant towns and villages results in the alienation of the countryside from the state. Despite detailed and large-scale control over various aspects of urban life, most praetorian states pay at best scant attention to the countryside. Most, in fact, neglect the economic development of rural areas and their political mobilization or at least pacification also. Even in instances where concerted efforts aimed at the political mobilization of rural inhabitants have been launched, large numbers of peasants continue to remain outside the influence of what often times turn out to be only halfhearted campaigns. The political vacuum thus created offers potential guerrilla leaders ample opportunity for recruitment and mobilization. In an environment of little or no official political presence of any kind, guerrilla leaders can recruit followers with relative ease. They can also conduct revolutionary acts, which, even if only symbolically important, may have a magnified effect. For guerrilla organizations, mere survival can be politically as important as it is to win battles. In the eminently political types of wars they wage, survival for the guerrillas is a victory in itself.[105]

Another reason for the attraction of revolutionary leaders to the peasantry is the supposed "ideological purity" of peasants because of their geographic and political distance from centers of power. Alienation from the state also entails estrangement from its ideology and values. Mao, who was perhaps the most astute observer of the peasantry's revolutionary potential, went so far as to label peasants – not the Communist Party – as "the vanguards of revolution," "blank masses" uncorrupted by the bourgeois ideologies of the city.[106] Moreover, not only is the peasantry ideologically unassimilated into the political establishment, its predicaments and objective conditions often closely match those of the revolutionaries. Most revolutionaries declare their aims to be the alleviation of misery and injustice, poverty, and exploitation, the very conditions that in one way or another are dominant in most rural areas. Coupled with greater possibilities for recruitment and mobilization, ideological compatibility with objective conditions draws most leaders of planned revolutions to remote rural regions and areas. There is thus a strong connection between the revolutionaries' ideology and dogma on the one hand and circumstances prevailing in the countryside on the other.

The development of the actual links that bind revolutionary leaders and guerrilla organizations to masses of peasants is important in determining the extent and effectiveness of revolutionary mobilization. The establishment of such links and the resulting mobilization are dependent upon several variables, some indigenous to local conditions and others dependent on the characteristics of the guerrilla leaders themselves. Chief among these determining factors are the extent to which local ruling classes dominate power sources, the nature and extent of rural coalitions and alliances, and the ability of guerrilla leaders to deliver the goods and services that others cannot. In most rural regions, pre-capitalist peasant small-holders, sharecroppers, and tenants are likely to enjoy cultural and social (as well as organizational) autonomy from ruling elites, despite their tendency toward localism and traditionalism.[107] This relative, built-in resistance to elite hegemony, and comparative receptivity to ideological and organizational alternatives, arises out of a sense of economic security and independence *vis-à-vis* the more dominant rural classes such as big landlords and estate owners. The spread of capitalism and the subsequent commercialization of agrarian society is also important in bringing about peasant rebelliousness.[108]

This increasing propensity toward revolutionary activity is not necessarily because of the increased exploitation of peasants due to the spread of capitalist relations. Instead, it is derived from a general breakdown of "prior social commitments" to kin and neighbors and, therefore, greater flexibility and independence to act as desired.[109] Even more important is the extent of direct government control over a region, or indirectly through landed proprietors acting as government proxies. Favorable political circumstances, the most important of which are the existence of weak states, are crucial in determining the feasibility of revolutionary activism and possibilities for peasant mobilization.

Another significant factor that determines the success of guerrilla leaders in mobilizing peasants is the guerrillas' ability to deliver goods and services, both actual and perceived. People will join or abstain from opposition groups based on the rewards they receive, both individually or as a collective whole. These rewards may be emotional – i.e., a sense of empowerment – or material.[110] In specific relation to rural areas, revolutionary movements have won broad support when they have been willing and able to provide state-like goods and services to their targeted constituents. The establishment of "liberated areas" that are secure from government attacks; the provision of services such as public education, health care, and law and order; and the initiation of economic reforms in the form of land redistribution or tax reductions are all particularly effective measures in drawing peasants closer to guerrilla movements. Revolutionary groups are especially successful in attracting peasant support when they provide local goods and services with immediate payoffs *before* attempting to mobilize the population for the more difficult task of overthrowing the government.[111]

The provision of goods and services may not necessarily be material. For most peasants and rural inhabitants, participation in an army-like guerrilla organization offers a way of escaping from disillusioning surroundings and finding purpose and meaning in a greater cause. Membership in an organization becomes an end in itself, a means to overcome powerlessness and to strive for higher goals and principles. To command and in turn to be commanded, to hold a gun, and to aspire for dreams and ideals are often mechanisms through which peasant revolutionaries, especially younger ones, try to shatter their socially-prescribed, second-class image and, within their own world, try to "become somebody."

Given his reluctance to veer too far off course from Marxist orthodoxy, of all revolutionary leaders Lenin had perhaps the hardest time justifying his attention to the peasantry. He therefore often couched his appeal to peasants with references to the proletariat. As one of his biographers has observed, Lenin "was an improviser; he worked by instinct as well as by doctrine. His agrarian project was unconvincing in its own terms, but his intuitive searching was understandable. He wanted the party, when finally it came into existence, to take account of the fact that 85 percent of the subjects of the Russian empire were peasants."[112] Lenin was keenly aware of the power of the peasantry as a potent revolutionary force, as evident from one of his writings in 1905:

> Today the question of the peasant movement has become vital not only in the theoretical but also in the most direct practical sense. We now have to transform our general slogans into direct appeals by the revolutionary proletariat to the revolutionary peasantry. The time has now come when the peasantry is coming forward as a conscious maker of a new way of life in Russia. And the course and outcome of the great Russian revolution depend in tremendous measure on the growth of the peasants' political consciousness.[113]

This political consciousness could only be harnessed and channeled for revolutionary purposes by peasant alliance with the working class. "Trust the workers, comrade peasants," Lenin wrote in 1905, "and break with the capitalists! Only in close alliance with the workers *can* you begin to carry out the programme set out in the [socialist] mandates."[114] Lenin believed that "the small peasantry can free itself from the yoke of capital only by associating itself with the working-class movement, by helping the workers in their struggle for the socialist system, for transforming the land, as well as the other means of production (factories, works, machines, etc.), into social property."

> Trying to save the peasantry by protecting small-scale farming and small holdings from the onslaught of capitalism would be a useless retarding of social development; it would mean deceiving the peasantry with illusions of the possibility of prosperity even under capitalism, it would mean disuniting the labouring classes and creating a privileged position for the minority at the expense of the majority.[115]

For Lenin, the coalition between the peasantry and the working class was a necessity for the revolution's success. On its own, the working class was too small in size and resources to win the revolutionary struggle. But it could not trust the bourgeoisie. As he wrote in a letter to *Pravda* in December 1917, an alliance between the workers and the bourgeoisie was inadvisable "because of the radical divergence of interests between these classes." However, an alliance between the proletariat and peasants was "an 'honest coalition,' an honest alliance, for there is *no* radical divergence of interests between the wage-workers and the working and exploited peasants. Socialism is *fully* able to meet the interests of both. *Only* socialism can meet their interests."[116]

Whereas Lenin saw the peasantry as a useful appendage to what should be fundamentally a workers' revolution, Mao, and also Ho Chi Minh, believed that real revolutionary potential actually lay with none other than the peasantry.[117] Both men saw the peasantry as a truly revolutionary force, especially prior to the capture of power, when the force of circumstances had left them with few options but to establish their base of operations in overwhelmingly peasant-dominated areas. For Ho, given the composition of Vietnamese society at the time, with some 90 percent being peasants, it was incumbent upon the party "to carry out *political agitation*" among the peasantry and to "stir them up." This meant awakening the peasants' political consciousness, tightly organizing and uniting them, and "leading them to struggle vigorously for their own interest and that of the fatherland."[118] Similarly, from the very beginning of his revolutionary career, Mao was also preoccupied with the mobilization of the "masses," which for him at the time meant the peasantry. "The revolutionary war is a war of the masses," he wrote in 1934, and "it can be waged only by mobilizing the masses and relying on them."[119] Mao considered "the masses" to be "the true bastion of iron," the real force on whose shoulder the revolution rests. True revolutionary potential, he argued, resides with "the masses, millions upon millions of people who genuinely and sincerely support the revolution."[120]

Chinese revolutionaries, Mao included, were aware that the peasantry in China was economically stratified and could broadly be distinguished into the categories of landless, poor, middle, and rich. As a result, in the early days of their movement most of Mao's contemporaries thought he overestimated the revolutionary potential of the peasantry. Mao, however, was unwavering in his belief in the peasantry's mobilizational and revolutionary capacities:

> In a very short time in China's central, southern and northern provinces, several hundred million peasants will rise like a mighty storm, a mighty hurricane, a force so swift and violent that no power, however great, will hold it back. ... All revolutionary parties and all revolutionary comrades will stand before [the peasants] to be tested, to be accepted or rejected by them.[121]

There was, by all accounts, more to Mao's statements than mere slogans meant to arouse passions and attract recruits. The journalist Edgar Snow, who spent time with Mao's army and followed it around for a number of years, had a similar assessment. "The Chinese peasant was not passive," Snow later wrote. "He was not a coward. He would fight when given a method, and organization, a leadership, a workable program, hope – *and arms*. The development of 'communism' in China had proven that."[122] Not surprisingly, Snow witnessed widespread support for the Communists among the peasantry. Communist initiatives such as land distribution, the introduction of more effective farming techniques, organizational skills, and the integration of women into the workforce were all highly popular among the Chinese peasantry.[123]

Perhaps no other revolutionary leaders romanticized guerrilla warfare as much as Fidel Castro and Che Guevara did. Both men, of course, were keenly aware of the critical role that peasants played in the guerrilla army, and agrarian land reform was one of the central goals of the Cuban revolution. Che Guevara went so far as to maintain that "important individual exceptions notwithstanding" – including, most notably, himself, Castro, and most other members of the July 26

Movement – "the combat nucleus of the guerrilla army should be composed of peasants."[124] And, to attract as many peasants to the revolutionary cause as possible, Castro constantly emphasized the humility of his movement: "The 26th of July movement is the revolutionary organization of the humble, by the humble, and for the humble."[125] Guerrillas found guilty of crimes and infractions were severely punished by the rebel army. On some occasions, the rebels even executed some of their own who had committed serious offenses such as treason or rape. By Castro's own account, over the course of two years some ten offenders faced the rebel group's firing squad.[126] But Castro's war in the Sierras was not a peasant war *per se*. In fact, a majority of the combatants were from the cities.

In his treatise on guerrilla warfare, Che outlined "three fundamental lessons to the revolutionary movements in the Americas": (1) popular forces can win a war against a regular army; (2) "the insurrectional *foco* [a small nucleus of revolutionaries] can develop subjective conditions based on existing objective conditions"; and (3) the underdeveloped countryside is "the fundamental arena for armed struggle."[127] Moreover, in the same tradition as Mao Zedong and Ho Chi Minh, Che Guevara saw guerrillas as more than mere armed combatants:

> As social reformers, guerrilla fighters should not only provide an example in their own lives, but should also constantly give an orientation on ideological issues, explaining what they know and what they wish to do at the right time. They should also make use of what they learn as the months and years of the war strengthen their revolutionary convictions, making them more radical as the potency of arms is demonstrated, as the outlook of the local people becomes a part of their spirit and of their own life, and as they understand the justice and the vital necessity of many changes, the theoretical importance of which they understood before, but perhaps not the practical urgency.[128]

While offering the ideal environment in which guerrillas can operate, fighters do have a responsibility to the local peasants. They must educate the peasantry ideologically and help radicalize them by demonstrating the efficiency of armed action:

> The guerrilla fighter is above all an agrarian revolutionary, who interprets the desires of the great peasant mass to be owners of

> land, owners of their means of production, of their animals, of everything they live for, which will also constitute their cemetery.[129]

He continues:

> Intensive work must be undertaken among the local people to explain the motives of the revolution, its goals, and to spread the incontrovertible truth that the enemy's victory over the people is ultimately impossible. *Whoever does not feel this indisputable truth cannot be a guerrilla fighter.*[130]

As it turned out, Che Guevara romanticized the fighting spirit of the peasantry and the life of the guerrilla fighter to a fault. Guevara believed that since there are certain fundamental laws to guerrilla warfare, both the conditions and the successful rebellion in Cuba could be replicated elsewhere in the Americas.[131] Following a series of high-level positions in the post-revolutionary government in Havana, including as minister of the economy (1960) and industry (1961), Che traveled first to Belgian Congo and eventually, in November 1966, to Bolivia, where he hoped to instigate the same kind of revolution that he had fought in Cuba. Less than a year later, he was dead.

Che's Bolivian venture was exceptionally difficult. He and his small band of Cuban revolutionaries had little success attracting local recruits and then integrating them into their cabal. The recruits initially numbered only four, soon to grow to six.[132] "Of everything that was envisioned," he lamented, "the slowest has been the incorporation of Bolivian combatants."[133] In fact, there continued to be divisions and tensions between the rebels from Cuba, to whom Che referred to as the Vanguard, and the local Bolivian recruits.[134] In April 1967, only a month after arriving in Bolivia and approximately six months before his capture and death, Che could hardly hide his despair:

> We are totally cut off; illness has undermined the health of some compañeros, obliging us to divide our forces, which has greatly reduced our effectiveness ... the peasant support base has yet to develop, although, it appears that the systemic terror they suffer will ensure the neutrality of most – support will come later. There has not been a single new recruit, and apart from the deaths, we have lost [fellow fighter] Toro, who disappeared after the action at Taperillas.[135]

The fact that the Bolivian army actively recruited peasant informants and brutally attacked those areas suspected of sympathy for the rebels greatly helped keep the number of local recruits down. By the following month, the rebels' predicament had grown even more dire:

> The only food we have left is lard; I felt faint and had to sleep two hours to be able to continue at even this slow and halting pace; in general the march has been that way. We ate soup made from the lard at the first water hole. The troops are sick and now many have edema.[136]

By the end of July 1967, Che admitted that "the gradual loss of men" was "a serious defeat" and that the band of rebels numbered no more than twenty-two.[137] A month later he made one last-ditch effort to rally his troops:

> I am beginning to lose control; this will be corrected, but we are all in this together and anyone who does not feel up to it should say so. This is one of those moments when great decisions have to be made; this type of struggle gives us the opportunity to become revolutionaries, the highest form of human species, and it allows us to emerge fully as men; those who are unable to achieve either of these two states should say so now and abandon the struggle.[138]

Betrayed by the very peasantry he thought he was saving, Che Guevara was captured by the Bolivian army and killed on October 9, 1967.[139]

Conclusion

> Revolutions, radical and accelerated social transformations, are made in specific circumstances. They rarely, if ever, emerge fully ripe, and not all their details can be scientifically foreseen. They are made from passion, from the improvisation of human beings in their struggle for social change, and they are never perfect. Our revolution was no exception. It committed errors, and some of these cost us dearly.[140]

Che Guevara perhaps could not have imagined how prescient his words would be. No matter how *planned* a revolution may be, it is still a messy, unpredictable affair. It takes tremendous commitment, herculean courage, and all too often enormous and sustained use of violence for a planned revolution to succeed. That success, of course, hinges on the military defeat and collapse of the state, often dramatically culminated in the flight or even death of a fallen strongman. Planned revolutions set out to weaken pre-revolutionary states either by chipping away at their power and their base, as in China and Vietnam, or by overwhelming them with brute force, as in Cuba. Most often, the revolution succeeds when both the support base of the state is too narrow and tenuous and its institutions are rotten and corrupt. If the rebel army can sustain itself and over time achieve military superiority over the forces of the government, then the revolution succeeds.

The rebel army, meanwhile, is made up primarily of the peasantry, at least in theory if not in reality. Revolutions are actually often waged and fought by the middle classes, who do so in the name of the peasants and workers and the downtrodden. Orthodox Marxism had no room for any revolutionary force other than the working class. No less a luminary than Karl Marx himself had referred to peasants as a "sack of potatoes" and mused about "the idiocy of rural life" due to the peasants' lack of political organization.[141] But his heirs came to discover that the master theorist had been wrong. Lenin only reluctantly, but Mao, Ho Chi Minh, and Che Guevara all embraced the peasantry wholeheartedly, aware of, or perhaps even resigned to, the fact that the industrial working class on its own was hardly numerous or foolhardy enough to take up arms against the establishment. It was among the peasants, who had the least to lose and the most to gain, the later revolutionaries reasoned, where real revolutionary potential laid.

There is, as the next chapter will show, a certain amount of contagion that a spontaneous revolution can emit, the mass exuberance of one population inspiring and spilling over to populations across the border or even further afield. But planned revolutions, which are essentially military and power contests between state elites and their opponents, do not necessarily have the same contagion affect. Instead, those who plan revolutions often build on the received wisdom of their predecessors from whom they learn ideological blueprints, tactics and strategies, popular mobilization techniques, and broader revolutionary objectives. Not all planned revolutions have the same cross-fertilization that existed between the Chinese and the Vietnamese people's wars. But there is accumulated knowledge – of how to affect a revolutionary capture of power – that is often passed on from one generation of revolutionaries to the next.

3 FROM SOCIAL MOVEMENT TO REVOLUTION

The revolutions that engulfed China, Vietnam, and Cuba were *launched*. Those in France, in Russia in February 1917, in Iran, and during the Arab Spring *happened*. These were spontaneous uprisings that were initially largely unorganized and haphazard. These uprisings were unpredictable, at first were not guided by any overarching ideological goals except vague ideals of redistributive justice and nationalism, and had neither clearly identifiable leaders nor pre-determined outcomes. Instead, they emerged as largely uncoordinated protests and only over time mushroomed into mass-based revolutions, some quickly and others more gradually.

All spontaneous revolutions tend to follow a broadly discernible pattern. The first development usually is an opening of political space in what turns out to be the final days of the pre-revolutionary state. This political opening is precipitated by the growing weakness and vulnerability of the state and its diminished authority, enabling social actors to advance specific goals and setting off a social movement. In spontaneous revolutions, this social movement begins to gather steam and eventually grows into a revolutionary uprising. In the process, amongst the multiple groups vying to place themselves at the head of the brewing movement, those best positioned with access to social institutions, or a culturally resonant message, or both, emerge as the leading voices of the "revolution" and begin to be seen as its leaders. Revolutionary populism sweeps over the country, and mob rule becomes the order of the day.

As elites begin to defect from the ruling coalition and state leaders become increasingly isolated, the role of the military assumes greater centrality in the unfolding political drama. If the military breaks down or defects, the state's collapse is irreversible. Under such circumstances, the once mighty and unassailable edifice of the state starts to crumble, steadily replaced by new institutions, some of which are mutations of preexisting ones, others borne out of the revolutionary process, and still others created anew. The individuals by now recognized as de facto leaders of the revolution take over. A new order is heralded.

This chapter begins with an examination of how weaknesses in pre-revolutionary states provide space and opportunity for social actors to express their grievances and anger. Even if not overtly political, the very expression of these grievances is itself an act of political defiance. Weaknesses on the part of the state, meanwhile, may be institutional – rooted in the inability of state institutions to adequately perform those functions for which they were designed – or they may be personal, with individual state leaders incapable of responding effectively to the mounting crises confronting them. Often times, state weakness is prompted and exacerbated by a combination of weak institutions and incompetent leadership.

Whatever the cause, state weakness provides the opportunity for the emergence of a social movement, which then grows into something bigger and stronger than the state can handle. Spontaneous revolutions, the chapter maintains, originate as social movements. Whereas social movements may be single-issue focused, their emergence and growth within the context of crumbling state authority gives them additional dimensions. They grow in scope and ferocity, encompassing within them greater demands that become politically more focused and less compromising. In the process, they attract a greater number of people and excite the public's imagination to think what was once unthinkable. Political targets now begin to be attacked directly and bluntly. Courage becomes contagious. The revolution becomes unstoppable, unless, that is, there is a massive commitment of force on the part of the military. In all cases in which the revolution has succeeded, the military has either sided with the protestors or, alternatively, it has been incapable of putting down the rebellion.

State Vulnerability and Collapse

Spontaneous revolutions begin when openings start to appear in the political space allowed by the state. Jack Goldstone has identified three conditions likely to push the state toward breakdown: fiscal crisis, precipitated by a decline in state resources relative to its expenses and commitments; elite alienation and conflict, setting off defections by key allies of the state; and a high potential for the mobilization of the populace, by rural or urban groups with economic and political grievances.[1] These conditions, no doubt, are of critical importance in seriously undermining the state's ability to govern effectively and even precipitating its collapse. But the actual health of nondemocratic states – more specifically, their institutional strength – and their willingness or reluctance to open up political space to social actors depend on a number of interrelated developments.[2] These developments include the state's position in the international system and the degree to which it is susceptible to or immune from international pressures to open up; the state's ability to stave off or to deal with a crisis of legitimacy; elite cohesion or defection in the face of mounting social pressure; the viability of state institutions and their efficacy in mediating elite conflict or ameliorating social pressures; and the role and position of the armed forces. In this section I will discuss each of these developments in some detail.

Let us begin with the proposition that all states operate in an international environment that directly impacts their power and the nature and extent of their relationship with the society over which they rule. Domestic developments are only one category of events that bring about the structural collapse of an existing state. International factors can be equally potent determinants of the viability of domestic institutions and structures. The prevalence of unequal economic and political relationships between peripheral states and more powerful ones only compounds the vulnerabilities of domestic political institutions to changes in the international environment.

The extent of domestic institutional responsiveness to international fluctuations varies according to levels of economic and political dependence. In overtly dependent countries, several factors make the domestic power structure particularly fragile and vulnerable to pressures from abroad. To begin with, the identification of state leaders as clients of one or more foreign powers substantially increases their perceptions of illegitimacy in the public's eyes and makes it difficult for them to justify their rule on historical and nationalist grounds. More specifically, dependence on a foreign power reduces the political maneuverability of incumbent elites and circumscribes the range of their potential responses in times of crisis.[3] For such elites, the conduct of domestic politics becomes diplomatically conditional: Domestic responses rely heavily on the diplomatic preferences of the patron state. Thus, pre-revolutionary regimes in Iran in 1978, in Philippines in 1986, and in Hungary in 1989 felt compelled, for one reason or another, to pursue domestic policies that were being explicitly or implicitly advocated by their much stronger patrons.[4] Whether actual or perceived, these states felt constrained by international dynamics in their ability to pursue policies that might otherwise have enabled them to remain in power.

In instances of outright colonial domination, ruling colonial institutions are not necessarily any less prone to revolutions as are weaker, dependent states. Similar to personalized and bureaucratic–authoritarian states, direct colonial rule often dispenses economic and political privileges to very few elite groups, often to settlers, and thus generates considerable anger and resentment, especially among the middle and upper classes.[5] As if the granting of special privileges on the basis of racial or ethnic characteristics, often the case in colonies, is not a sufficient precondition for widespread animosity toward the colonial establishment, nationalist sentiments and demands for self-government further fan the flames of anti-colonial revolutions.[6] Furthermore, again similar to personalized states, colonial administrations are highly visible targets for economic and political frustrations. They serve as focal points that draw together groups with diverse social, economic, and ethnic backgrounds whose unity would not have been so easily achieved otherwise.[7]

The foreign relations that can potentially lead to revolutions need not necessarily be of the type found between patron and client states. The outbreak of revolutionary circumstances in one country may lead to similar developments in another through imitation, instigation, or even contagion.[8] Insecure about the extent of their newly acquired powers and paranoid about the conspiratorial designs of outside forces, revolutionary states often try to foment revolutions in neighboring countries in order to enhance their own legitimacy and power base both at home and abroad. Also prevalent are the contagious effects of revolution in one country on events occurring in another. These "inter-societal" connections, as George Lawson observes, take the form of connections and flow across borders, through which "relations among people, networks, institutions, and polities drive revolutionary dynamics."[9] In particular, people can feel empowered as they see others in a neighboring country mobilize, overcome fear, and bring down a dictatorship. Besides Eastern and Central Europe in the late 1980s and the early 1990s, the most dramatic effects of revolutionary contagion could be seen across the Arab world in 2010–2011, where, fueled by Facebook and other digital media platforms, revolutions jumped across national borders first from Tunisia to Egypt, and then on to Libya, Syria, Bahrain, and Yemen. Once the Tunisian revolution got going, there was no telling where it might go next or when it would stop.

Insofar as dependent states are concerned, relations with a more powerful foreign patron can have either negative consequences for the viability of domestic structures or, as the case might be, a reinforcing, positive effect. For decades, for example, the overwhelming shadow of the Soviet Union, backed up with military might under the Brezhnev Doctrine, kept together the seams of East European states and repeatedly suppressed emerging revolutions such as the ones in Hungary in 1956 and in Czechoslovakia in 1968. In the 1960s, the Kennedy administration's policy of "Alliance for Progress" was similarly designed to curtail the emergence of revolutionary circumstances in Latin America.[10] This policy of containment was once again pursued with great zeal in the 1980s under the auspices of what came to be known as the Reagan Doctrine. In speech after speech, President Reagan warned of "a mounting danger in Central America that threatens the security of the United States" and spoke of the necessity to contain it.[11] "Using Nicaragua as a base," he declared,

> the Soviets and Cubans can become the dominant power in the crucial corridor between North and South America. Established there, they will be in a position to threaten the Panama Canal, interdict our vital Caribbean sealanes and ultimately move against Mexico.[12]

The pursuit of such a foreign policy by the United States resulted in heightened American economic, diplomatic, and even military presence throughout Latin America, from Mexico down to Grenada, El Salvador, Honduras, Panama, Colombia, Chile, Brazil, and Argentina. In one way or another, whether militarily or through economic aid, American efforts in Latin America were designed to strengthen incumbent states and to stem the tide of revolutions threatening the governments of the region.[13]

The relationship between international relations and the fate of autocracies is complex and multi-dimensional. Given the book's focus, much of the discussion here revolves around the international forces that strengthen social movements and help undermine state power. But the inverse of this phenomenon can be equally powerful: Autocracies can derive great power from their international connections and, by doing so, successfully weather challenges posed to them by their own social actors. Paradoxically, despite their lofty rhetoric, Western liberal democracies have a particularly tormented history of supporting many of their authoritarian allies as they have sought desperately to cling to power.[14] But Western states are far from being the only culprits in this respect. Like birds of a feather, in moments of need friendly authoritarian leaders tend to stick together. The 2011 Arab uprisings saw the particular reinvigoration of authoritarian support networks both within the Middle East and between Middle Eastern dictators and their American, European, and Russian patrons. Saudi Arabia, for example, launched a frontal assault on the Arab Spring.[15] And, not to be left behind, Iran did what it could to prop up Bashar Assad's bloody rule during the course of Syria's civil war.

Even when international actors wish to help a social movement, they may inadvertently undermine its chances of success. International sanctions, for example, often make life more difficult for the urban middle classes and further squeeze the private sector without seriously eroding the state's ability to stay in power. This is amply evident in Iran, where the Islamic Republic state has for decades successfully withstood the force of comprehensive international sanctions as the country's middle classes have suffered.[16] Sanctions had similarly unintended consequences in Panama and Kenya, where, as Sharon Erickson Nepstad has demonstrated, they were used as neither successful nor appropriate sources of leverage over political incumbents.[17]

Turning to domestic dynamics, revolutions are brought about through a confluence of political developments and social dynamics that weaken the powers of governing incumbents and at the same time enhance the capabilities of those seeking to replace them. The political dynamics at work involve the incumbents' loss of legitimacy, coupled with a growing weakness and vulnerability of the institution and structures they have at their disposal. Equally significant are the activities of revolutionary groups aimed at exploiting these emerging exigencies and the resulting mobilization of the masses toward revolutionary goals.

A number of social and cultural conditions make revolutionary mobilization possible, be they a general sense of deprivation among various urban groups or pervasive unhappiness over prevailing economic and political circumstances. Also important are the means of access that revolutionary groups have to the general population, determined in turn by either existing social organizations or by alternative nexus that are specifically forged for this purpose.

With this in mind, it is important to remember that the key to all successful spontaneous revolutions, the catalyst that sets into motion all of the other dynamics that produce revolutionary circumstances, is the political incapacitation of the ruling elite. Revolutions are in the first order developments that result from the political crises that engulf those in power. This centrality of state power arises out of the state's control over the various instruments of political control. In authoritarian polities, the state not only has power over the army, the police, and the bureaucracy, it also controls, directly or indirectly, various aspects of economic life, including resources and services. It is also the beneficiary of many of the economic activities that occur within its national borders. In short, the state seeks to control most if not all of the essential tools and resources that enhance its powers and are necessary for the running of the country. Unless and until this control is somehow weakened and the state is made vulnerable, aspiring revolutionaries will not find sufficient space or resources with which to mount and to maintain a political takeover.

The political weakening of pre-revolutionary states can be caused by a number of developments. Most directly consequential in bringing about revolutionary situations, and by far the most common of developments weakening state power, are those with direct negative bearings on the state's institutional cohesion and organizational viability. These are developments that lead directly to the institutional weakness of the state. Developments as diverse as wars, economic bankruptcy, or the death of a central figure in a personalized system can dramatically reduce the state's continued ability to control the resources needed to stay in power. I will have more to say about these and other similar developments shortly. First, however, it is important to highlight a notion that has long been part of the study of revolutions and remains one of the central causes of state weakness, namely the state's crisis of legitimacy.

The relationship between a state's crisis of legitimacy and its institutional weakness and vulnerability is particularly strong. In fact, these two developments are frequently interrelated and reinforce one another. This relationship of mutual reinforcement assumes special importance in nondemocratic and developing states, where the very process of economic development can create crises of political legitimacy for political incumbents. As classical developmentalists argued some time ago, questioning the legitimacy of political leaders is an inevitable ramification of the intertwined processes of industrial growth, social change, and political development. The development syndrome results in a widening of gaps in popular perceptions toward political ideals versus political realities as practiced by state leaders.[18] What occurs is a "dissynchronization" between the values that political leaders uphold as compared to those commonly held among the urban middle classes.[19] More specifically, crises of political legitimacy arise when the claims of current leaders to power are based on socially unacceptable historical or ideological interpretations, when the degree of political socialization has not been sufficient to convince the people of the legitimacy of existing political arrangements, and when there is excessive and noninstitutionalized competition for power.[20] In essence, a legitimacy crisis arises out an absence of consensus over the rules of the game and what legitimate power and authority mean. Thus, any analysis of the weakness of pre-revolutionary states must necessarily examine the legitimacy crises that concurrently accompany them.

Legitimacy crisis signifies the inability of state leaders to justify their continued hold on power.[21] As mentioned earlier, legitimacy crisis is inherent to the process of development. However, a number of specific dynamics exacerbate the withdrawal of the proverbial "mandate of heaven" and heighten a sense of regime illegitimacy among the population at certain historical junctures. The state's problem is one of inability to deliver the goods promised or in demand, be they economic, political, or emotional.[22] Lack of responsiveness or political acumen by state leaders, continued and persistent demands for greater political participation or increased economic expectations by the urban classes, or a neglect or abuse of sources with symbolic importance, such as religion and nationalism, can all significantly accentuate popular perceptions about a state's illegitimate claims to power and its lack of fitness to govern. The weakness or inefficiency of state institutions also add to perceptions of illegitimacy by seemingly corrupt and incompetent leaders.

It is no accident that revolutions have historically taken place in decidedly antidemocratic, authoritarian states. Exclusionary states, which do not seek to mobilize popular support in order to justify their narrowly based sources of authority, are seen as particularly illegitimate and are most vulnerable to the outbreak of revolutions. Such states are often based on the rule of a single, all-powerful individual or a narrow ruling clan, and rely largely on three central pillars to stay in power: the security forces and intelligence services; fear among subjects of the high costs of nonconformity; and a narrow alliance of key elites held together through an intricate network of patronage and mutual economic interests. The blatant corruption of the elite that is frequently endemic to these states, the control of the economy by a few families and their conspicuous consumption, and their frequent neglect of national interests in preference over their own interests and the interests of outside patrons all combine to significantly increase the likelihood that such polities experience crises of legitimacy.[23] Nevertheless, even these narrowly based political systems can stave off revolutions if they secure the patronage of a sufficiently broad segment of the population, especially those within the urban middle classes.[24]

The relationship between political leaders and legitimacy crisis extends to more than the mere maintenance of popularly acceptable political practices and interpretations. Political leaders can significantly enhance or harm perceptions of their popular legitimacy depending on how they treat those resonant cultural symbols that are valued by the social classes. Most notably, the political leaders' neglect or offensive treatment of widely held cultural values, traditions, and religious beliefs and symbols can greatly harm the ways they are perceived by the population. In order to make their political ideologies and practices seem in line with prevailing cultural values, state leaders often interpret socially pervasive symbols in a manner that would fit their political purposes, regardless of how twisted or even offensive those interpretations may be. In particular, interpretations ascribed to specific historical episodes and to religious values, in particular, are used extensively in augmenting the legitimacy of existing political institutions and practices.

Nationalist feelings can be equally consequential in undermining the legitimacy of state leaders, especially when their rule is seen as inimical to national interests. Colonial or neocolonial relations tend to generate the most potent sense of nationalism and are most conducive to legitimacy crises for colonial powers or their local proxies. Other forms of less dependent relationships are also instrumental in causing the legitimacy of ruling elites to be questioned by heightening perceptions of their subservience to foreign powers.[25] Nationalist sentiments can be agitated through the appearance of economic and industrial subservience to a foreign country. State leaders may effectively cultivate nationalist sentiments for their own political purposes. However, the economic policies that they pursue, especially if their strategy of economic development is one of import–industrialization substitution, can give rise to sentiments of economic nationalism and undermine their legitimacy.[26] Large discrepancies between the cultural values espoused by state leaders and the sensibilities of their subjects can have similar consequences.

In addition to demands for greater political participation and the upholding of cultural values commonly seen as important, crises of legitimacy can arise out of a government's inability to meet evolving economic demands and expectations. The inability to "deliver the goods," politically and normatively, represent only two of the shortcomings that lead to legitimacy crisis. A state's inability to deliver the economic goods, those that directly affect the well-being of the population, can have even more direct bearing on its perceptions as legitimate or not. One of Theda Skocpol's early insights is worth remembering: Those countries that are in a comparatively disadvantageous economic position in the international system are more prone to revolutions.[27] Not unlike growing demands for political participation, the transitional nature of economic development breeds rising expectations, thus accentuating the legitimacy crisis of those states unable to meet such expectations.[28] In instances where "there is the continued, unimpeded opportunity to satisfy new needs, new hopes, new expectations," the legitimacy of political leaders is greatly enhanced and the probability of a revolutionary outbreak is reduced.[29] When there is widespread economic deprivation, however, whether actual or perceived, in absolute or relative terms, the likelihood of opposition to a state increases significantly, especially when the state is seen as an obstacle to continued economic mobility.[30]

Lastly, the sources and the means through which a sense of the illegitimacy of political leaders is instilled and popularized among the people is important. A general feeling of unacceptability regarding the political and ideological justifications of state elites may already exist among the population. But how are these negative sentiments given sufficient potency and direction to be usefully channeled into revolutionary agitation? The issue is not merely one of overt revolutionary mobilization. Before large-scale mass mobilization toward avowedly revolutionary goals can be achieved, and even before the social and cultural conditions conducive to mass mobilization can appear in a society, there must be voices of dissent, no matter how faint and silent, bringing to light the illegitimate premises on which the incumbents' rule is based.

The growing sense of unease with the legitimacy of the body politic is further compounded by the institutional paralysis of the political system itself. A group of politicians who are unable to deliver the political, cultural, economic, and normative goods that are in demand are considered as being even less justified in their rule when the very institutions through which they govern start to fall apart. Again, the contextual relationship between legitimacy crises and the state's institutional weaknesses are crucially important. Spontaneous revolutions, as mentioned earlier, are precipitated by institutional weaknesses within states that provide space and opportunity for expressions of dissent against the political establishment. Only after the state has already lost a substantial part of its coercive abilities due to various debilitating developments, such as military defeats or bureaucratic collapse, have revolutionary groups found an opportunity to carry forward their agendas and to gain widespread popular support. Reinforcing and in fact expediting this break-up are popular perceptions of state leaders as unfit to rule and unjust in holding on to the reins of power.

Closely related to the state's legitimacy, or lack thereof, is its institutional composition. Almost all authoritarian systems feature limited political participation, forcible political demobilization, and, often times, widespread apathy.[31] Devoid of an elaborate or guiding ideology, in such systems "a leader or occasionally a small group exercises power within formally ill-defined limits but actually quite predictable ones."[32] Moreover, in authoritarian states there is often "relatively low specificity of political institutions."[33] Most state organs in one way or another penetrate the life of society in order to suppress impulses for political expression or to forcibly incorporate social groups or institutions, such as religious or labor organizations, into the orbit of the state.

Personalist systems, in which political rule is concentrated within an individual or one family, are particularly susceptible to revolutions. Such systems tend to breed an atmosphere in which otherwise nonpolitical grievances become politicized. Those individuals or groups that are excluded from the political process and are not beneficiaries of its patronage are especially likely to blame the state for shortcomings that may or may not be political in nature, such as economic difficulties or sudden social and cultural changes that cause widespread disillusionment. Particularly in closed, authoritarian systems, political leaders see themselves as the primary protectors of the social and economic good. They behave as if they are omniscient and that all power emanates from them. Eager to ascribe to themselves all benefits accrued to their population through their rule, these leaders are similarly blamed by their public for discomforts that may not necessarily be the fault of the state. Precisely because of this overwhelming role played by the autocrat in all affairs of the country, or at least due to popular perceptions of such a role, personalist leaders represent highly visible and resented symbols of authority, targets that are not only easily identifiable but also serve to unify protestors with different grievances and from diverse backgrounds. Also important is the tendency of such regimes to valorize political opposition and, by virtue of their repressive characters, to turn even moderate opposition into radical acts of revolutionary heroism.

Autocratic, sultanistic systems that are ruled by an all-powerful ruler or a family, found in pre-revolutionary France and Russia and perhaps Iran, are few and far between. Far more common are neopatrimonial states, which are characterized by partial and skewed modernization of bureaucratic institutions and procedures that exist alongside personalist and patrimonial ones. In such systems, often times "a single powerful person rules society through an extensive system of personal patronage, rather than obedience to impersonal laws."[34] At the same time, the burgeoning state machinery is replete with ostensibly modern agencies and institutions. These neopatrimonial states are particularly vulnerable because they are often unwilling or incapable of facilitating alliances with the various elite groups, many of whom tend to be highly politicized. The loyalty of the armed forces and the elites are secured through continuous patronage, any disruption to which could jeopardize the state leaders' narrow base of support. Bereft of mass support, state leaders rely extensively, often exclusively, on small but influential elite groups to maintain power. If and when these elite groups become alienated from the state, they could potentially mobilize movements against state leaders.[35]

Neopatrimonial and other authoritarian regimes rely on what Juan Linz sees as "mentalities" in order to rule. "Mentalities," Linz argues, "are ways of thinking and feeling, more emotional than rational, that provide noncodified ways of reacting to different situations."[36] Mentalities are formless and fluctuating, best conceived of as intellectual attitudes and psychic predispositions. As such, the state seeks to depoliticize, de-ideologize, and politically demobilize its population. The state's primary objectives, in fact, are shaped and guided by two central problems. One is the problem of authoritarian control – i.e., how to rule over the people – and the other is the problem of authoritarian power-sharing. Authoritarian leaders face the challenge of not only falling out with their subjects but also of having a falling out amongst themselves. To help address these challenges, they often create an elaborate network of institutions meant to devise ways of power-sharing. Some institutions – such as parties, elections, and the armed forces – may matter more than others. Others may be merely cosmetic, designed more for symbolic consumption rather than for actual functional purposes.

Creative institutional arrangements meant to enhance durability have resulted in a proliferation of hybrid authoritarian states that feature some competitive politics. Such hybrid states, however, may be vulnerable to change because of the very same tools for political inclusion they have devised for purposes of durability.[37] Legislatures and parliamentary elections, for example, offer autocratic states a form of controlled bargaining and an opportunity for policy concessions in return for political support.[38] Controlled elections can also serve as safety valves, but they may also unwittingly empower disenchanted elites. Elections, in fact, can either lead to durable authoritarianism or to democratization opportunities.[39] Sometimes elections bring out into the open contradictions that are present but latent in authoritarian states by polarizing factional differences and tensions among different groups. In general, since institutions require regular interactions between the dictator and his allies, they can foster greater transparency, making it easier to detect the dictator's non-compliance with power-sharing arrangements.[40]

In addition to formal institutions, dictatorships often govern through creating and then manipulating cleavages between various institutions, even within various factions of the army, and are highly dependent on the loyalties they forge through patronage and manipulation.[41] Bereft of popular legitimacy, state leaders need key allies among elite groups – oligarchs and entrepreneurs, coopted intellectuals and opinion-makers, religious leaders, sports and artistic figures, and the like. Elite support is of critical importance as elites can enhance the repertoire of resources, support base, and skills available to state leaders. But even more significant is the societal base of the elite. Linkages between the elites and their constituents can be a source of constraints as well as support and power.[42] At the same time, state leaders are constantly on guard against possible conspiracies by their allies, or at least a waning of loyalties, loyalties that frequently wear thinner as crises set in. Elite defection is one of the first signs of state trouble. Revolutions, in fact, become likely when multi-elite coalitions appear that oppose the state.[43] Combined with the sovereign's loss of legitimacy and popular unrest, the defection of the state by its elite allies makes its breakdown nearly inevitable.[44]

In all dictatorships, regardless of their precise makeup, institutions will be ineffective or will breakdown if not backed by credible use of force.[45] In fact, compared to all the other dimensions of authoritarian rule discussed here – international dynamics, legitimacy crisis, elite cohesion, and institutional configuration and efficacy – the position of the armed forces is the most consequential factor in the durability or collapse of the regime. The response of the armed forces to an uprising is critical in determining the success or failure of the uprising. In fact, no matter how massive or widespread, no insurrection is likely to succeed when confronted with the full strength of the military. As social movements grow and evolve into something bigger, the army's disposition toward the revolution becomes the most important predictor of the revolution's outcome, with the military's support being a necessary, if not sufficient, condition for the success of the revolution.[46]

Militaries are likely to either support uprisings, suppress them, or be split by them. In his study of how militaries respond to revolutions, Zoltan Barany maintains that the response of the military to an uprising depends on factors such as the military's internal cohesion; its composition from volunteer versus conscript soldiers; the state's treatment of the military; the generals' view of state legitimacy; the size, composition, and nature of protests; and the potential for foreign intervention.[47] To these we can also add the commercial interests and economic strength of the armed forces. Ultimately, then, the military's actions are driven by its interests and its composition. If the armed forces have a unified command structure and their rank-and-file are not riven by multiple ethnic or other divisions, the military's response is determined by its corporate interests: Defection from state leaders or sticking with them depends on what the military determines to be in its institutional, political, and economic interests. If the military lacks a corporate structure and its esprit de corps is weak, either because of its reliance on conscript soldiers or because its top commanders have divided loyalties, then the military is likely to either crumble and disintegrate or to splinter into smaller armies.

In his comparative study of Egypt and Syria, Joshua Stacker has shown that pre-uprising levels of power centralization are key to explaining different state responses to popular uprisings. In Egypt, political power within the state was centralized, and therefore the transition that ensued was smooth. All political power was concentrated within a narrow inner circle clustered around the family of President Hosni Mubarak, who ruled through an extensive neopatrimonial network of patronage and clientelism, backed up by police suppression and fear. The army, meanwhile, remained united and cohesive, had strong corporate interests given its multiple and lucrative commercial revenue streams, and exhibited a strong esprit de corps. When the wave of popular protests hit, the army broke away from President Mubarak in order to protect its interests, leaving the presidency and its patronage network without the protection they needed to stay in power. Although not part of Stacker's study, the very same process unfolded in Tunisia as well.

In Syria, by contrast, state power was diffuse and decentralized, spread among a number of institutions in which elite allies of President Bashar Assad had vested interests. When popular protests erupted in March 2011 and quickly gathered pace, elites coalesced to protect their interests. The army's high command did not defect, seeing the uprising as inimical to its interests. The state, or whatever of it remains after years of bloodbath, remains largely intact. The outcome of the Syria transition has therefore been anything but smooth, so much so that the social movement ended up in a civil war.[48]

The armed forces tend to respond differently in cases where they actually run the state and control its various institutions. Unlike most other nondemocratic states, military dictatorships are not as readily susceptible to revolutions, although they are inherently just as unstable politically. Institutionally, the precise roles of the armed forces and the security services are central to the survival of different authoritarian states. In all nondemocracies, repressive institutions such as the military and the police are central to maintaining the political status quo. In fact, coercive institutions in such systems tend to be among the most sophisticated and organizationally viable of the state's organs.[49] Nevertheless, in military dictatorships, the police and the army are often more capable of supporting the political order in times of crisis and turmoil than they are in personalized systems. This discrepancy in the effectiveness of coercive institutions in maintaining the status quo arises out of the different structural relationships they have with the various governing bodies. In bureaucratic and military dictatorships, the army and the police are often the very institutions that occupy the seat of power and themselves form the state elite. Even if not directly part of the establishment themselves, the relationship between these institutions and the ruling elite is at a much more intimate level than is the case in personalized systems. There is thus a lot more at stake for them in ensuring the survival of the political order than might otherwise be the case.

We see different elements of state breakdown and vulnerability in the various historical cases in which spontaneous revolutions have occurred. Not all dynamics discussed previously were present in all prerevolutionary states, and contextual differences account for significant variations from one case to another. Nevertheless, in all cases we see parallel developments starting with stresses on the state that result in an opening of political space, followed by missteps by state leaders in responding to the brewing crisis – or not responding at all – followed by and reinforced through steady institutional atrophy, elite defections, and, in most instances, decisive action by the military.

In France, the dismantling of royal authority was slow and gradual though steady. The immediate causes of the French revolution were the crown's economic bankruptcy and ill-fated attempts to reform the administration.[50] In the years leading up to the revolution, the state had experienced repeated strains arising out of rapid population growth, drought, and foreign military adventures. The population had shot up from 18 million inhabitants in 1715 to 26 million in 1789. This population rise was the greatest among the rural and the urban poor. The state's finances were further stressed due a series of droughts, and also competition in the textile industry, despite the fact that French industry was experiencing a period of growth.

The state, or more accurately the royal court, meanwhile, remained ill-equipped and incapable of handling the approaching crisis. The king and the queen were neither politically savvy nor popular. As one observer has noted,

> Louis XVI was not a great king: kindly, devout, no lady's man, bored with politics, sleeping at Council, he was more interested in clocks and in his passion for food and the chase … He was also to show both weakness and strength at just the wrong moments. He lacked political judgement.[51]

Intrigue and scandals among the nobility and irresponsible courtiers only further weakened the royal court.

Although the king remained personally popular, by the time the revolution approached, the monarchy, and even its spiritual pillar the church, had both become largely devoid of legitimacy. As protests grew in frequency, the state saw itself defected by some of its traditional allies, especially the nobility. Some nobles, fearing a loss of privilege and hoping to preserve whatever they could, defected from the regime and actually joined the revolution. Many simply packed up and left France, abandoning the monarchy at a time when their support was needed the most. In the summer of 1789, French authorities issued some 200,000 passports, mostly to the nobility, who were streaming out of the country as the revolution was gathering steam.[52]

The collapse of royal authority was steady, and relatively rapid. On July 14, 1789, a crowd stormed the Bastille, long a symbol of royal despotism.[53] That same summer a new Parisian government formed a force of citizen-soldiers, called the National Guard, to "ensure and protect property." Soon the king recognized the National Guard, effectively ending royal authority in the capital.[54] Food riots broke out in October amid persistent rumors that the king would either mount a coup to crush the revolution and roll back its gains or escape from the Versailles Palace. A large crowd of about 7,000 marched on Versailles and forced the king to accompany them to Paris on October 6. What came to be known as the October Days appeared to have significantly pushed the revolution forward.[55] By now the revolution appeared to have reached a point of no return. As royal authority crumbled, it was steadily replaced by institutions evolving out of the revolution itself.

Developments in the summer of 1789 transformed the political landscape beyond anyone's expectations. No one had foreseen the outcome when the king initially made the decision to call elections to the Estates General.[56] It took another two years for the monarchy's collapse to take place, punctuated in June 1791 by a desperate attempt by King Louis XVI to save his family by escaping from Paris, resulting in his capture and further humiliation. By the time the ill-fated Flight to Varennes occurred, the days both of the monarchy and of the lives of the king and queen were numbered.

Similar to France, Russia experienced rapid economic growth in the three decades before the 1917 revolution. At the same time, the conditions of the Russian peasantry steadily deteriorated and in fact became dire.[57] As the intelligentsia zeroed in on the misery of the peasantry as a rallying cry against Tsarist rule, developments both exogenous to the system and within the system itself hastened its demise. Perhaps the biggest shock came in the form of the humiliating military defeat in the 1905 Russo-Japanese war, from which the Tsarist regime never quite recovered. After 1905, the Tsar became increasingly distant from the rest of society, his image of "little father" steadily eroding among his loyal subjects.[58] All the meanwhile, thanks to the indiscretions of others in the royal household, especially the queen and the soothsayer Rasputin, the reputation of the Romanovs was even more tarnished and Tsarist legitimacy further undermined.

This loss of legitimacy, as we shall see more fully soon, was further deepened through uneven and skewed processes of social change. Russia's urban society featured what one scholar has called a "schizoid nature," with some characteristics that can be described as "modern" and some ultraconservative.[59] This provided a fertile breeding ground for the Russian intelligentsia, which was often Western educated, alienated from the rest of Russian society, and often radical. The more radical elements of the intelligentsia connected with the working classes, whose peasant background – many having been former peasants who had only recently joined the industrial workforce – made them receptive to militant ideologies. As we saw in the last chapter, this helped the Bolsheviks attract more support among the working classes, especially between 1910 and 1914, as compared to their main competitor, the Mensheviks.

The humiliation of the 1905 war, meanwhile, forced the Russian government to make a number of concessions, including the convening of the parliament, the Duma, whose work Tsar Nicholas II did everything to undermine and obstruct. Reforms, when they are meaningful enough to address the underlying cause of popular grievances, can serve to abort revolutions. But when reforms are superficial and only enable political opponents to more effectively articulate their sentiments and to attract more supporters, they expedite revolutions. The Tsar's superficial reforms only helped to push the revolution further along. After the 1905 war, Nicholas not only gave in to the establishment of the Duma, he also allowed the creation of political parties and trade unions. That is where his flexibility ended. Adaptability helps autocrats maintain power. But that was not the case with the Tsarist state. By the time the Great War erupted, the Russian autocracy was in a highly precarious condition, its bureaucratic structure highly fragile and strained, and the state "vulnerable to any kind of jolt or setback."[60]

The war, and the disintegration of the Tsarist army as the war progressed, was the state's death knell. The Tsarist state's final collapse, in February 1917, ushered in a situation of "dual power" among competing heirs to the post-revolutionary era. But dual power was only illusory as it masked a real power vacuum. The popular revolution, in the meantime, was becoming increasingly more radical. It was only a matter of time before the Bolsheviks wrested control over the unfolding revolution through their October putsch.

The monarchy's collapse in Iran followed along similar lines. In the 1970s the Shah became increasingly distant from his subjects, and his attempts at enhancing the operations and legitimacy of the state, such as the 1975 establishment of the official Rastakhiz Party or the anti-profiteering campaign of the same year, only further alienated and antagonized the urban middle classes.[61] The monarchical state had little understanding of the society over which it ruled and even fewer answers to its multiple social ills. As rapid social and economic change created dissonances in Iranian society and heightened rural–urban migration, unemployment, and cultural alienation, the state came to rely more and more on the secret services to stifle dissent, convinced that before long Iranians would come to see the wisdom of the state's "march toward Great Civilization."[62] Superficial reforms, such as greater media freedom and futile, at times comical, efforts to make the ruling family seem more accessible to the general public only helped further fuel popular anger and the spread of anti-government demonstrations from one city to another. The army, meanwhile, comprised of conscript soldiers, experienced desertions of no less than 1,000 to 1,200 walkouts a day, crumbling like a house of cards.[63] On January 18, 1979, sensing that his time was up, the Shah left Iran, never to come back. Within weeks, the monarchical state, already in tatters, experienced a total collapse.

Similar to the Shah's reign, the steady crumbling of Ben Ali's rule in Tunisia and Mubarak's in Egypt began at the very top. Also similar to Iran, in both Tunisia and Egypt the years preceding the revolution had witnessed astounding growth in the powers and pervasiveness of the security services throughout the various echelons of the state and across most social institutions.[64] In the process, in both countries the army underwent increasing degrees of depoliticization, focusing on enhancing its professionalism and, especially in Egypt, deepening its corporate interests through involvement in a myriad of economic sectors and industries. When the wave of popular protests hit, the two militaries had a simple choice to make: remain loyal to the ruler and risk the consequences of an open-ended mass movement, or side with the protestors and abandon the costly affiliation with highly despised leaders. Both opted for the latter option. And once they did, there was nothing that Ben Ali or Mubarak could do to save their rule. In the process, both militaries emerged as beloved, national institutions that had acted to protect the aspirations of millions of people. As history would have it, the people's love affair with the Egyptian military waned quickly after 2013, when General Abdel Fattah el-Sisi bloodily suppressed mass demonstrations and launched a coup to take over power.

Social Movements

When political challenges and opportunities allow for it, people engage in contentious politics. By taking part in collective action, people can create new opportunities and widen the space for a cycle of contestation. When they can build on cultural symbols, construct dense social networks and "connective structures," and when their struggles revolve around broad cleavages in society, that is when people are engaged in a social movement.[65] Commonly referred to as *people power*, this form of collective action has also been variously labeled as "civil resistance" or "unarmed insurrection."[66] My preference here has been to employ the concept of *social movement* to refer to popular forms of collective action that are inspired by one or more political objectives and are driven by dynamics that are both internal to the movement and are exogenous, such as state reactions, elite defections, and intersocietal connections. They are initially largely nonviolent, involve mobilization at the local level, and provide space and opportunity for acts of political defiance and nonconformity. Although social movements do not always grow into something bigger, all spontaneous revolutions start out as social movements.

Precisely when or why social movements break out are difficult to predict as people tend to falsify their preferences both before and after engaging in contentious politics. As Timur Kuran has argued, "Before a revolution, preference falsification conceals the potential for a successful revolt."[67] Nevertheless, the appearance of several successive developments in spontaneous revolutions, in roughly the same order, is difficult to discount. Crises of legitimacy undermine the state's ability to justify its sources of authority and its continued hold on power, compelling it to rely more and more on brute force. Political challenges and difficulties, often precipitated by economic exigencies, push the state toward opening the political space in order to mollify some of the social pressures from below, only to inadvertently fan the flames of what is emerging as a popular uprising. Along with state breakdown, or at least state vulnerability, the other key dimension of spontaneous revolutions is the eruption of a social movement, one that then mushrooms into a full-scale uprising.

The state's crisis of legitimacy is based on the perception that the current political values and practices on which the state relies are not legitimate, whereas some other alternatives are. It is more than coincidental that almost all legitimacy crises that precede revolutions occur along with a general "intellectual rebelliousness," a series of ideas that criticize the normative status quo and propose alternatives. The proliferation of intellectual activities that occurred before the revolutions in France, Russia, Cuba,[68] Iran,[69] and Hungary,[70] to mention a few, all had the effect of heightening popular perceptions of illegitimacy attributed to incumbent states. All too often, these sudden outbursts of intellectual activism are scattered, unorganized, and uncoordinated, without a coherent doctrine or theoretical framework emerging until sometime later. But they do contribute to a general atmosphere in which the state and its leaders find it increasingly difficult to sell their own ideas and to justify their paternalistic approach to society. Revolutions by definition question and disrupt tradition and authority, and among the first values questioned are traditional and existing sources of authority.

In France, in the 1700s, *salons* grew in numbers and became gathering places for discussion and debate, especially among the more abstract and philosophically minded *philosophes* and the more practical *physiocrats*. Much of the writings of the early *philosophes* was a literature of protest. Many criticized clerical intolerance, and, steadily, anticlericalism became widespread. Cumulatively, such writings and the resulting "ferment of ideas" inspired "a general spirit of criticism hostile to existing institutions."[71] This pervasive spirit of debate did not always mean democracy. Rousseau's *Social Contract*, for example, was not widely read before 1789.[72]

Tsarist Russia also had its own revolution of ideas in the 1910s, expressed mostly through a highly amorphous literary movement. Ideas that purported to forward scientific progress and questioned superstition and backwardness became particularly appealing among the more educated strata of the middle classes. Not surprisingly, Bolshevik "scientific Marxism" fit extremely well with the cultural and political tenor of late imperial Russia.[73] A similar intellectual movement of sorts occurred in Iran in the 1970s, inspired mostly by the African liberation movements of the 1960s, and, at the same time, seeking to inject a more revolutionary spirit into Islam.[74]

Intellectual movements reinforce and provide the larger cultural contexts within which social movements occur. According to Sidney Tarrow, social movements are a form of contentious politics that "are backed by well-structured social networks and galvanized by culturally-resonant, action-oriented symbols [that] lead to sustained interaction with opponents."[75] They are based on common purposes and social solidarities. Social movements combine three claims – program, identity, and standing – and they help assert popular sovereignty.[76] Moreover, once established in one setting, social movements can be adapted and adopted in other settings, and therefore their form and personnel can vary and evolve over time.[77] Those who take part in social movements not only demand change, but also operate within the context of "inherited understandings and ways of doing things." They operate on "the boundaries of constituted politics, culture, and institutions."[78]

Social movements are often influenced by the interactions between those involved in it and the state, as well as by the larger institutional context (e.g., firms, schools, places of worship, etc.) within which they take place.[79]

Social movements create moments of great enthusiasm, when what was once impossible is now both possible and, in fact, probable, when thanks to the power of the crowd, the crumbling image of the once invincible despot has made the present historic moment possible. Social movements and citizenship are intimately connected. In social movements, conceptions of citizenship, often implied and unspoken, are broadened so as to become inclusive as well as active and empowered. The individual is no longer a mere recipient of state power. "I am a citizen" means I can control my own destiny – *I am empowered.*

This sense of empower often bestows social movements with a self-perpetuating dynamic. To begin with, as compared with other, especially more violent forms of political activism, the moral, physical, informational, and commitment barriers to participation tend to be much lower in social movements. This "participation advantage" is reinforced by a number of internal mechanisms that reinforce solidarity within social movements and help their success, including enhanced resilience, higher probabilities of tactical innovation, expanded civic disruption, and loyalty shifts among state supporters.[80] Ironically, state repression against an expanding social movement, especially if that social movement is at first avowedly nonviolent, could potentially backfire as it often expedites elite defections and provides the movement's emerging leaders with a larger menu of tactical and strategic choices.[81]

Social movements can, nevertheless, mutate into some other form of politics, or disappear altogether. While mobilization at the local level is often a more reliable source of power, movements that cannot overcome the challenges of participation are likely to peter out and fail.[82] Social movements initially appear because of favorable structural conditions. Once they get underway, it is largely strategic factors – namely the tactics and maneuvers employed by activists and by the state, and also by their respective outside supporters – that shape their outcomes.[83] More specifically, the trajectory of social movements depends on the extent to which they can undermine state capacity, the internal dynamics that shape their cohesion and group solidarity, and the external influences that produce shifts in the balance of power between state and society.[84] Pervasive state repression or its absence are, of course, critical factors as they determine the opportunities or the risks and costs associated with activism. But factors internal to the movement itself, and the broader context within which it emerges and develops, can also significantly influence its expansion into something bigger or its devolution.

In spontaneous revolutions, social movements grow into full scale, mass-based rebellions. But even before that happens, for a social movement to sustain itself it needs political entrepreneurs who would expand its scale and ensure its durability and effectiveness. Actors must find ways of organizing themselves and sustaining their mobilization through reliance on existing social networks and building internal capacity.[85] The relationship between social movements and their leaders is complex and often paradoxical. On the one hand, social movements can provide opportunities for individuals with greater ambitions, or better resources and opportunities, to be propelled into positions of leadership. Aspiring leaders, in fact, can create social movements if they tap into and expand deep-rooted feelings of solidarity and identity.[86] On the other hand, social movements can sweep aside and overwhelm the very people who seek to lead them. Moments of enthusiasm make heroes out of ordinary individuals. But of these heroes only a few survive, victim to either the wrath of the state, or to competition with other aspiring leaders, or both. Revolutions, as the next chapter starkly reminds us, all too often devour their children.

One of the central resources that propel individuals into positions of leadership is access to social institutions through which they can connect with potential followers, be they *salons* in France in the 1780s or mosques in Iran in the 1970s. These social institutions are often important sources of information and networked connections. As events unfold rapidly and the flow of information is often nonexistent or opaque at best, average participants in the movement find it challenging to develop appropriate strategies for furthering their objectives.[87] Access to information, and therefore the ability to strategize accordingly, is often one of the leaders' greatest assets.

By the time the twenty-first century rolled around, *salons* had given way to virtual space. In recent years, the spread of social media has facilitated the formation of demands, their spread, and the mobilization of the masses. As the 2011 Arab uprisings demonstrated, social media and communications technology help facilitate the emergence of virtual networks that enable activists to communicate and mobilize. Social media has made mobilization broader, but also less predictable.[88]

By all accounts, social media played a critical role in the astonishingly rapid spread of social movements in Tunisia, Egypt, and elsewhere in the Middle East. Linda Herrera's insightful account of how a Facebook page, named after one of the victims of the Egyptian state security, spearheaded anti-Mubarak protests is worth retelling here:

> In the wake of Tunisia's revolution, the "We Are All Khaled Said" Facebook page issued a call for an event, the "January 25 Revolution," which was to be Egypt's own revolution. The page did not cause the revolution, and youth of the internet (*Shabab al-internet*) were not the only groups active in it, but it is hard to imagine the revolt being put into motion without, firstly, the Tunisian revolution, and, secondly, the changing political culture, mentality, and networked behavior of Egypt's wired youth.[89]

Today's Middle Eastern youth, as Herrera correctly observes, "has experienced exponential rates of connectivity while suffering from systematic disenfranchisement, especially when it comes to the institutions of the state and the economy."[90] Prior to the Arab Spring, the countries of the Middle East had experienced a digital "cultural spring" of sorts. The example of Egypt prior to the country's 2011 revolution is instructive. With a population of approximately 83 million, the country's internet users went from a mere 300,000 in 2000 to 6,000,000 in 2006, 10,500,000 in 2007, and more than 17,000,000 in 2010.[91] For its part, the US State Department sought to make the most of the digital explosion in the Middle East as a tool to expand US interests in the region, in 2008 launching an initiative called the Alliance of Youth Movement (YAM). In the process, the American initiative expedited, both deliberately and inadvertently, the political potency of the internet as a supposedly "democratic society."[92]

Exactly when and how social movements grow into something bigger and more lethal is as difficult to predict as is the initial appearance of a social movement. During social movements, the first time the word "revolution" is used it is often for symbolic purposes, more a metaphor than an actual blueprint for what is about to happen. It is used not so much to arouse passions for a better, ideal future, but to evoke symbolism, sometimes mockingly, sometimes as a historical reference. It is only slowly that the word gets widespread currency, develops actual and temporal meaning, and begins to refer to an actual process and an objective endgame rather than a symbolically evocative but substantively hollow figure of speech. In Egypt, a Facebook page called "The Revolution of Silence" was at first mocked when it was initially set up. Until it wasn't irrelevant any more.[93] The initial hesitation by Wael Ghonim, a well-known internet activist in Egypt's 2011 uprising, to use of the word *revolution* was shared by many others like him. "I found myself unable to resist the word *revolution*," he wrote in 2012.

> Every time I attempted to steer away from it in my thoughts it kept coming back. The decaying regime had become Egypt's main problem, and the only way forward was to remove it. This was ironic, given that I had clearly stated on more than one occasion that I was not a revolutionary.[94]

As *social* actors become *revolutionary* actors, state leaders tend to remain completely detached from and unaware of the reality unfolding around them. In Iran in the late 1970s and in Egypt, Libya, Bahrain, and Syria in 2010–2011, state leaders dismissed the people's anger as the machinations of provocateurs and foreign governments, a negligence of the people's grievances that was only at their own peril. The more politicians ignore popular grievances, or dismisses them as the work of foreign agents, the more determined people become to press their case.

Gradually, a revolutionary narrative emerges, a storyline that captures the sense of angst, a collective unease as "perceptions accumulate that something has 'gone wrong.'"[95] Just as power takes many forms and has many "capillaries," so does resistance: "It forms part of the narrative of everyday life that gives meaning to encounters with power."[96] Eric Selbin captures this in what he calls "stories":

> stories of resistance, rebellion, and revolution, the tales that are told (and retold), the songs that are sung or played, or the places or objects that are shown, quietly, confidently, with commitment and conviction and, sometimes, but not always, with passion or something even harder to describe but which anyone who has talked to someone who has been involved in the revolutionary process has seen, heard, and felt: an expression on someone's face, a swell or catch in their voice, a shift in posture, a gesture with head or hands, perhaps a lapse into silence in reverie or frustration, of sorts, at trying to convey to the interloper something so profound.[97]

Selbin continues:

> Revolution does not occur without the articulation of compelling stories that enable, ennoble, and empower people who seek to change the material and ideological conditions of their lives. People draw on the past to explain the present and predict the future, forecast a future predicated on the present and refashion the past as necessary to fit the exigencies they face. The result is an array of stories which compete to become the story of the moment, a process in which people rely on a complicated and complex combination of myth, memories, and mimesis which they use – consciously or not – to tell a story of who they are and where they have been, of who and where they are now, of who and where they want to go and be, and of how they will get there.[98]

Stories and narratives are precursors to ideologies. By and large, in spontaneous revolutions ideologies do not become clear until after the revolution's "leaders" have emerged and have taken charge of the revolutionary narrative. If initially there is an ideology that guides the uprising, it is a negation of the status quo: Everyone knows they are united in their condemnation of the current crop of leaders, their policies, and the institutions through which they rule.[99] But an alternative ideology, a blueprint for the politics of the post-revolutionary era, they do not have. When such ideologies do emerge and capture the imagination of the mobilized masses – Puritanism, Jacobinism, constitutionalism, variations of communism, and Islamic fundamentalism – they all share a number of broad themes around which revolutionary coalitions unite: rectification of the current circumstances, more equitable redistribution of goods and services, and nationalism.[100]

More common than ideologies are *slogans*, catchy phrases that capture the mood of the masses, and increasingly their rage, without necessarily offering a how-to or a sober assessment of the day-after. But slogans are important because they are vague enough to attract broad spectrums of societal groups: "peace and land" in Russia, "Somoza must go" in Nicaragua, and "death to the Shah" in Iran.[101] In the Arab Spring, the slogan that traveled from one country to the next was "the people want to bring down the regime."

Slogans also serve to build coalition, tenuous at first and built around a negative of what ought not to be rather than united by a common vision of the future, but a *revolutionary* coalition nonetheless. Before long, "opposition groups" begin to coalesce around what is by now a full-blown mass uprising. This is occurring at a time of increasing defections of the state by elites who see it in their interests to abandon rather than to stay with the regime. In France, what began as an aristocratic protest movement out of fear of losing privileges soon developed into a cross-elite coalition, propelled forward by ideological commitments forged by academics, philosophical societies, and Masonic lodges, which demanded equal representation for the commoners.[102] Similarly, in Nicaragua in 1977 a group of radical entrepreneurs and clergy formed the Group of 12 (G12), and steadily came to represent an alternative authority structure that provided support to the anti-Somoza alliance.[103]

As this is occurring, we see the emergence of what John Foran calls a "political culture of opposition and resistance," one in which "broad segments of many groups and classes must be able to articulate the experiences they are living through into effective and flexible analyses capable of mobilizing their own forces and building coalitions with others."[104] This political culture of opposition, along with the networks of activists to which it gives rise, facilitates the birth of "groups that are highly organized at the outset of the revolutionary crisis, and can more effectively deploy their resources to take advantage of opportunities" that present themselves. These regime opponents "have a better chance of defeating other contending groups. In addition, groups that develop an attractive, synthetic ideology are likely to gain resources and supporters. In particular, radical and nationalist ideologies are liable to be more successful in this regard than moderate, merely formal rectification programs."[105]

Protests become widespread, frequent, and often uncontrollable through conventional military means. Reflecting back on the country's Arab Spring, one Tunisian activist recalled how he and his fellow protestors "felt it necessary to inform, mobilize and counter State propaganda all at the same time so the protestors in Sidi Bouzid would not find themselves alone and vulnerable."[106] Such activists are moved by a sense of the possible. Courage and hope replace fear and cowardice. The same Tunisian activist recorded the following:

> I experienced moments of epic heroism by students, union members and female activists as they confronted the clubs and

> sticks of the thuggish police . . . In the eyes of my fellow citizens I saw an extraordinary determination to confront the forces of repression. I got the feeling that I was witnessing a movement that – as no other before – would shake the regime to its foundations. The protestors' eyes gleamed with resolve and courage, their raised palms and V-signs waved tirelessly and their throats bellowed out the slogans of freedom and dignity.[107]

By the end of 2010, the Egyptians' hope and sense of the possible was equally compelling. As Wael Ghonim, one of the hero activists of the Egyptian uprising, recorded at the time,

> Today empowered young Egyptians know that they are capable of shaping the future of their country, truly believing that it is *theirs*.[108]

A spirit of cooperation also becomes pervasive: "We worked in a wonderfully sharing atmosphere and the way we complemented each other was truly incredible."[109] Before long, fallen comrades become "martyrs" for what by now had become a revolutionary cause. In Tunisia, soon slogans recalled the fallen: "The martyr has left his will: never abandon the cause."[110]

Culture and ideology are important because they help explain why some groups and elites come together during revolutionary periods and others do not. Political activists often cluster around a perceived "leader," a savior, someone who says the right things, has the right background and credentials, and, most importantly, has the best access to means of communication with the broader masses, be they mosques and cassette tapes in Iran or the internet and the social media in Tunisia and Egypt. In most cases, the emergence of a revolutionary hero, someone who personifies the hopes and aspirations of the protesting masses and represents the best chance of ushering in a new tomorrow, is only a matter of time. Given the pervasiveness of state repression and the constrained and charged circumstances within which regime opposition takes place, the personalization of the opposition, or at least the emergence of an opposition hero to the state, is almost inevitable. According to Foran, "Rapid modernization and autocratic repression cut the intelligentsia off from society; the intelligentsia become oppositional though dogmatic and rigid, highly sectarian and polarized, and in the end personalistically organized around a leader."[111]

In Poland in the late 1980s that hero was the union organizer Lech Walesa. In Czechoslovakia it was the playwright Vaclav Havel. In Iran it was the cleric Ayatollah Ruhollah Khomeini. And in Egypt it was the diplomat Mohamed ElBaradei. As with most other aspects of spontaneous revolutions, who emerges and who remains as the revolutions' leaders are hard to predict. Walesa, Havel, and Khomeini ended up being not just leaders of the popular uprising but also victors in the post-revolutionary era; ElBaradei did not. And, as it happened, most of Nicaragua's Group of 12 fell out of favor with the Sandanista leadership and were soon sidelined or left the country.

Spontaneous revolutions are often helped along and are triggered by a catalytic event. In France, there appear to have been several such catalytic events: the storming of the Bastille; the mass gathering at Versailles in October 1789, when the king and queen were forced to travel to Paris; and the royal family's ill-fated escape attempt in 1791. A devastating earthquake in Nicaragua in 1972 had exposed the depth of the Samoza regime's incompetence and the scale of corruption that permeated it. An equally disastrous earthquake in Iran in September 1978 had much the same affect. Also in Iran, an ill-advised article in January 1978 in one of the country's most widely read newspapers identified Khomeini by name and propelled him to the leadership of the movement that was brewing. The article, written by someone at the royal court, was meant to discredit Khomeini as an archaic reactionary, but it had the exact opposite effect. In Tunisia it was the self-immolation of the Mohammed Buazizi in December 2010 that led to the resignation of President Zein el Abidin Ben Ali less than a month later. And in Egypt, it was the circulation on the internet and social media of the bloodied, mutilated body of Khaled Mohamed Said, a young internet activist who had been beaten to death by the police in Alexandria, that set into motion the country's version of the Arab Spring.[112] Revolutions, invariably, "generate knock-on effects that spread well beyond their point of instigation."[113] On January 14, 2011, the day after Ben Ali fled Tunisia, open calls for a "revolution" became widespread in Egypt.[114]

Conclusion

Spontaneous revolutions initially have neither a plan nor even leaders, and grow, if allowed by circumstances and by the state's response, from an accumulation of collective displays of anger and frustration against political targets. What we have is the gradual but steady emergence of revolutionary populism that appeals to and reinforces mass sentiments about economic mismanagement, corruption, redistributive politics, egalitarianism, and nationalism. There is an unmooring of society, whether through social change, relative depravation, feelings of despair and hopelessness, and a general sense of unease and unhappiness, deepened through and in turn reinforcing frequent eruptions of wildcat strikes and protests. What occurs is the capture of these amorphous, scattered feeling by a group well positioned to articulate, focus, and politically channel them.

The state, meanwhile, often has a discourse of authoritarian nationalism, and places great emphasis on law and order. State leaders try to capitalize on those facets of popular culture that they see as politically salient and beneficial, but seldom do they gain much political capital by doing so. The message is increasingly hollow and void of social resonance, their rule bereft of legitimacy. They have coercion and fear to rely on. And once the wall of fear cracks, their days are numbered.

Political aspirants, particularly those who find themselves as a more cohesively defined "political opposition," make use of what is available to them in the cultural resource pool. If they have the right resources – a social message that resonates widely among the people, access to means of communications through social institutions or old and new media, and the ability to evade state censure and repression at least long enough until they become untouchable – then they have the best chances of emerging as the revolution's leaders.

During revolutionary times, prevailing circumstances can change quickly and in unforeseen directions, and with them so do the fortunes of those riding the revolutionary wave. Today's leaders may be tomorrow's outcasts, heroes one day villains the next. Revolutions are not for the faint of heart, and the fainthearted and the idealists unwilling to use force to outmuscle opponents are likely to be the first ones purged.

As some of the spontaneous revolutions of the late twentieth century showed, not all have to necessarily end up in a reign of terror. In the late 1980s in Eastern Europe, in the early 1990s in South Africa, and in Tunisia in 2010–2011, pre-revolutionary states weakened, and social movements appeared, gathered steam, and became revolutions. But the outcome was far from the brutal elimination of former comrades that we saw in post-revolutionary France, Russia, Iran, and Egypt. The revolutions of Eastern Europe, South Africa, and Tunisia empowered society enough to challenge the regime but not to overthrow it. At the same time, the pre-revolutionary state in each was weakened just enough not to be able to ignore popular demands for change. So the revolution was settled in a most unrevolutionary way, through negotiations and elections.

Spontaneous revolutions are mass movements that unleash popular and populist forces, whose containment frequently requires resort to massive force and repression in the post-revolutionary era, as new state leaders seek to consolidate power, eliminate rivals, and impose their own vision of the ideal polity. But sometimes, when the state retains enough power to still enforce law and order and to dictate the tempo of political life, the revolutionary transition is necessarily less chaotic, less violent, less brutal. It requires dialogue and compromise by state leaders willing to compromise in order to salvage some possible advantages, and by revolutionary leaders for whom the bitter pill of talking to state leaders offers the only viable means of capturing political power. In such a scenario, in which we have negotiated transitions, the outcome involves little or no violence, with the elimination of opponents taking place through the ballot box, or around the negotiating table, rather than through purges, the guillotine, or firing squads.[115]

The non-ideological character of these negotiated revolutions, and their focus on and preoccupation with establishing inclusive practical political arrangements, enable them to avoid the patterns of domestic and international terror, counter-revolution, and anarchy and war that are so common to spontaneous and planned revolutions. Instead, the most likely outcome of negotiated revolutions so far have been political systems that are largely liberal democratic, feature economic liberalization and privatization, have relatively free media and educational systems, and uphold social equality.[116] Spontaneous revolutions, if they don't end up in a reign of terror, are likely to end up in a democracy of sorts, of the kind we see today in eastern Europe, South Africa, South America, and Tunisia.

4 REVOLUTIONARY STATES

Revolutions give rise to popular euphoria, to collective displays of heroism and courage, and to the release of mass energies long suppressed by autocrats and their cronies who are now on the run. Quite often, in the days following the revolution's victory, mob rule reigns. Old laws have been broken but new ones haven't been devised yet. There is chaos everywhere. Local youths, some with dubious pasts and suspect intentions, organize themselves into neighborhood governing units. The day after – the day that many dreamt about but few actually imagined – has finally arrived, and few know what to do with it. Invariably, sheer force is applied to restore law and order. Who applies that force, and how they go about doing so, is the subject of this chapter.

More broadly, the chapter explores the question of what happens when revolutions succeed. The focus here is on planned and spontaneous revolutions, whose end and success are more nebulous as compared to negotiated revolutions, which invariably result in controlled transitions that culminate in elections. As George Lawson observes, negotiated revolutions, which arise out of state weakness instead of state collapse, often entail "festivals of hope" instead of "festivals of violence," are concerned with non-ideological compromise and consensus instead of pursuing a utopia, and feature roundtables instead of guillotines.[1] In negotiated revolutions, elections determine who leads the new state. But that determination is far less clear in other revolutions, especially in spontaneous ones, in which the revolution's leaders do not emerge until after the revolutionary process is well underway.

Before examining how post-revolutionary leaders go about institutionalizing their powers, it is important to consider the question of when revolutions actually end. Any discussion of post-revolutionary states must necessarily entail an examination of the point at which revolutions are thought to have succeeded. This is a risky venture, for the success of a revolution is, by its very nature, elusive and almost impossible to pinpoint. The question of exactly when revolutions succeed is complicated by the proclamations of new political leaders and actors who frequently claim to have accomplished one revolutionary goal after another. For the vast majority of leaders of post-revolutionary states, particularly those who took active part in the revolutionary struggle, the revolution never ends. Whether due to political prudence or a matter of genuine commitment, for the likes of Lenin, Mao, and Khomeini the end of the revolution never came, the fruition of their ultimate dreams and ideals having been superseded by their own deaths.[2] Fidel Castro's fiery speeches and his unendingly passionate stewardship of Cuba epitomized more than just bombastic rhetoric. They give insight into his conviction that the Cuban revolution continued decades after he came to power. Historians may choose different dates to denote the end of one era and the start of another. But at least as far as revolutionary leaders are concerned, revolutions never end. It is often only with the coming to fore of second- and third-generation revolutionary leaders, the children and disciples of the original victors of power, when new, revolutionary institutions have been consolidated, that the fervor of revolutionary change eventually simmers down and gives way to routine patterns of political interaction between post-revolutionary leaders and the people.

Even before the ascension of new generations of leaders, revolutions are seen to have fully succeeded when the political sentiments to which they have given rise are translated into actual political arrangements that are successfully superimposed on existing ones. More specifically, a revolution can be considered to have succeeded when post-revolutionary political actors have established new political institutions, have operationalized working arrangements within and among these institutions, and when they have consolidated them in relation to social groups and classes. In other words, once the tasks of political institutionalization and consolidation have been accomplished, the revolution has succeeded. These are not necessarily overnight processes. They often take considerable time, sometimes years, given that revolutions release pent up pressures and are, all too frequently, immediately followed by periods of chaos and lawlessness. There are also few revolutions that are not met by attempts at counter-revolution, either by remnants of the old state or by foreign powers, or, as is often the case, by a combination of both.

In her analysis of the French, Russian, and Chinese revolutions, Theda Skocpol makes a similar case for when each of these three revolutions succeeded. She argues that the three revolutions "were fully consummated only once new state organizations – administrations and armies, coordinated by executives who governed in the name of revolutionary symbols – were built up amidst the conflicts of revolutionary situations."[3] "In all three revolutionary situations," she argues,

> political leaderships and regimes – the Jacobins and then the Napoleonic in France, the Bolshevik in Russia, and the Communist in China – emerged to reestablish national order, to consolidate the socioeconomic transformation wrought by the class upheavals from below, and to enhance each country's power and autonomy over and against international competitors.[4]

The success of revolutionary movements in capturing political power, whether they are planned or spontaneous, changes the world of politics. The mandate of government changes, leaders having promised a universe of new realities and followers having risked their lives for those promises. Upon seizure of power, the revolutionary project is itself at once revolutionized: No longer is the task one of achieving state paralysis but rather one of power consolidation. Political power, once the focus of anger and anti-government sentiments, is now the embodiment of the ideals for which the masses rose. The new state must now deliver the world that was promised. Its leaders and their agendas, its institutions and their organs, its ideals and their audience, and the manner and the means with which it conducts itself are all products of a revolutionary struggle, one in which the world of politics was turned upside down. The day now belongs to a new cadre of leaders. Their concern is not only to carve out a new national identity, to create the ideal society in which they invested the hopes of the masses, but at the same time to popularly legitimize their rule and to live up to their revolutionary rhetoric. Their efforts are thus directed at expanding the various linkages and connections between the state and society, incorporating the popular strata into the process of state rule, and concurrently solidifying their own hold on power through institutional consolidation and political centralism.

Ironically, in their attempt to forge a new society and to make good on their revolutionary promises, post-revolutionary states often inadvertently accentuate economic hardships. The economically redistributive character of most revolutionary states, despite the loudly proclaimed goals of the actors involved, do not always enhance the economic lot of their target audience. Indeed, as will be shown shortly, the results are often the opposite.

Post-Revolutionary Leadership

The success of the revolutionary struggle brings to the fore a new cadre of leaders, men – and, in a few instances, women – for whom the revolutionary project now becomes one of governing rather than capturing and destroying. Who are these men, and why do they emerge as the revolution's eventual or temporary victors? And, why, as is often the case, do some leaders of post-revolutionary states show greater resilience and survivability than others? The question of who assumes the leadership of the post-revolutionary state depends largely on the nature of the revolutionary movement and the manner in which the revolution succeeded in overthrowing the ancient regime.

The direction, intensity, and leadership of the revolutionary struggle shape the post-revolutionary state. More specifically, insofar as the leadership composition of post-revolutionary states are concerned, the rise of particular actors to leadership positions depends on whether a revolution was planned or spontaneous. In planned revolutions, the leadership of the post-revolutionary state is assumed by leaders of the guerrilla organization that spearheaded the struggle against the old order. Without exception, in successful, guerrilla-fought (and thus planned) revolutions, yesterday's rebels become today's leaders. History provides numerous examples of successful guerrilla revolutions in which post-revolutionary leaders were drawn from the ranks of the guerrilla organization. Mao and other leaders of the Chinese Communist Party, for example, subsequently assumed leadership of China's post-revolutionary, communist state. Similarly, post-revolutionary leaders of Algeria, Cuba, and Vietnam all came from the ranks of those who had been directly involved in the revolutionary struggle. Unlike leaders of spontaneous revolutions, most former guerrilla fighters have shown remarkable resilience in holding on to power in post-revolutionary states.

The emergence of post-revolutionary leaders in spontaneous revolutions takes a slightly different course, although the underlying dynamics that lead to their ascent are not fundamentally different from those at work in planned revolutions. Many of those who rise to leadership positions after the success of spontaneous revolutions are also figures once prominent in the revolutionary movement. Their ultimate success and survivability in the post-revolutionary era are, however, less predictable and depend on evolving and changeable circumstances and dynamics. Consequently, leaders who eventually come to claim the leadership mantle of states that have emerged from spontaneous revolutions are often not the same as those who provided leadership to revolutionary movement. In these instances, ascension to positions of leadership depends on the characteristics, qualifications, and situational opportunities of the individual leaders themselves, as well as on prevailing social and political dynamics. Before examining in detail the forces instrumental in the shaping of post-revolutionary states in both spontaneous and planned revolutions, let us examine some of the alternative explanations of revolutionary outcomes.

"The revolution, like Saturn, devours its children."[5] So is the dominant theme of Crane Brinton's classic work on revolutionary outcomes, arguing that the initial victory of revolutionary leaders is but a brief "honeymoon" by relative moderates before they are themselves overthrown by the "illegal government" of extremists. Revolutions follow an almost unilinear path, starting with the honeymoon of the moderates, moving on to a Reign of Terror, eventually settling down during a "Thermodorian" reaction, "a period of convalescence from the fever of revolution."[6] "There is a tendency," Brinton argues,

> for power to go from Right to Center to Left, from the conservatives of the old regime to the moderates to the radicals or extremists. As power moves along this line, it gets more and more concentrated, more and more narrow, its base in the country and among the people, since at each important crisis the defeated group has to drop out of politics.[7]

The consolidation of power by extremists is brought on by their superior organizational skills and their greater ability to fight foreign and domestic wars, which, Brinton claims, are natural derivatives of revolutionary movements.[8] In an environment polarized by "heated debates, attempted repression, (and) a steady stream of violent propaganda," the extremists find the political arena particularly hospitable to their own ends.[9]

These are "heaven-storming idealists, scornful of compromise," disciplined ideologues particularly adept in dealing with crises.[10] They have all the means and the determination that their moderate counterparts lack. Their ultimate victory, however, often comes in the form of a *coup d'état*, a final *putsch* through which the "illegal government" capitalizes on the incapacitation of the moderates and establishes itself as the sole, legitimate heir of the revolution.[11] Nevertheless, the extremists' reign is impermanent, for "most men cannot long stand the strains of prolonged effort to live in accordance with high ideals."[12] Eventually, "after a revolution has undergone a crisis and the accompanying centralization of power, some strong leader must handle the centralized power when that mad religious energy of the crisis has burned itself out."[13] Oliver Cromwell, Napoleon Bonaparte, and Josef Stalin were more than mere men of ambition. They fit into a specific pattern in post-revolutionary states, epitomizing centralized power and a semblance of return to social and political normalcy.

Other studies of revolutionary outcomes have been less deterministic. One of the most thorough attempts at constructing an analytical framework for the study of revolutions and their outcomes is that of Theda Skocpol, who originally concentrated on class and structural dynamics as pivotal forces in determining the character of post-revolutionary states. While recognizing the importance of revolutionary ideologies and popular commitment to them as one of the "necessary ingredients" of major, historical revolutions, Skocpol argued that the "cognitive content of the ideologies in (no) sense proved a predictive key to either the outcomes of the Revolutions or the activities of the revolutionaries who built the state organizations that consolidated the Revolutions."[14] Instead, "ideologically oriented leaderships in revolutionary crises have been greatly limited by existing structural conditions and severely buffeted by the rapidly changing currents of revolutions."[15] Two specific sets of factors, the structural circumstances within which revolutionary struggles are waged and the features and relations of the various classes, determine the ultimate outcome of revolutionary episodes.

> Revolutionary struggles have emerged from crises of state and class domination, and social-revolutionary outcomes have been powerfully shaped by the obstacles and opportunities offered by those crises. Likewise, social revolutionary outcomes have been shaped and limited by the existing socioeconomic structures and international circumstances within which revolutionary leaderships have struggled to rebuild, consolidate, and use state power ... Variations in revolutionary conflict and outcome (can be) explained partly in terms of the specific features of each revolutionary crisis: exactly how each old-regime state broke apart; exactly what kinds of peasant revolts were facilitated by existing agrarian structures. And variations (can be) also ... explained partly by reference to the specific socioeconomic structures and international situations carried over, more or less from each old to new regime ... [E]xplanations of the conflicts and outcomes of social revolutions best flow ... of the prior understanding of the structures and situations of old regimes and from a prior analysis of the causes of social-revolutionary crises. Revolutionary changes are accomplished upon such foundations and within such circumstances.[16]

Skocpol continues to assert that

> both the occurrence of the revolutionary situations in the first place and the nature of the New Regimes that emerged from the revolutionary conflicts depended fundamentally upon the structures of state organizations and their partially autonomous and dynamic relationships to domestic class and political forces, as well as their positions to other states abroad.[17]

While Skocpol's analysis significantly enhanced the understanding of revolutionary eruptions and outcomes, her strict emphasis on pre-revolutionary, structural arrangements as determinants of outcomes of revolutions was soon challenged by others and revised by herself. Structural and class dynamics may indeed be of paramount importance in certain revolutions. However, as the Iranian revolution so starkly demonstrated, forces other than the structural and class arrangements of pre-revolutionary states, such as culture and newly emerging organizational capabilities, may prove to be equally important in determining the leaders of post-revolutionary states.

As a result, an analytical framework somewhat different from Skocpol's was forwarded by S. N. Eisenstadt. Eisenstadt argues that revolutionary outcomes are

> not necessarily given in the prerevolutionary structure of society but ... [are] the product of interaction among prerevolutionary characteristics, the forces of change – most notably, international forces – and the revolutionary process itself. Only through such interaction do coalitions of broad classes and coalitions between them and their major types of institutional entrepreneurs arise and change.[18]

In a later article, Skocpol sharpened the focus of her original analysis of revolutionary outcomes. She argued that

> to understand which political leadership will win out in (at least the initial stages of) the consolidation of state power in a social-revolutionary situation, one must ask *not* which leaders are most "modern" by some Western or technical standard, but which possess, or can easily develop within given historical circumstances, the appropriate political resources.[19]

While paying greater attention to the importance of access to specific political resources, Skocpol also argued that there may well exist "moral symbols and forms of social communication" that *may* result in a culture conducive to challenges to authority. These cultural dynamics warrant greater attention in certain revolutions, such as the one in Iran, where cultural forces played a central role in shaping the revolution's overall character and ultimate outcome.[20]

The analytical approaches of all three authors discussed here find partial or complete applicability to the historic examples that they set out to examine. Brinton, a historian, carefully charts his discussion of the revolutionary moderate's "honeymoon," the emerging "crisis of extremists," and the subsequent "Thermidorian reaction" by analyzing the English, American, French, and Russian revolutions.[21] Skocpol similarly examines the French, Russian, Chinese, and later the Iranian revolution with considerable skill and historical accuracy.[22] Eisenstadt's analysis involves less overt reliance on historical examples and is more thematic, his primary concern being the overall nature of post-revolutionary states rather than the particularities of their leaderships.[23] All approaches are credible scholarly explanations for the study of outcomes of revolutions, at least insofar as the *political institutions* of post-revolutionary states are concerned.

Nevertheless, in one way or another these analyses mostly leave unanswered certain specific questions about the nature of post-revolutionary leadership. Specifically, the issue of exactly how the "moderates" (to use Brinton's term) or the initial victors of the revolutionary struggle assume power is at best treated with scant attention.[24] Only Skocpol mentions, in passing, that "during revolutionary interregnums, political leaderships rise and fall according to how successful they are in creating and using political arrangements within the crisis circumstances that they face." She continues:

> Struggles over the most fundamental issues of politics and state forms go on until relatively new state organizations have been consolidated; thereafter political struggles continue about how to use state power in its broadly established forms.[25]

While these lines of analysis may not necessarily be inaccurate, they do not adequately deal with the questions of exactly how and why specific individuals ascend to leadership positions in post-revolutionary states while others do not. What is necessary is an analytical framework that not only discusses the overall characteristics of post-revolutionary states but also takes into account the nature and character of forces that lead to the emergence of particular leaders. It is here, in examining post-revolutionary leaderships as well as revolutionary causes and processes, that a distinction between planned and spontaneous revolutions further demonstrates its analytical utility. Leaders of successful planned revolutions almost invariably end up leading the states that emerge subsequent to their victory. This almost-assured ascendance arises from the fact that guerrilla-based revolutions are largely battles between competing power centers, struggles involving the organized forces of the government versus armed guerrilla groups. When the government's forces are defeated and its institutions are captured, the only viable means through which political power can be exercised are at the disposal of the former guerrillas. They have captured the state and are therefore in control of is institutions. It is important to remember that in pre-revolutionary societies, the establishment and activism of guerrilla organizations are intended to bring together otherwise disparate and uncoordinated political tendencies. The aim is to forge institutional venues for political expression and mobilization in settings where such institutions either altogether do not exist or if they do, they operate under tight government control. Thus, during and immediately after the revolutionary struggle, guerrilla organizations are the only viable means through which popularly legitimized political power can be exercised. As a result, guerrilla leaders become heads of the newly emerging political establishment. The consolidation and monopolization of power by all post-revolutionary states merely reinforce the political survival of former guerrillas as new political leaders.

The emergence of leaders following successful spontaneous revolutions, in which disciplined and organized political parties by and large do not play an overwhelming role, follows a path different from that in planned revolutions. Before revolutionary victory, leaders of spontaneous revolutions emerge relatively late in the movement, when the anti-regime struggle has already gotten underway, albeit in an uncoordinated and haphazard fashion. The ascendance of some activists to positions of leadership, as mentioned in the previous chapter, is facilitated by the cultural communicability of the emerging leaders' message in relation to the larger society and the means of access they have. Either through formal organizations or by virtue of their social positions, these activists-cum-leaders can communicate with large numbers of people in a relatively free manner. However, unless they give political substance and institutional backing to their positions, they will not be able to maintain themselves as leaders of the post-revolutionary state. Culturally compatible ideological messages and access to means of mass mobilization are important in mustering support against a regime. These factors do not lose their importance in the post-revolutionary period. But to bear actual political fruit they now need to be transformed into institutional means of exercising state power, means that can help achieve explicitly political ends and objectives. What is important, in Skocpol's words, "is that which political leaderships in revolutionary crises are above all *doing* – claiming and struggling to maintain state power."[26]

Here the role of institutions established immediately prior to or right after revolutionary victory assume particular importance, especially if their establishment took place with an eye toward wresting political power from other, competing centers. The collapse of the *ancient regime* and the resulting release of revolutionary energies give rise to a multiplicity of groups and organizations seeking to fill the prevailing political vacuum. Of these different groups, the ones with the most effective mobilizational abilities have the best chances of assuming leadership positions in the new order. Since most institutions of the former regime are no longer viable due to their defeat or collapse in the revolutionary struggle, especially the military command and the top echelons of the bureaucracy, the new political aspirants need to establish their own control over them or to have at least comparable institutions of their own. It is access to and control of these "appropriate political resources" that ultimately determine the leaders of spontaneous revolutions.[27]

The importance of access to resources and institutions is borne out by various historical examples. The conflict between the Girondins and the Jacobins, both of whom claimed to be the rightful heirs of the French revolution, was eventually settled in favor of the latter only after they had placed themselves at the helm of the *sans-culottes*.[28] The Jacobins were at times reluctant to cultivate ties with these revolutionary foot soldiers, whom they considered too fanatical in their adherence to moral purity and too extremist in revolutionary fervor.[29] Nevertheless, control over the *sans-culottes* proved highly beneficial in enabling the Committee of Public Safety to consolidate its rule during what came to be known as the Reign of Terror.[30] Similarly, the Bolsheviks' leadership of Russia's revolutionary movement and of the emerging ruling system was largely the result of their extensive control over the soviets, thus giving them significant organizational leverage as compared to other, competing revolutionary groups.[31] At the same time, patronage of the peasantry, epitomized by Lenin's program of "Peace and Bread, Peace and Land," deepened the Bolsheviks' support base among an increasingly important segment of Russia's revolutionized society.[32]

In the Iranian case, the clerical establishment, one among the many groups that had in one way or another "led" the revolution, quickly used its popular support base to gain control over the many local revolutionary committees (the *komitehs*) and the irregular militia revolutionary guards (*Pasdaran-e Enghelab*) that had sprang up throughout the country soon after the collapse of the shah's regime.[33] Soon thereafter the Islamic Republic Party was established, giving institutional viability and cohesion to the clergy's populist ascent to power.[34] The outcome of the Nicaraguan revolution, meanwhile, which fell somewhere in between the planned and the spontaneous models, was largely the result of widespread and grassroots support for the principal revolutionary party, the FSLN, and its affiliated organizations at the expense of potential rivals.[35]

In all these examples, the determining factors were both institutional and political: Groups and individuals became leaders because of access to organizations and institutions through which they could communicate with their respective revolutionary audiences. These institutions soon became significant administrative arms of the states that were subsequently established. For those groups and individuals who did not have access to equally viable institutions, or who saw no need for institutional anchors of any sort at all, political leadership became less and less of a lasting reality, particularly as the revolutionary process continued to steam ahead.

The revolution's intellectuals and "the moderates," as Brinton calls them, are among the first ones to go. They are overly philosophical in orientation and temperament, men more of letters than the sword.[36] Their concern is with generalities, the overall quality of the new universe that the revolution has brought about, not with the details of political organization.[37] Brinton correctly observes that revolutions eat their own children, and that the moderates are soon overthrown by the "illegal government" of extremists. Revolutions, at least in their immediate aftermath, result in an atmosphere of uncertainty and competition, and an uncapping of forces long suppressed and eager to make their political mark. At their height, when the regime is weakest and its opponents the loudest, revolutions have numerous self-proclaimed leaders, men (women have been historically absent from the scene) of different ideological persuasions, skills, and political inclinations. It is those with the most viable, emerging institutions at their disposal, political, military, and otherwise – revolutionary committees and *ad hoc* organizations, self-appointed policemen and irregular militia – who are able to hegemonize the institutional mechanisms used for governing society and, as a result, usurp the revolution, justly or unjustly, in their own favor. These are pragmatist politicos, hardened by the realities of trying to govern a society made ungovernable by the tumults of revolution. They are men adept at praxis, aware of those intricate nuances of daily life that assume such overwhelming significance in the extraordinary circumstances of the revolutions. They are, by nature, different from the well-meaning idealists who were, along with others, vociferously heard from in the earlier phases of the revolution.

The extremists' affinity with cold, pragmatic concerns often translates into more than merely superior organizational abilities. It frequently manifests itself in the form of a lack of compunction about the violent use of terror in attaining short-term results. "The logic of the situation," according to the social anthropologist Ernest Gellner,

> imposes a kind of ruthless eliminatory struggle on the participants. One can see this re-enactment in any society in which a revolution destroys the old recognized center of legitimacy and the old circle of mutually reinforcing convention: competing new self-proclaimed authorities emerge, none of which is yet hallowed by age. The one which can destroy or intimidate the other most effectively eventually concentrates power in its own hand.[38]

As one biographer has observed of Lenin, for example, "Lenin's acceptance of the need for executions and the use of terror was not something he agonised over. He had grown up in a world where such methods were often taken for granted."[39]

The endemic eagerness to use violence later leads to an unprecedented level of political centralization in post-revolutionary states, as we shall see shortly. But insofar as the more idealistic, moderate elements are concerned, it is not surprising that they find their political space increasingly narrowed in the post-revolutionary government, eventually so much so that they cease in any way to be a part of it. Brinton argues that revolutions move from the extreme right to center to the extreme left.[40] This is a product of the political and institutional resources at the disposal of the revolution's initial victors. As many revolutionary experiences have demonstrated, there is a tendency in post-revolutionary governments to use gratuitous violence as a necessary end to reach higher ideals. The first victims of such violence, sanctioned as it is by groups of leaders within the evolving state, are themselves revolutionaries who do not necessarily agree with the direction in which the revolution is evolving. To their opponents, they tend to pose the most potent threat. Their stature and popularity have been enhanced by their participation in the revolutionary struggle, and their ideologies and dogma have had some support among those who poured into the streets. They are, indeed, the children of the revolution, placed in the unfortunate position of being unable to shape it to their own liking and thus falling to its wrath.

Just as the leadership of the post-revolutionary state becomes clearer, so is the new political order that it leads cleansed of nonconformist threats. Once the new state has filtered out its ideologically less-reliable elements, then the focus of political correctness shifts to society. The new state seeks to eliminate actual or perceived threats by clamping down on politically excluded groups and those with doctrinal tendencies different from its new leaders. One after another, political parties are banned, free-thinking intellectuals harassed, and dissenters terrorized. All of these developments – from the emergence of winning groups from among revolutionary leaders to the brutal campaigns of social purification – deepen the institutionalization of the new order. They point to the steady consolidation of the revolutionary establishment, a process whereby the new leaders' hold on power is strengthened and their network of supporting institutions are expanded. It is to these developments that we next turn.

Institutionalization

Planned and spontaneous revolutions often result in a proliferation of state institutions. In the process, the expansive post-revolutionary state becomes far more intrusive into the lives of citizens than the previous state had ever been. One of the most pressing problems of post-revolutionary states is that of routinization, of transforming destructive revolutionary energies into politically constructive tasks. Having eliminated potential sources of competition, the leaders of the emerging state now turn their attention to strengthening and expanding the institutional mechanisms through which they rule. These new institutions, and the ground rules that govern their conduct and their relationship with the larger society, form the very basis of post-revolutionary states.[41] The primary task of state leaders becomes one of institutionalizing and consolidating their newly acquired powers.[42] Doing so requires taking a number of complementary steps: ensuring that their new institutions function effectively and as designed; inculcating a new sense of legitimacy and shaping new perceptions of political and national identity; and incorporating the popular classes into the political process. Rhetoric, terror, and the threat of coercion do not necessarily subside, but now they are complemented by various institutions designed to perpetuate the new order and to provide direction and substance to the wishes of the new elite.

Reinforcing the need for new institutions is the impermanent nature of charismatic authority, on which the legitimacy of most revolutionary states is, at least initially, based. Charisma is an inherently unstable form of authority, eventually giving way to routinized forms of political conduct.[43] At some point in the life of post-revolutionary states, the charismatic foundation on which the state's legitimacy is based, one derived from the efforts of specific figures during the revolutionary struggle, will sooner or later wane due to natural deaths or political purges.[44] Even if the charismatic leader continues to remain at the helm of the post-revolutionary state for some time, as for example was the case with Fidel Castro and the Cuban state, the need to complement charismatic appeal with political institutions soon becomes apparent. Not surprisingly, even during the active leaderships of charismatic, revolutionary founding fathers in the Soviet Union, Cuba, and Iran, for example, political parties and affiliated organizations were created with the specific aim of institutionally enhancing the rule of the state.

Moreover, the popular excitement generated as a result of the revolution is bound to subside at some point, even in instances when domestic revolutions spill over into international wars and result in a surge of nationalist sentiments. The new state cannot count on an indefinite expression of enthusiasm by the popular classes alone as a viable source of power. With extra-institutional sources of authority being by nature impermanent, those institutions that will perpetuate the longevity of the new order assume particular importance. In fact, post-revolutionary elites often view their survival as dependent on their control of some of the key institutions of power. Institutions involving the military, youth, culture, religion, education, and the economy are either brought under the state's direct influence or, if previously nonexistent, are established for the specific purpose of enhancing state power.[45]

The overall nature of emerging post-revolutionary institutions, as well as the manner of their conduct, largely depend on whether the revolutions that bring them about are more planned or involve greater spontaneity. Planned revolutions are based largely on premeditated programs devised by revolutionary actors who know precisely what they want and have a clear idea of the ways and means to achieve their goals. Their efforts are undertaken with clear goals in mind. If successful, there is often little disparity between their previously proclaimed goals and their newly initiated policies. Spontaneous revolutions, on the other hand, are more often the outcome of developments that at first look hardly revolutionary. They involve neither formulated programs nor planned initiatives. Their leaders emerge relatively late, and those leaders formulate and announce their exact goals even later. The revolution's goals and ideals are initially elusive at best, summed up in dogmatic slogans and vague promises. Each cadre of leaders promises such appealing alternatives as democracy and equality, principles that are left open to different interpretations. In these instances, the outcome of the revolution is likely to turn out differently from the ideals that originally inspired it. This contradiction is more than the result of the inherent fluidity of the revolutionary process itself rather than the sinister manipulations of revolutionary turn-faces.

Nevertheless, with remarkable uniformity and regardless of whether spontaneous or planned, revolutions give rise to populist, inclusionary states. Leading a revolution, it is often said, is like riding a bicycle; one has to keep peddling hard to avoid a nasty fall. By nature, revolutions involve the patronage of masses of people. The relationship between revolutionary leaders and followers is essentially one of patrons and clients, with the group most capable of catering to the needs and wishes of the widest spectrum of people emerging as their leader during the revolutionary process. Once the revolution has succeeded and former opposition activists become new state leaders, their reliance on the patronage of the masses does not dissipate. In fact, it is often deepened. Their mandate is no longer to oppose the state but to make good on the numerous promises they gave before the revolution's success. To sustain power, they now need to deliver the goods they promised, or to at least divert attention from them by fomenting popular anger against enemies of the new order, real or imagined. Efforts at directing the people's attention often take the form of politically sanctioned post-revolutionary violence, wars and other international disputes, and purges and the elimination of alleged "counter-revolutionaries." But even if only symbolic, a token delivery of the goods promised is necessary to maintain the viability of the new system. The result is populist and politically inclusionary states in which streets and city squares become primary arenas for revolutionary mass mobilization and for keeping the public excitement going.

Various means of garnering public support, such as economic reforms, programs for public welfare, and greater political participation, no matter how farcical and cosmetic, heighten the new state's sense of legitimacy among the population. Moreover, post-revolutionary states, which in any event owe their very genesis to violence, feel less inhibited to use coercion in order to preserve their newly acquired powers than would otherwise be the case. The constant identification of counter-revolutionary elements as the public's enemy, the perpetual sense of besiegement and threat from outside forces, and the unending rhetoric of denouncing the morbid past all make post-revolutionary states more prone to using violence against actual or perceived sources of opposition. Crushing those who oppose the new order is in fact one of the very sources upon which its legitimacy is based. Interconnected as they often are, new forms of legitimacy and an uninhibited reliance on violence are often readily employed by post-revolutionary states. At the same time, and largely as a result of these developments, the powers and the structure of the state become highly centralized, leading to a much higher concentration of power in state hands as compared to pre-revolutionary times.

Much of the efforts of post-revolutionary states can be understood as attempts to find new means of political legitimation. These new means of legitimacy may come in different forms, from engagement in international conflicts to attempts to incorporate the masses into the political process and suppress dissenters. On a most fundamental level, the legitimacy of new ruling elites depends on their ability not just to lead revolutions but also to deliver on the promises they made during the revolutionary struggle. The economic performance of the post-revolutionary state is thus instrumental in enhancing its legitimacy, particularly since the hopes of its participants (who are now its clients) had been raised to a high pitch during the struggle.[46]

In some instances, however, revolutionary movements were neither the result of gross economic disparities within society, nor did, as a result, revolutionary figures promise extensive restructuring of economic relations. Instead, the wrath of the revolution was directed at those perceived to be corrupt and governing the country illegitimately. In these cases, the most striking of which occurred in Iran, the values attached to new political institutions and practices, and the manner of conduct of individual actors themselves, assume legitimizing functions. Ethics and vaguely defined notions of ethnicity become important sources of legitimacy. Symbols and symbolic actions also become highly significant, often giving rise to political rituals that are rich in symbolism. Steadily, as the next chapter elaborates, the foundations of a new political culture are laid down. Often, the memory of fallen revolutionary heroes is kept alive and is used by the state as a source of legitimation. These and other mechanisms are designed to enhance the legitimacy of the new order among the various social classes, particularly those whose support was essential to the success of the revolution.

The inclusion of previously politically disenfranchised groups into the political process, even if more cosmetic than substantive, is also a major source of legitimacy for the post-revolutionary state. Whereas bureaucratic–authoritarian states rely on the exclusion of the masses from politics, post-revolutionary populist states deliberately set out to use mass politics as a source of political support. Along with authoritarian mechanisms, popular mobilization is used as an important tool for state-building.[47] Emphasis is put on the symbolic dimensions of public affairs, manifested in the form of street marches, demonstrations, and collective outbursts of political jubilation and support. Participation enhances the citizen's subjective sense of state legitimacy by the very fact that one feels involved in the act of governing.[48] Although such ritualistic ceremonies are often "little more than a cheap means to achieve political acquiescence," they are intrinsically valuable as they often bestow on people a sense of political empowerment.[49] For the masses once excluded from the political process, participation in events heavily pregnant with political symbolism results in a sense of enhanced popular involvement in national political life. Although such states may be as dictatorial as any other authoritarian variety, their incorporation of the masses into the political process makes them appear as popular democracies. In this sense, populist states enjoy a degree of popular legitimacy unsurpassed by others. It is this heightened sense of political legitimacy, brought on by the ostensibly democratizing effects of mass mobilization, that enables such states to motivate their population to make supreme sacrifices for the nation.[50]

Significantly, post-revolutionary polities invariably assume the form of populist, inclusionary states. In such political systems, mass mobilization is achieved even before the formal establishment of new institutions, and at a time when emotional and ideological bonds linking revolutionary leaders with the masses are strongest. Such links are greatly strengthened with the acquisition of power by the revolutionaries, reinforced by an increasing, mutual reliance by each side on the other. The new leaders need their supporters more than ever before in order to strengthen their hold on power, while the masses rely on their leaders to deliver the promised goods for which they endured the traumas of revolution.

What thus emerges out of revolutions is ideologically reconstructed national identities involving the sudden incorporation of formerly excluded popular groups into state-directed projects.[51] Such projects frequently include economic self-help plans, intense efforts aimed at inculcating a new culture and national identity, and, in certain instances, international wars. Historically, many post-revolutionary states have also excelled at channeling popular participation into international wars. Because of the way that revolutionary leaders mobilize popular groups during their struggle for power, the new state can tackle mobilization for war better than most other tasks, including the promotion of economic development. The realization of this potential depends on threatening but not overwhelming geopolitical circumstances.[52] By their very nature, post-revolutionary states are more prone to engage in international wars, or at least give off the impression that an attack by a hostile foreign power is imminent. Vilifying international actors as patrons of the state's internal enemies gives post-revolutionary states justification for repressive policies and campaigns of terror. The likelihood of engaging in international conflicts is further increased because most post-revolutionary states voice challenges to the regional status quo, seeing prevailing international arrangements as inimical to their new, "radical" priorities. And, of course, such states have plenty of enemies, whether made up of counter-revolutionaries seeking to reverse the course of the revolution or neighbors seeking to take advantage of the chaos next door.

Wars are materially and humanly costly ventures and are, as a result, impermanent. Even the longest of the protracted wars in which post-revolutionary states engage, such as Iran's war with Iraq in the 1980s, eventually die down. Even more common are efforts by state leaders aimed at redefining national identity and the citizens' perceptions of themselves and of their nation. In its ambitious quest to create a new citizen, the state micromanages politics. It initiates various plans and projects – through the media, the sponsorship of various acts of collective behavior, and "educational" efforts of varying subtlety – in order to enhance its own legitimacy by minimizing state–society gaps and, in the process, creating a new political culture suited to its own purposes. As one observer of Cuba's post-revolutionary politics noted more than two decades after the revolution's success, even the apparently spontaneous demonstrations of support for the state were staged and carefully coordinated.

> What may appear to the untrained eye as an immense sea of anonymous faces of persons temporarily detached from their customary social relations to participate in the *jurnadas* of the revolutionary calendar is instead a publicly acknowledged, carefully rehearsed, and studied choreographic exercise of groups who are firmly attached to existing institutions and occupy clearly specified and lasting niches.[53]

The conventionalization of collective behavior is a particularly rewarding practice for keeping the new elite's ideology alive and for maintaining elite–mass linkages. By encouraging mass participation, state-sponsored collective behavior separates the devout from nominal followers. Moreover, it perpetuates the legitimacy of the state by keeping the revolutionary spirit alive.

The cornerstone of the legitimacy of post-revolutionary states is the popular cultivation of a new national identity. The question of what it is to be a citizen of Russia, China, Cuba, Iran, or any other country where a revolution might have occurred, assumes a completely different answer after the success of the revolution and the subsequent establishment of the new order. By incorporating formerly excluded popular groups into state-directed projects, revolutions promote "ideologically restructured national identities."[54] This new identity is anchored in the revolutionary struggle, and now, due to its apparent or actual participation in the political process, is empowered with a new sense of authority and mission in life. "What revolutionaries offer themselves and their own societies," according to one observer, "is above all else an image of power, control, certainty and purpose in a world in which impotence, incomprehension and terror of sheer meaninglessness are permanent threats."[55] The poor and the politically servile, previously conditioned to a self-acceptance of inferiority and subordinate status, acquire a new sense of power and significance. At least insofar as the symbolic aspects of politics are concerned, the state and society are drawn closer together, the former deliberately forging new cultural and emotional bonds with the latter.

An additional element that significantly enhances the powers of post-revolutionary states is their greater willingness to rely on coercion and brute force in order to retain power. Post-revolutionary states, emerging as they often do in the midst of violent inter-elite struggles, wars and other forms of international conflict, are much stronger and politically more centralized in comparison to the states they replace. This relative strength and centralization is due not only to the popular support that such polities cultivate but also a result of the ease with which they employ violence in order to stay in power. Success in the violent pursuit of power habituates leaders to the political use of violence. "Elites who have secured state power and have maintained their position by violent means are disposed to respond violently to future challenges."[56]

The steady elimination of political nonconformists is part of a broader process of institutionalization, the end result of which is highly likely to be a police state, at least in the short run. The bloody and savage purges that invariably follow every major revolution, from the infamous purges of the Stalin era to those that followed the Chinese, the Cuban, and the Iranian revolutions, are more than mere historical coincidences. They demonstrate a preoccupation on the part of new state elites to secure their powers against alleged and real counter-revolutionaries and other domestic opponents. Having relied on violence to acquire their new powers, and in the process having risked a great deal, revolutionary elites seldom have any inhibitions about continuing to rely on violence in order to protect their new privileges.[57] As a result, emerging post-revolutionary states are often far more brutally coercive than the ones they replace, suppressing actual or perceived sources of opposition with considerably less restraint than did their predecessors. In some instances violence is so endemic – as in China, for example, where an estimated 100,000 people were executed in the first half of 1951[58] – that certain forms of violence are symbolically upheld and even assume a measure of popular cultural acceptability.[59] The ends, often visions held in high esteem by the new ruling elite, justify the means regardless of how violent and brutal they may be. Terrorist assassinations, firing squads, summary executions, and torture all become commonplace.

Political centralization, mass politics, and inclusionary institutional arrangements frequently give rise to one-party systems. As discussed earlier, access to institutional means of mobilization is often crucial in facilitating the hegemony of one group of leaders over others. Thus, even in spontaneous revolutions, the seeds of post-revolutionary parties are sown early on. Single, highly centralized political parties are often the most visible institutional manifestations of post-revolutionary states. At least initially in the life of post-revolutionary states, single, official parties play a pivotal role in their institutionalization. This central role is played at two specific levels. First, the political party is designed to enhance the institutional reach of the new state at a time when existing state organs, such as the bureaucracy and the military, are undergoing purges and being revamped. The party does not so much set policy as it serves as an auxiliary to institutions that have been paralyzed by the weight of the revolution. Its specific intent is to give direction to the new state's many goals and agendas. As such, these parties at once perform a multitude of functions through which the new state's ties with society are strengthened. With the political party in place and at work, the raw, largely uncoordinated energy of mass demonstrators can be channeled in the direction of enhancing the strength of the new order. Through providing for a means of participation, albeit in a highly controlled fashion, the party also enhances the new order's legitimacy.[60] By virtue of its ideology, agendas, and organs, it becomes the most popularly inclusive institutions of the emerging inclusionary state. The party becomes the principal venue for political participation. Its cells and affiliated organizations, blessed with official backing and immune from criticism in the stifling post-revolutionary environment, grow both in their geographic purview and in membership. It thus becomes a pivotal instrument for recruiting leaders for both the intermediate and the top echelons of the state.[61]

Second, the official party serves as an instrument of ideological legitimacy for the new power elite. It becomes an instrument of propaganda for the new state, a means through which the ideology of new political actors is popularized among the people. Accordingly, the party plays a highly significant role in helping articulate and propagate the ideologies of new state leaders. To begin with, the ideological platform of the party is part of the dominant dogma of the day. Thus, membership in the party, or even mere participation in its activities, entails a significant amount of political socialization. Importantly, official state parties, particularly post-revolutionary ones, resort to a number of forms of ideological propaganda. They frequently sponsor lectures and forums for the study and discussion of the dominant ideology.

More often, they print various publications, from books and essays to newspapers, which are heavily tainted with the ideology of the day. In most post-revolutionary states, the most dominant daily newspapers are those published by the state party. Such newspapers as *Pravda*, China's *Peoples' Daily*, the Cuban *Granma*, and Iran's *Jomhouri Islami* all served functions deeper than formulating state policies. More importantly, at least at the outset of their publication, they were intended to be further means of political indoctrination.

For the most part, official post-revolutionary parties are largely discarded once they outlive their practical and ideological utility. Initially, state parties serve as means of attaining institutionalization through facilitating mobilization, legitimacy, indoctrination, and recruitment. They also serve as surrogates for the bureaucracy at a time of partial or complete bureaucratic paralysis. But once institutionalization is achieved and the new order is on solid organizational and doctrinal grounds, when the bureaucracy is on its feet again and the previously tenuous ideology of the elite has become an integral feature of the establishment, the official state party can potentially pose a threat by becoming a powerful and autonomous base for specific individuals within the elite. This is particularly the case in non-communist states, where official parties are not necessarily embedded in the revolutionary ideology itself but are rather more of a practical tool for furthering the revolution. Once the revolution is achieved and in the eyes of its leaders victorious, there is now less of a need for the organization that had spearheaded it. Many single parties, therefore, become more bureaucratic appendages to the state, their functions bureaucratized, and turn into an important bastion of the status quo. In so many African states in the 1970s, the parties that had valiantly headed wars of national liberation were left to languish once independence was at hand.[62] Many linger in shadow of a glorious past, becoming empty symbols.[63] In Iran, the once mighty Islamic Republic Party was ordered to disband altogether by Khomeini in 1987.[64]

The fate of official political parties in post-revolutionary states is to some extent related to a broader process that such states almost invariably undergo, namely factionalism. The appearance of factional groupings within a political system may either be a product of the skewed evolution of post-revolutionary institutions or, as is often the case in non-revolutionary regimes, a result of purposeful political engineering. A variety of political establishments, particularly those that embody various forms of patrimonial rule, deliberately encourage the existence of different political factions, whose competitive efforts against each other are designed to ensure the security of the leader at the top.[65]

Even after purges and the elimination of opponents within the leadership, there is still a likelihood that factions may form within the new state. Individuals emphasizing a specific aspect of the dominant ideology may become concentrated in one particular institution – the army, the official party, or a specific ministry, for example – while others with different doctrinal priorities may be clustered in another institution. At times factions form around clashing personalities. Often personal differences are reinforced by differing doctrinal interpretations within the broader context of the governing ideology. These factional tendencies often persist despite repeated and at times brutal purges. In broad terms, all factions adhere to the revolution and its ideals. They do, however, seek to pursue specific agendas within the general contours of the post-revolutionary environment, agendas that may or may not find equally enthusiastic supporters among other political leaders. Some of the more common doctrinal issues that frequently lead to factional divisiveness include different views over the future direction of the revolution, the economy, and relations with other countries. The Trotskyite position of exporting the Russian revolution abroad, exemplified in the slogan "World revolution now!," and subsequent factional struggles within the Bolsheviks have parallels in the post-revolutionary states of China, Cuba, and Iran, along with those that follow virtually every other major revolution.[66]

Apart from factionalism, post-revolutionary states face enormous challenges when confronted with a need to transfer power from one generation of leaders to the next. At stake is the future course of the revolution. Because there are factions within the leadership with subtle but pronounced ideological agendas, and because a consensual process for the selection of new leaders is conspicuously absent, with the change of leaders the revolutionary state *may* take a dramatic turn in direction, as it did with the passing of successive Soviet leaders, as occurred in China with the death of Chairman Mao, and in Iran with the death of Khomeini. In Cuba, the departure of the Castro brothers Fidel and Raúl from the political arena has yet to result in significant changes to the Cuban polity, a product, perhaps, more of American policy toward the island state than domestic political dynamics. And in Nicaragua, Daniel

Ortega manipulated electoral rules in order to remain president long after the Sandanista revolution swept him into power.

The Economy

In their efforts to foster institutionalization and at the same time perpetuate their legitimacy, post-revolutionary states often initiate a number of popular economic reforms. Most revolutionary movements, in fact, particularly planned ones, base much of their legitimacy on promises of redistributing wealth and reformulating economic relationships. Whereas some revolutions may be "authenticating" in the sense of emphasizing the legitimacy of new symbols and new forms of identity, as was the case in Iran, many other revolutionary movements put greater emphasis on the need for a redistribution of economic goods among the popular classes.[67] This was especially true of the French, Russian, Chinese, and Cuban revolutions. By nature, such revolutionary movements and the post-revolutionary states to which they subsequently give birth are strongly committed to enacting redistributive economic policies.

All post-revolutionary states, of course, have much at stake in ensuring the economic well-being of their new constituents. For such regimes, much of their legitimacy and popular support depends on their ability to make good on the promises of the revolution, on ensuring that their followers' actual economic status improves and that they no longer feel completely disenfranchised from society. Particularly in planned revolutions, where the banner of revolution is raised in the name of particular social classes – the Cuban peasantry being a prime example – the bulk of the post-revolutionary project is devoted to enhancing the economic positions of those classes. Traditional oligarchs are replaced through a "continuous process of replacement and restructuring of elites" that brings to the fore a new, ruling counter-elite.[68] Regardless of their dogma and zealous rhetoric, the seemingly major economic restructuring efforts undertaken by most post-revolutionary states are as much products of immediate political necessities as they are a result of ideological goals and agendas.

Efforts by post-revolutionary states aimed at achieving economic reforms and restructuring often manifest themselves in the form of confiscations of land, assets, and other forms of capital. The state also nationalizes many privately owned enterprises and introduces mechanisms designed to control the flow and concentration of capital. The confiscation and redistribution of land from proprietors to peasants and serfs is by far the most dramatic manifestation of economic transformation under post-revolutionary regimes. At the same time, the process of land reform is itself at once economically, politically, socially, culturally, and psychologically transforming and, at times, violent. It creates and reinforces bonds between the state and a segment of society whose support is central to the new political establishment. With the old elite physically eliminated or at least economically immobilized, those previously left out of the economic mainstream – peasants and the proletariat, laborers and industrial workers – are made to feel that they are now the new elite, the state directing its boisterous economic propaganda toward them instead of capitalists and industrial magnates, feudal lords, and aristocratic families.

Even in instances where land reform is carried out halfheartedly or is aborted soon after a noisy start, post-revolutionary states invariably attempt to redirect the flow of income and capital away from certain classes and toward others. The principal means of such efforts at economic redistribution are the introduction of extensive regulatory policies and widespread nationalization, with the state retaining control over the confiscated assets. The primary targets of nationalization are often those profitable enterprises through which wealth was accumulated in the most conspicuous manner. Large factories and successful firms, privately owned banks and insurance companies, import–export businesses and larger stores, all are among the first wave of establishments to become nationalized by post-revolutionary states.

Often specific agencies are set up to coordinate the redistributive economic agendas of the new state or to manage and run the new state-owned enterprises. State cooperatives are established in order to overlook the production and sale of agricultural and other consumer goods. Large private enterprises are turned into parastatals and become an integral part of the new state's economic plan. Through these and other initiatives, post-revolutionary states often try to penetrate into deeper levels of economic activity and, consequently, further centralize power by assuming an increasing array of economic responsibilities.

Ironically, attempts to enhance the living standards of a substantial portion of the population and to concurrently expand the state's involvement in the economy take place within a context of declining state abilities and mounting economic difficulties. Because of the very redistributive goals that post-revolutionary states set for themselves, coupled with the limited and often depleted pool of resources they have at their disposal, post-revolutionary states invariably face a compendium of economic problems, exacerbating their own difficulties, particularly in the short run, as they attempt to remedy them.

Such economic quandaries are to a large extent inherent to the nature of post-revolutionary states, although they are also accented by dislocations resulting from the revolution. To begin with, the state's efforts aimed at achieving greater dominance in the economic sphere lead to apprehensions and uncertainties in the private sector and foster a general tendency to pull capital and investments out of the market for fear of partial confiscation or outright state takeover. At the same time, managerial and restructuring changes in the newly nationalized enterprises can lead to declining productivity and dwindling surpluses.[69] The negative economic ramifications of such an environment are aggravated by policies pursued by post-revolutionary states themselves. At a time when economic realities lead to declining living standards, attempts are made to enhance the people's economic largess. Often large increases in money wages are allocated, food and other basic goods are subsidized, and social security nets are expanded. However, while these and other similar policies, designed especially to help the needy, absorb large amounts of resources, they do little to raise the level of economic output and in fact merely stretch the state's stressed resources even thinner. While the lower classes are likely to see gains and improvements in their purchasing power, local producers and industrialists, as well as domestic and foreign entrepreneurs and investors, see themselves constantly threatened by the possibility of nationalization or, at best, by state harassment designed to win over the support and sympathy of consumers.

Combined, these policies and the broader context within which they are formulated often lead to serious economic crises or, at least, exigencies of one kind or another. Invariably, post-revolutionary polities encounter significant difficulties in the economic domain. Increased concern over the repercussions of poor economic performance often result in the allocation of resources in ways inconsistent with revolutionary rhetoric. Certain policies may also be devised and implemented based not on their revolutionary merits but on their attractiveness to foreign, primarily Western, creditors and banking agencies. Moreover, due to the tenuous nature of political institutions in initial phases of the revolution, many of the regime's far-reaching economic reform projects lack the necessary political muscle needed to ensure their full and unimpeded implementation.

By and large, the economies of post-revolutionary states need to be examined within the context of embryonic processes of political institutionalization, inclusionary political arrangements, and the contradictory forces of supply and demand in relation to the state's capacities and its aspirations. All too often, the economic logic of post-revolutionary states is guided by an impulse of political centralization. States emerging out of successful planned revolutions, which by nature embody previously devised economic platforms, have far more pointed economic agendas compared to other post-revolutionary states, at least initially, because they made specific promises to specific groups during the revolution and now have to make good on them. Much of their legitimacy and continued popular support now depends on their ability to make good on the economic promises made during the revolutionary struggle. That is largely why extensive efforts at land reform were launched following the Chinese, Cuban, and Nicaraguan revolutions, during each of which peasant support was sought through promises of economic betterment and redistribution of land. States emerging out of spontaneous revolutions also attempt to better the lives of previously disenfranchised popular classes. Despite laudable intentions and extensive measures designed to restructure economic relations and redistribute available resources, however, the structural limitations that entangle post-revolutionary states invariably lead to economic slowdowns and at times even serious crises. Attempts to address such politically troublesome economic shortcomings, often coupled with stringent conditions set by international patrons or creditors, frequently lead to a mutation of the economic agendas of post-revolutionary states and a gradual return of less restrictive regulatory policies.

Conclusion

By definition, revolutions give birth to political systems that are radically different from the ones they replaced. New symbols and values, new forms of identity and modes of conduct, and new organizations and institutions emerge and replace those of the old order. In short, revolutions lead to changes in both the subjective as well as the objective aspects of political life. Within this context, the most noticeable change in the political character of post-revolutionary states occurs in the composition of their leaders. The leaders of post-revolutionary states are determined not necessarily by virtue of their revolutionary credentials, political wiliness, or charisma – although these are often crucial auxiliary factors – but primarily by the extent and viability of institutions at their disposal that enable them to form effective links between them and the larger society. At a time when existing political and nonpolitical institutions of the old order have fallen under the weight of the revolution, when society is left with at best tenuous forms of political leadership, the factors that determine the eventual composition of new and emerging political elites are ultimately institutional in nature rather than dependent on such extra-institutional dynamics as charisma and political skill.

In the politically volatile atmosphere that immediately follows revolutions, what counts are the various links and connections that bind new political aspirants to those segments of the population whose political input matters. In planned revolutions, these mobilizational links are invariably established through the very organization that defeated the government and established itself as its rightful successor, namely the revolutionary guerrilla party. Once the forces of the Old Order are defeated and incapacitated, the only viable institution that can penetrate society and lay claim to its political mantle is the party organization that spearheaded the revolution. In fact, the party's very revolutionary victory attests to the viability of its links with the popular classes, links whose purpose becomes one of channeling destructive revolutionary energies into politically constructive goals.

Spontaneous revolutions, in contrast, initially lack existing institutional linkages between emerging leaders and the larger society. Compared to planned revolutions, these institutional links between the new elites and the masses emerge somewhat later in spontaneous revolutions. Frequently, new political institutions, often in the form of organized parties, are quickly formed with the aim of institutionalizing the newly won clout of segments or individuals within the band of revolutionary leaders. The new institutions of the regime itself – its military, legislature, or bureaucracy, for example – may also be turned into de facto centers of power and influence for specific individuals or factions hoping to enhance their own position in the post-revolutionary period.

Significantly, the changes that result from revolutionary transformations extend far beyond the mere format and functions of political arrangements. The very nature of emergent post-revolutionary institutions differs. They are inherently much stronger and more centralized, are less hesitant to rely on violence as a means of political sustenance, and are married to the society in much more direct ways than pre-revolutionary states. They are, concurrently, transformative in nature, driven by goals of inculcating new symbols and forms of identity among the masses, altering established patterns of social and political behavior, and giving substance to the economic promises of the revolution.

"Revolutions will come and revolutions will go, but I will continue with mine," said the defiant Mexican revolutionary hero Emiliano Zapata as he flaunted Mexico's post-revolutionary government.[70] There comes a point in the life of every post-revolutionary polity when it needs to realize that it is no longer *revolutionary*, that it needs to get on with the conduct of politics free of rhetoric and zeal, albeit still under different auspices. Zapata's refusal to let go of the Mexican revolution was as much symptomatic of an instinctive need by revolutionary leaders for the continuance of their cause as it was a result of the frustration of his hopes for agrarian reforms.[71] In the same way that wars never end for warriors, revolutions never end for revolutionaries. But the popular fervor of revolution is inherently impermanent, bound to eventually subside because of its very intensity and scale. Street demonstrations, marches, slogans, and bombastic rhetoric may be good for the upkeep of symbols, but they do not necessarily enhance the people's economic lot. Everyday life has to somehow return to normal; society cannot run on a permanent revolutionary footing.

Accentuating this need for a return to social and political normalcy is the inevitable waning of charismatic authority and the need to eventually replace it with regularized procedures and institutionalized forms of power. The invisible bonds that glue the masses to their revolutionary heroes need to be transformed into actual political institutions, be they new political parties and organizations or preexisting institutions modified accordingly. To maintain that revolutions die is to overlook their lingering legacies as manifested in the institutions, political cultures, and patterns of practice to which they give birth. These new characteristics permeate every aspect of post-revolutionary states, and, by all indications, never completely cease to be a part of them. But they become routine, losing their zeal and ferocity over time. Successful revolutions do not die; they first give birth to post-revolutionary states and then slowly subside.

5 REVOLUTIONARY POLITIES

Revolutions transform not just political actors and institutions but also symbolic sources of political legitimacy. In essence, the legitimacy of the revolutionary state rests on society's attitudes and perceptions at a much more fundamental level than would otherwise be the case. States cannot operate in a social vacuum and, even if exclusionary in character, they are invariably linked to society through a variety of ways and means. Whether through sheer coercion or a facade of legitimacy, even the most narrowly based states need somehow to retain ties with specific segments within the larger society in order to survive and remain functionally viable. The inclusionary nature of post-revolutionary states, coupled with their need to provide for systemic means of mass-based political input, significantly increases the importance of both the institutional and symbolic means through which the state and society interact.

Moreover, precisely because both the state and society have become *revolutionized*, the nexus between the two assumes particular characteristics. Chapter 4 examined the states that emerge following revolutions and their influence on society. The present chapter focuses on society, analyzing those trends and dynamics within post-revolutionary societies that give the entire polity – not just the state but non-state actors as well – the peculiar characteristics that they acquire after revolutions. Having been through an event as traumatic as a revolution, do post-revolutionary societies in fact embody features that in one way or another influence the body politic? If that is indeed the case, it is then important to examine the nature of the interaction between a revolutionary society and a revolutionary state. It is to these questions that this chapter turns.

The chapter examines the changing nature of state–society relations in the aftermath of revolutions. In specific, the chapter focuses on how the emerging leaders of the new state impose their own vision of the revolution on social actors, not all of whom may share the same vision. New state leaders often suppress or altogether eliminate nonconformists while at the same time continuing to keep the momentum of revolutionary mass mobilization going. This has consequences for the emerging political culture, which is often polarized, revolves around zero-sum assumptions, and is therefore antidemocratic. The ingredients for political opposition are abundant, and often extremist, though the prospects of yet another revolution are dim.

Post-Revolutionary Societies

A revolution is a movement from within society to wrest power from the state. As such, the launching of a revolutionary movement, and particularly its success, involves considerable adjustments and disturbances on the part of society. Whether the product of collective efforts by large cross sections of society, as in spontaneous revolutions, or the result of initiatives by specific groups, as is the case in planned revolutions, the revolution is brought on and won through the efforts of groups from within society. Apart from the complex and varied bonds that link the emerging revolutionary states and societies together, post-revolutionary societies acquire additional features that they would not have had had they not experienced a revolution. The revolutionary movement, in sum, gives rise to specific characteristics within post-revolutionary societies.

In the lead-up to and in the immediate aftermath of the state's collapse, there is a likelihood of chaos and lawlessness in most urban centers. At the very least, political activity takes place within a context of changing social and political symbols, with the very perceptions that society has of the state having greatly changed. Increased political participation aimed at capturing state institutions in turn polarizes different preexisting social and political cleavages. Efforts aimed at wresting political power away from the state, meanwhile, result in the resurgence of a number of cultural norms and values supporting political struggle. Specifically, a heightened sense of nationalism and a symbolic upholding of the value of sacrifice for the greater good become strikingly prevalent, particularly among those social groups who were at the forefront of the political struggle. Society, in essence, becomes just as revolutionized as the state.

On a most general level, revolutions result in changes to the ground rules of social interactions and, subsequently, in the structural and institutional manifestations of these ground rules.[1] Social institutions that previously may have been considered politically marginal could rise in social significance and power and prestige – religion in Iran, for example – while others may be adversely impacted, as was the case with the nobility and the clergy in France. Cultural orientations, mores, and norms change, particularly those that relate to political activity, with new symbols replacing the old. A new political culture emerges, and is in turn cultivated by new state leaders, with mass-based political activism as one of its core values. Political input is, on the one hand, encouraged by the emerging inclusionary state and, on the other hand, desired by masses unwilling to forfeit their newly found political liberties.

The mutual desire on the part of both state and social actors to continue the populist impulse for as long as possible has the potential of engendering state–society tensions. While the inclusionary state seeks to foster *controlled* forms of participation, not all social actors desire to partake in guided displays of political expression. The internal conflicts among competing heirs to the revolution that characterize post-revolutionary states early on often manifest into open clashes between followers of emerging state leaders and those finding themselves increasingly marginalized. Since revolutions lead to a temporary collapse of the repressive capacities of the state, they invariably result in a period of nonexistent or at best minimal social control.[2] Society has become liberated, not just politically but culturally as well. It is embroiled in a process of formulating new values and symbols, new patterns of conduct, and new expectations.[3] But the eventual victors of the revolutionary struggle, those who can outmuscle and outmaneuver their former comrades and wrest control over the post-revolutionary state, are willing to support such new cultural symbols and values only insofar as they suit their immediate political ends. In fact, post-revolutionary societies are often marred by coercive and brutal attempts on the part of new elites to establish social control. With a zeal and determination uncharacteristic of the former regime, new elites seek to inculcate among the populace those values and norms that they consider to be the correct ones. These new values form the basis of their legitimacy, and their popular acceptance is central to the success of the new regime.

The inherently conflictual nature of the relationship between post-revolutionary states and societies does not, at least initially, necessarily translate into political violence. What occurs is more a clash of political values, a conflict between the specific values being promoted by the political elite on the one hand and those expressed during the rebellion on the other. Especially during spontaneous revolutions, people are often united not by what they want but rather by what they do not want. They know they do not want the present regime. What comes after is seldom discussed or theorized; it is simply assumed to be better. In the enthusiasm of the moment, there is no time for serious thought and contemplation, with visions of a better tomorrow frequently summarized in catch-all slogans. When that tomorrow actually arrives, and when those on top of the revolutionary coalition put their own vision into effect, then the realization sets in that the revolution is being "hijacked," its ideals corrupted, its vision diverted in a direction few anticipated. What transpires is a new round of violence, with new state leaders pushing through their own vision and agendas, and those not sharing that vision trying to keep the struggle alive. The overt violence that plagues post-revolutionary states is often also a product of internal squabbles among various political elites. Post-revolutionary states, for whom coercion is frequently synonymous with the process of institutionalization, often do not hesitate to force conformism on nonconformists and to resort to violence in order to eliminate opponents.

Crane Brinton argued that post-revolutionary states try to "enforce a life without the ordinary vices within a fairly short time."[4] The goal of the state is actually more than merely enforcing revolutionary ascetism and sobriety. It also has a cultural component, one that is intimately tied to processes of political consolidation. All too often, the post-revolutionary state's ostensibly cultural campaign is in reality a political effort aimed at deepening its consolidation and, in the process, eliminating its opponents.

The reigns of terror that follow revolutions are not just dark political experiences; they are as much projects designed to eradicate nonconformity with the new political as well as social and cultural orders. Calls for cultural vigilance become part and parcel of post-revolutionary life. Attempts at creating a New Man, socialist or otherwise depending on the revolution, become as much socially and culturally intrusive as they are politically stifling. Stalin's Cultural Revolution was meant to eradicate "enemies of the people." China's Great Leap Forward, from 1958 to 1962, was designed to abandon the Soviet model in favor of a Chinese way to accomplish socialism politically, culturally, and economically, all in one giant leap.[5] Mao soon launched a Cultural Revolution of his own, this one directed against "class enemies." The launch of the new campaign was a surprise to most regime insiders. It was meant to "revolutionize" Chinese society by purging an ill-defined "bourgeoisie within the party." By 1967, Mao's own views on the Cultural Revolution seemed to have reached a point of endorsing the destruction of the party organization itself.[6] In Iran, meanwhile, Khomeini empowered a so-called Hanging Judge to stamp out "corruption on Earth."[7] Other revolutions had similar cultural agendas, though perhaps less violent in nature and implementation. As Arshin Adib-Moghaddam has observed, whereas the Iranian revolution sought to create a *homo Islamicus*, the ultimate Islamic man, the Arab Spring paved the way for *homo Pictor*, "a transgendered subject that is not devoid of choice."[8]

In each of these cases, the success of the cultural dimensions of the state's campaign are difficult to measure. But the political consequences of revolutions are undeniable. Few post-revolutionary leaders can resist the temptation of placing themselves – or being placed by others – at the center of a new cult of personality. For most, their personality cult dies down when they depart the scene, by force or natural retirement. Mao's case, though an extreme example, represents the view of most other leaders in comparable positions. While the Chairman's continued radicalism and the elimination of some of his oldest revolutionary comrades had disillusioned many party cadres, and many ordinary Chinese were disillusioned with Mao's rule, at death he still retained the status of legitimate emperor.[9] To varying degrees, the same could be said about Robespierre, Lenin, and perhaps even Stalin, Ho Chi Minh, Khomeini, and Castro. Nelson Mandela, of a different caliber and in a different context altogether, remained universally beloved until his passing in 2013, years after having left office in 1999.

While the goal of political consolidation may be central to such projects, their penetrative social and cultural affects cannot be overlooked. Nevertheless, post-revolutionary societies succumb to the cultural edicts of their new rulers only grudgingly at best, the threat of being branded "counter-revolutionary" hanging over the heads of all nonconformists. Nevertheless, outbursts of defiance and overt opposition do exist. The violence that accompanied the imposition of moral codes by Iran's victorious revolutionaries is a striking illustration of culturally based frictions which entangle post-revolutionary polities.[10] The forced imposition of veiling by Iran's post-revolutionary government, for example, was part of a more comprehensive program designed to ensure the moral purity of the citizenry.[11] But it encountered vociferous opposition from large segments of Iranian population, for whom the action contradicted much that the liberating promises of the revolution stood for.[12]

The tensions accompanying the inculcation of a new cultural frame of reference are compounded by characteristics that post-revolutionary societies themselves assume as a result of the revolutionary experience. Specifically, the divisions that invariably characterize all societies become polarized as a result of the revolutionary experience. Frictions and subtle maneuvers, carried out with a sense of gentility for the sake of a semblance of post-revolutionary unity, soon give way to conflicts that become steadily more intense. As the revolution progresses, the stakes become higher. What were once faint and muted differences – be they ethnic, social, cultural, political, or religious in origin – become increasingly sharper, mutually exclusive tendencies, each hardened with time. Unspoken pacts and implicit arrangements that previously kept disparate social, ethnic, and economic groups in seeming harmony begin to break up and often degenerate into open warfare, the political glue that once kept the revolutionary coalition together rapidly coming apart.

Polarization occurs at two particular levels. On a general level, the advent and course of the revolutionary movement politicizes the population and, even after a post-revolutionary state has been firmly established, intensifies political beliefs and orientations. Polarization also occurs on a more fundamental level, involving the various tendencies that differentiate the various cultural orientations of post-revolutionary societies. Often after much disquiet, the ensuing political chaos is finally subdued as the new order consolidates itself. But because social and cultural values are deeply held and concern people's private attitudes and thoughts, it takes longer for new, dominant cultural forms to emerge, and even longer for them to become socially routinized. Social mosaics break apart, not to be reconstructed until well after new leaders can enforce their own cultural hegemony. People with different political values vie for greater cultural hegemony, attempting to mold the emerging norms of the New Society according to their own values and perceptions of right and wrong. Apart from the new political direction in which post-revolutionary states try to lead their societies, there is an attempt from within post-revolutionary societies to rethink cultural priorities, reformulate dominant values, and redirect social energies. At the very least, there are efforts by some social actors, especially those with deeper convictions, to impose their own cultural values and perceptions on the larger society.

A polarization of social and cultural differences occurs concurrent with, and mutually reinforces, a dramatic rise in the overall level of political awareness and activity by the general population. Revolutionary mass mobilization, polarity of cultural values, and inclusionary political practices, all of which combine to give post-revolutionary polities an intensely charged character, lead to the "politicization of traditionally nonpolitical social sectors."[13] Observations by one of the chroniclers of the euphoric days of the Egyptian revolution are worth quoting here:

> The street-side vendor suddenly had an Egyptian flag; the taxi driver had an opinion; the young man on the street was no longer scared to say that there was something he didn't like; the tree trunks were painted red, white and black; the youth, once skulking, were now handing out flyers, forming political parties and collectives, chanting, discussing, planning, hoping, for those better lives. For every emotion, every thought, every idea, now, there was an audience, and on the same street corners that were once host to dejected, possibility was being born.[14]

This politicization is achieved not only through the attempts of revolutionary leaders to mobilize previously docile masses through propaganda and manipulation, but also through the self-perpetuating nature of political participation. Political participation, and at its heart exposure to political information – tainted and biased as that information may be – enhances the ability to conceptualize and develop more abstract understandings of the political system.[15] What results is not necessarily a "superior capacity for political discernment,"[16] but rather a greater willingness to partake in political activities. The post-revolutionary society as a whole thus becomes more politicized, more willing and able to take a critical look at the political environment. In a paradoxical development, this politicized society becomes politically more charged, with its political senses having grown sharper due to the revolutionary experience, while at the same time it becomes more dogmatic, with the rhetoric of revolutionary certainty replacing reasoned political discourse. The level of debate and argument rises, but the underlying ideological dogmas remain unchanged. Likening post-revolutionary Egypt to "a republic of arguments," Nathan Brown writes the following on the outcome of the Arab Spring:

> Arab politics – *in the sense of discussions and arguments about public affairs* – has been reborn. It is pursued, sustained, and developed in many overlapping institutions and practices. The structures of political arguments do not merely overlap. They interact in novel ways that, while they hardly replace older hierarchies and structures of authority, still mollify, steer, and even occasionally undermine or limit them. An authority figure who would brook no public dissent a generation ago now finds his words moved into media where they are easily mocked.[17]

The relationship between mass political participation and the rhetorical demagoguery that permeates political life in post-revolutionary societies is an important one. Mass mobilization, acts of valor and heroism, a sense of certitude and self-righteousness, the semblance of participatory democracy, and the sheer weight of the revolution as a dramatic historical event all lead to the development of a collective identity and solidarity arising out of the revolutionary experience. As William Gamson has observed, "Movement identities create boundaries between an 'us' and a 'them.' From the beginning, [there are] sharp distinctions between two types of critics: those who [are] part of the movement and those who [are] not."[18]

In the process, "movement participants construct a 'we' that becomes, in varying degrees with different individuals, part of their own definition of self."[19] At the core of this identity are the ideals around which the group originally mobilized. When confronted with risks, the group's identity becomes all the more pulverized, its ideals assuming an almost sacred character. In post-revolutionary societies, the solidarity of mobilized groups is reinforced by having withstood the harsh tests of the revolution. Even for those revolutionary groups for whom control over the state remains elusive, their ideals have achieved a measure of victory over those prevalent in the *ancien regime*.

Under such circumstances, the identity of the group supplants and replaces the identity of the individual. "When a collective identity becomes a central part of one's personal identity, group solidarity and personal honor become indistinguishable."[20] Belief in certain values and political doctrines become central to the self-perceptions of most citizens in post-revolutionary societies. They identify themselves, and are in turn identified by others, by virtue of their positions on the burning political questions of the time. The identity of most becomes that propagated by the emerging post-revolutionary state. In name if not in spirit, the Russians became staunch Leninists, the Chinese devout Maoists, the Iranians "Followers of the Imam's Path," and the Cubans all "Fidelistas." For the doctrinal diehards who refuse to recognize the legitimacy of the new victors' ideals, political dogmas become an even more central part of their identity. They consider the revolution to have been rightly theirs but usurped by others along the way. The most potent weapon these aspiring revolutionaries have is their ideology, the physical battle having been ruthlessly won by the revolution's hijackers. In the uncompromising, indeed stifling, atmosphere of the post-revolutionary environment, ideological demagoguery is all but inevitable.

Increased politicization, collective identity, mass participation, and demagoguery are in turn perpetuated by the self-sustaining nature of revolutionary mobilization itself. Even after the revolution's success, people who were mobilized toward revolutionary goals tend to have a romanticized image of their "mission" and of the actual process of mobilization itself. Specifically, they tend to idealize the quality of social relationships in their movement, "at times reflecting wishful thinking about the way things ought to be."[21] The propaganda and inclusionary policies of the new government are not ineffective. They are, however, greatly complemented by the impulse of the populace to maintain their newly found sense of self-worth and empowerment. Especially among formerly marginalized groups, many want to maintain a "sense of non-private, extra-familial worth: a sense that one must be recognized as having intrinsic value and worth, not just to family and friends but to others in the larger society."[22]

The glorification of the masses reaches into the arts and the popular culture. Similar to post-revolutionary Russia and China, for example, by the 1950s, in Vietnam the all-consuming rubrics of "people's art" and "socialist realism" pervaded the arts and literature. In all cases, the people's continued struggle was mythologized, romantically upheld for others to emulate.[23]

Moreover, especially among those who took part in the revolutionary struggle, continued mobilization and choreographed demonstrations become ends in themselves.[24] The sacrifices for the revolution are not easily forgotten, particularly among those with fallen comrades. "The dead live," it is said of revolutionary martyrs, "and, recognized by the revolution, continue to work on its behalf."[25] Political participation is, in itself, perceived to be one of the fruits of the revolution. Efforts to halt it or to gain control over it are bound to meet with determined opposition. Instead, as part of their consolidation efforts, post-revolutionary states reinforce and manipulate it.

There is, lastly, a marked rise in the nationalistic sentiments that permeate post-revolutionary societies. Considerable euphoria is generated with the success of the revolutionary movement, the public frenzied with a sense of power rarely experienced before. For everyone involved, the "motherland" becomes the main source of inspiration and the principal reason for embarking on political activity. The term "motherland," or some glorified version of it, becomes part of the routine vernacular of the day. Long-gone historic figures are resurrected and upheld as heroes of the revolution's antecedents. Stalin went so far as to justify the actions of the most notorious of Russian leaders, including Ivan the Terrible. Mao, perhaps independently, glorified Genghis Khan, and Castro, somewhat less perniciously, upheld the memory of José Martí.[26]

For the newly emerging political elite, love of the motherland becomes a particularly important means of maintaining popular support. In cases where international wars occur, whipping up nationalist sentiments becomes a crucial part of the political project.[27] But the manipulation of popular nationalist feelings becomes central to the consolidation of power against domestic enemies also, with nonconformists and dissidents branded as traitors working to undermine the motherland. More importantly, nationalist sentiments are often called on to justify the economic sacrifices that post-revolutionary states demand of their citizens. At the same time, groups for whom the revolution has been hijacked justify their continued, extralegal pursuit of power not on grounds of merely wanting power but on grounds of a better vision of what is right for the country. Whether truly a pawn of the state's propaganda or genuinely taken in by the euphoria of the revolutionary experience, the public is, in the meanwhile, also caught up in the nationalistic frenzy. State-articulated nationalism, as defined by state leaders in a manner that suits their political purposes, finds a receptive ear among the urban masses. For once, official and popular perceptions of nationalism complement and reinforce one another.

It is within this overall context that post-revolutionary societies operate, at least in the immediate aftermath of revolutions. But for how long? Do societies endlessly experience these phenomena once they have undergone a revolution? There are no definitive answers to these questions, for a revolution or a specific aspect of it cannot be said to have necessarily ended say five or ten years after its success. Some revolutions never die, or at least unleash dynamics whose effects touch generations of lives. Most do, nonetheless, peter out at some point or another, their lingering social, cultural, and emotional – if not political – effects eventually routinized by the force of time. The polarization of the masses, both culturally and politically, eventually subsides. As wars end, whether fought domestically or internationally, so does euphoric nationalism subside and turn into an ordinary sense of attachment to the country. Demands for continued participation in the political process become routinized under inclusionary systems, concern with the symbolism of mass participation giving way to the realities of everyday life. The level of political discourse and debate remain high, at least compared to pre-revolutionary times, but still carefully eyed by the political establishment. Perhaps most importantly, the conflictual relationship between the state and society becomes less conflict ridden, even if because of state coercion rather than voluntary compliance by otherwise noncompliant social actors. In other words, a new political culture begins to take hold, providing the milieu within which state–society relations are formulated.

Political Culture

Simply put, political culture is made up of the intersection of culture and politics. Politics and culture have a mutually reinforcing relationship. This relationship assumes particular characteristics in post-revolutionary circumstances. At the most basic level, political culture refers to the cultural values that govern political behavior.[28] In their pioneering work on the subject, Gabriel Almond and Sidney Verba defined political culture as the "particular distribution of patterns of orientation toward political objects among members of the nation."[29] They saw political culture as the connecting link between micro- and macro-politics, with popular political perceptions and orientations having direct bearing on a country's political institutions and prevailing patterns of political behavior.[30] Political culture affects "the conduct of individuals in their political roles, the content of their political demands, and their responses to laws."[31] In short, political culture is made up of the sum total of popular perceptions toward the body politic.

Not surprisingly, in revolutionary circumstances significant changes occur to the political culture. In fact, a mutually reinforcing relationship develops between the post-revolutionary institutions on the one hand, and the new, emerging political culture on the other. Political initiatives by the new elites foster new and radically different ways in which they are perceived by the public, while cultural traits with roots in both the ethos of revolution and the pre-revolutionary era in turn nurture and strengthen evolving political forms.

Revolutions, it was earlier mentioned, are caused and in turn bring about a collapse of social control. This is reversed by the reestablishment of the repressive capacities of the state, which, coercively if need be, devises, implements, and reinforces new norms for political conduct. In a sense, the post-revolutionary state becomes domestically powerful enough to be able to impose its tailor-made political culture on society. This new political culture is not completely alien to the populace and its many nuances are, in fact, much more in tune with the sensibilities of the people than was the case with the political culture of the *ancien regime*. This is a political culture borne out of a mass-based revolution, embodying the ethos of popular struggle. It is one that by necessity harnesses politically inclusionary principles, ceaselessly striving to minimize any gaps that may appear between the masses and the political establishment. The distinction between the rhetorical "government of the masses" as a tool for political gimmickry and an actual reality becomes increasingly blurred. Popular identification with the state in fact becomes the most marked characteristic of the system.[32] The apparent marriage of society and the body politic at times becomes so pervasive that those subject to it cannot help but to idealize their predicament, perceiving of themselves as participants in a highly democratic political culture. Street democracy, choreographed as it may be, becomes a source of empowerment. The following passage, written by two scholars of Cuba, is representative of this type of idealization:

> The very evolution of citizen's political culture under the strong impact of the revolution has essentially modified the conditions for the exercise of participatory democracy and popular power in Cuba. The Cuban citizenry, independent of its ideological diversity, shares a complex political culture born out of the country's singular historical experience and developed and refined over three decades and has achieved a superior capacity for political discernment. These values, reinforced or constructed by the revolutionary process, are the fundamental substrate of potential change.[33]

As the preceding discussion has shown, post-revolutionary political cultures generally embody features that are conducive to mass political participation and collective behavior. Amid a highly charged political atmosphere, the state shows sensitivity toward popular political sentiments, all the while propagating and trying to instill its own values among the population. In his discussion of the political culture of post-revolutionary China, Lucian Pye has presented an analysis that, despite its contextual specificity, applies to most other post-revolutionary political cultures. Chinese political culture, he argues, is marked by

> sensitivity of authority to matters of "face," the need for authority to omnipotence, the legitimacy of bewailing grievances, the urge to monopolize virtue and to claim the high ground of morality, the drive to try to shame others, an obsession with revenge, the inability to compromise publicly, and so on. All of which come down to a basic problem in Chinese political culture, the management of aggression. Any conflict arouses hate; it becomes almost impossible to disagree politically without becoming disagreeable.[34]

These traits are not necessarily unique to the Chinese example. They are, to one extent or another, found almost universally in all post-revolutionary political cultures.

Two characteristics particularly stand out. The first is the all-engrossing nature of the political domain. In post-revolutionary circumstances, nearly every facet of life, from the most mundane to the most personal, somehow becomes political. This is brought on by a confluence of government initiatives as well as general popular perceptions. On the one hand, post-revolutionary states are determined to give popular currency to their new values and symbols. Their zealous drive for symbolic legitimacy often touches the most personal aspects of the lives of their citizens. From marriage ceremonies to funeral processions, from naming newborn babies to choosing places of residence, everything becomes tied into the symbolic legitimacy of the new, revolutionary order. In post-revolutionary Iran, for example, during the country's war with Iraq from 1980 to 1988, official condolence messages for war casualties that appeared in newspapers often congratulated the family of the deceased for having contributed a "martyr" to the revolutionary cause.

A second feature of post-revolutionary political cultures is their decidedly zero-sum nature. These black-and-white political cultures are not conducive to shades of gray. Despite the rhetoric of the revolution, such political cultures are, in fact, highly rigid and dogmatic. The underlying reasons for the appearance of inflexible political cultures after revolutions has to do with the sense of certainty and moral righteousness that permeates them. Revolutionary leaders are, by nature, certain of what they want, often believing their cause to be sacred. They talk, act, and conduct themselves as if their mission is messianic and their message celestial. Many go so far as to deify themselves, trying, as Mao did, to become immortal by fusing their ego with the collective imagination.[35] Revolutions involve mass mobilization, and mass mobilization involves belief, certainty, and conviction.

Those who show devotion to the cause of the revolution after its success are true believers, often imbued with a strong sense of moral righteousness, a stern belief in a unique understanding of truth. Considering the drama and intensity of revolutions, there often develops a sense that idealistic, revolutionary ends justify the means. In the process, most of the original ideals for which the revolution stood are ignored or modified. A cultural milieu is formed in which ideological rigidity, dogmatism, cults of personality, messianic tendencies, and the justification of ends by means become acceptable. Democracy is preached by the revolutionary government but is practiced only in city streets and public squares rather than the ballot box. Inclusionary policies perpetuate a semblance of democratic practices, but as an actual, culturally accepted and ingrained force, democracy remains at best an elusive ideal.

The persistence of antidemocratic trends in post-revolutionary political cultures does not automatically mean that political cultures do not undergo far-reaching, revolutionary transformations. Indeed, *revolutionary* political cultures are often just that, revolutionary. They are considerably different from the cultures they replace. Not only are their symbolic representations different, but so are their basic tenets in terms of popular perceptions of the body politic. In the inclusionary political systems that develop after successful revolutions, people often conceive of themselves as participants in a democratic process, although the political arena may indeed be highly rigid and stifling. The political culture, those popular perceptions that people have of the political establishment, is dramatically changed. People perceive the political system much more favorably, and in fact see the act of engaging in politics in a completely different light. No longer is "politicking" frowned on as it was prior to the revolution, no longer are politicians seen as vain and corrupt. Politics becomes a passionate field of activity devoted to the betterment of mankind; its artisans, the politicians, are revolutionary heroes committed to bringing about a better life. People identify with these rebels-cum-leaders much more readily. They feel, on the whole, closer to the political establishment, indeed perceiving themselves as an integral part of the political process. Post-revolutionary leaders also often have a greater degree of what one scholar calls "solidary relations with the broader strata."[36] Even if they find it necessary to resort to violence and coercion to legitimize their newly won powers – which they frequently do – they still retain a much closer relationship to the masses than pre-revolutionary leaders ever did.

Dissent and Opposition

Given the nature of post-revolutionary systems, societies, and political cultures, is the formulation and development – if not necessarily the expression – of dissent and opposition possible? The break-up of the successful revolutionary coalition and the ensuing violence during the reign of terror is a "natural corollary" of the revolutionary process.[37] But are opposition movements emerging outside of the revolutionary coalition also possible? Post-revolutionary political systems are inclusionary at best and totalitarian at worst, supported by political cultures with antidemocratic tendencies. With the state embarking on an intense propaganda campaign in order to attain legitimacy, supported by liberal use of violence in order to eliminate opponents, political opposition is stifled and not given much breathing room. Opposition is also stifled culturally, its message finding little purchase in a cultural environment permeated by rigid and inflexible dogmas. Is there, however, still a possibility that moves to oppose the revolutionary establishment might be made by the various social actors?

Opposition to revolutionary establishments is, indeed, a distinct possibility. In fact, despite, and often because of, the rigid conformism that characterizes post-revolutionary polities, flares of opposition to the political establishment commonly appear, at times with great intensity. Even if the new regime can effectively suppress the expression of oppositional sentiments, there are still dynamics at work that allow such sentiments to be formulated amongst certain groups. These underlying sentiments often boil into the surface and, even if for only a brief interlude, result in intense and violent conflicts. Among these potential sources of opposition to the post-revolutionary state, two stand out. They are, broadly, members of the old elite seeking to restore the previous regime, and former members of the revolutionary coalition who do not agree with the evolving direction of the revolution. Either individually or combined, potential efforts by these state opponents deepen the volatility of the political atmosphere following a revolution. The sense of siege felt by new state leaders has consequences for the profile and policies they adopt in relation to the larger society.

There is, nevertheless, a clear difference between the nature and extent of anti-government sentiments before the revolution as opposed to afterward. Prior to the success of revolutionary movements, anti-state sentiments are relatively widespread and, even if at times muted by the coercive arms of the state, they are held deeply enough to facilitate mass mobilization and revolutionary agitation. After the revolution, however, anti-state sentiments are often narrowly based, with state opponents all too often being a small minority among a vast majority of vocal and active pro-government supporters.

The politicization of previously nonpolitical groups has been previously alluded to but is worth recounting here. Following revolutions, the political atmosphere is intensely charged and polarized. This polarization is further accentuated by the incessant propaganda of not only the new political elite but also those of revolutionary hopefuls who find themselves excluded from the new institutional arrangements. Inclusionary practices are adopted not only by the state but also by the various politicized, non-governmental groups. Groups left out of the political formula carry forward their campaign to muster public support more zealously than ever before, in the process finding the charged political environment conducive to their ends. New political parties emerge, each claiming to spearhead an ostensibly revolutionary cause. Many such parties concentrate on peripheral issues, taking advantage of the tenuous position of post-revolutionary states in order to press for specific, narrowly based ethnic and regional demands. Resenting the efforts of post-revolutionary states to re-impose central authority on the country, such parties, even if not necessarily regionally based, often spearhead the cause of regional issues – autonomy, the right to teach the local dialect in schools, the right to control the local police force, refusal to be conscripted into the national army, and so on. These regional rebellions take place at a critical time in the life of the post-revolutionary state, when their powers are still being institutionalized: immediately after they have been established but before having had sufficient time to consolidate themselves. For a time, civil wars and the disintegration of the nation seem imminent. Civil wars, or at least armed secessionist movements, were indeed part of the immediate aftermaths of the French, Russian, Chinese, Vietnamese, and Iranian revolutions. In all cases, however, these regionally based conflicts were settled in favor of revolutionary elites once they had fully consolidated their powers.[38]

Apart from the possibility of opposition by elites seeking to share in the political fruits of the revolution, opposition is also likely from those remaining elements that were in one way or another tied to the *ancien regime*. When politically active, such elites are, by nature, counter-revolutionary, their prime purpose being the containment and eventual reversal of the revolution. Counter-revolutionary opposition to the post-revolutionary state is an inevitable phase of the revolutionary process. This is, however, an opposition that is neither forceful nor determined, its cause being one with little popularity and few supporters. Its task is to reverse the course of history, but its effort is faint and uninspired. As the military ventures of the White Russians showed, the efforts of such counter-revolutionaries are more cause for celebration among the revolution's foreign enemies rather than a real domestic threat.[39] These are, after all, members of the former elite, accustomed to a pampered life, not political activism and revolutionary agitation. Their main strength is neither their resolve nor their popularity but rather their once vast financial resources. Even with their economic power, they are hardly in a position to finance acts of violence against the revolutionary regime. Most are, in fact, no longer a real force inside their own country, having often been compelled to leave for exile or a safe haven. The most they can do is to use their money to fuel their propaganda campaign against the new order, a campaign with more listeners and adherents outside of the country than inside.

As the foregoing analysis demonstrates, dissent and opposition within post-revolutionary regimes is politically possible, and in fact prevalent, but socially and culturally vacuous. Despite its vibrancy and newly found zest, the post-revolutionary political culture is too much a captive of the new power elite to allow for unsolicited expressions of political opinion. The level of public debate may have changed. The caliber of political discourse may have progressed. Counter-revolutionaries sing their usual songs; long suppressed regional demands find temporary breathing room. But the underlying characteristics of the political establishment, those that nurture dogmatic tendencies and disallow the expression of conflicting views, remain the same. Dissidents are crushed with an intensity rarely seen in the pre-revolutionary era. Counter-revolutionaries and would-be separatists are punished harshly, all victims of a burgeoning police state.[40] The post-revolutionary state eventually triumphs, subduing all social groups that seek its overthrow. In the process, it shapes the social and cultural forces that govern the lives of its citizens.

Conclusion

Revolutions alter not just political institutions and practices but the very inner reaches of civil society as well. They change the ground rules on which social interactions are based, the perceptions that society has of the state and the manner in which the two interact, and the very direction in which social and cultural norms point. Revolutions consume the polity in totality, not just politically or socially but also culturally and emotionally. Few citizens are left untouched by the enormity of the revolution, their lives having been changed forever by its deeply penetrating effects. They not only see political objects differently but have a different perception of themselves and of their place within the political drama. People think differently, having achieved a measure of intellectual sophistication due to the sheer weight of the revolutionary experience.

Admittedly, the most conspicuous of revolutionary changes occur in the symbolic representations of the political establishment. They are, however, by no means the only changes that engulf the post-revolutionary polity. The dominant frames of political and cultural reference become unsettled, necessitating considerable normative and practical adjustments on the part of the general population. People need to learn and be familiarized with new political forms and symbols, accept their legitimacy, and make them part of their routine interactions with the body politic. This is at best a somewhat uneasy experience, involving fundamental shifts in the way people perceive and relate to the political universe around them. Many, in fact, resist adopting the new values attached to politics despite an overwhelming campaign by the state to give currency to its new political and cultural medians.

These new political values are radically different from the ones they replace. Regardless of what the pre-revolutionary political culture may have featured, the new values governing the post-revolutionary society are decidedly more puritanical, with much greater pretense to upholding the betterment of the entire society. But most revolutionary elites do not stop here. For many, the actual physical elimination of those related to the former rulers becomes a main revolutionary project. Guillotines, labor camps, hangings, and firing squads become the order of the day.

To avoid persecution, those members of the former elite who have the ability to do so emigrate. Many flee from real danger; many others flee because of the possibility of danger. Still others leave because they find the new political and cultural environments unbearable. These emigrants invariably make their way into countries where they find the political establishment sympathetic to their plight. Cultural proximity, if not outright similarity, does not hurt. What results is a growing community of *emigres* largely made up of wealthy former elites. They are, by nature, invariably opposed to the revolutionary system in place back in their mother country. Similar to despotic systems and counter-revolutionaries, *emigre* communities soon become a natural by-product of revolutions. Just as the French and Russian revolutions led to the appearance of *emigre* communities in Austria-Hungary and Germany, so did the Cuban and Iranian revolutions lead to the development of *emigre* communities in the United States. Similarly, an *emigre* Algerian community formed in France soon after Algeria's revolutionary war of independence.[41] Regardless of their specific predicaments, most *emigres* are soon resigned to the fact that their place in history has forever been lost, and they adopt their new place of residence as their own. A few, however, continue to entertain thoughts of defeating the revolution and become members of a vocal but ineffective counter-revolutionary movement.

Vociferous propaganda by counter-revolutionaries is only one of the less significant ramifications of the old elite's flight abroad. Their emigration can potentially have much more immediate negative ramifications for the fledgling political system they leave behind. They do, after all, tend to form the wealthiest segment of the population, often controlling key industries and sources of investment. Their flight may expedite the institutionalization of new political elites, but it also results in a direct and very conspicuous flight of capital. Whether through voluntary departure from the country or forced property confiscation, many of the country's economic magnates are dispossessed, no longer capable of supporting the economic networks that often revolve around them. The economic consequences can be multi-faceted and dire.

These difficulties are further compounded by a brain-drain, with the elite's most educated and skilled members leaving for safe havens. Doctors and engineers join the wave of wealthy merchants, industrialists, and high-ranking military and civilian officials streaming out of the country.[42] The consequences of such wholesale immigrations for the revolutionary country's economy and welfare are highly detrimental.

The second ramification of the forced imposition of revolutionary norms and values is far less tangible, and thus harder to discern. It involves a "psychic split," a dichotomy of the citizen's self-identity between ardent supporters of "the cause" on the one hand and ordinary individuals on the other. Similar to those living under totalitarian systems, the individual develops what one observer calls a "true" and a "false" self.

> An appropriately modulated false self protects the true self from environmental threats; the false self permits the true self to act only during those moments when success, if not assured, is probable; it allows the true self to live secretly, silently. In this sense, the false sense encompasses an appropriate and necessary "polite and mannered social attitude." After all, the "spontaneous gestures" may not always be functional. More colloquially,

> at times the true self needs a mask behind which to hide. Therefore, individuals quite naturally have a public and a private self.[43]

Political prudence often dictates behavior that may not necessarily be heartfelt, or a behavior that, even if voluntary, is intensified by the force of circumstances. In post-revolutionary circumstances, the split between the public and the private selves may not be as accentuated as is the case in totalitarian systems, of the kind that existed in Eastern Europe before 1989, for example, but it does, nonetheless, exist. Post-revolutionary societies are characterized by a new sense of identity wrapped in nationalism, revolutionary symbols, and the worship of revolutionary heroes, both dead and alive. The new, post-revolutionary political culture does support these principles, giving them a genuine measure of popularity among the population. However, as the revolution ages and its zeal subsides, as its message begins to tire, even the most devout, whole-hearted adherence to its ideals becomes more and more of a facade. To survive, those who engage in overt political activity have no alternative but to adopt a split self, whether consciously or subconsciously.[44]

The development of a "psychic split" serves to epitomize the very depths to which revolutions affect and change the polities in which they occur. Revolutions may be initially sparked by distinctively political phenomena, but their affects and ramifications are in no way limited to the political domain. They touch societies both as a whole and at a personal level, altering the individual lives of citizens. Whether making them political activists for the first time or enhancing their ability to think and conceptualize politically, be it subjecting them to a split personality or forcing their emigration, in one way or another revolutions change people's daily lives. Because of the revolution, many feel better about themselves, having achieved the impossible and in the process acquiring a new sense of identity and self-worth. Others feel betrayed, angered at their former comrades for stealing the harvests they feel rightly belong to them. Still others seek to reverse the tide of the revolution, scheming ways to restore past glory and power. A few stand on the sidelines, marveling at the perceived savagery of the drama being played out around them. And yet, like it or not, they too are players in this drama, unwittingly pushing forward the historical journey of the revolution.

6 CONCLUSION

Revolutions are dramatic episodes in the political history of the countries in which they occur. They alter fundamental aspects of not only prevailing political, social, cultural, and economic arrangements but the very personal lives of the citizens involved as well. As the preceding chapters demonstrated, revolutions are caused primarily by a coalescence of political, social, cultural, and diplomatic factors. Politically, revolutions will not succeed unless the state in which they take place is confronted with fundamental systemic problems that make its collapse possible. The mobilization of broad strata of society toward specifically revolutionary goals is equally important, brought about by situational links between revolutionary groups and the general masses on the one hand, and deep-seated grievances that make society susceptible to revolutionary mobilization on the other. Once they succeed, revolutions bring about political systems that are inherently more expansive and more reliant on coercion than the ones they replace. New leaders emerge following what is often an extremely brutal and violent struggle among former comrades, forging new institutional and cultural norms as part of a campaign to establish a new order. They often confront determined dissent and opposition from groups whose hopes had raised greatly during the revolutionary process. Seldom, however, are post-revolutionary systems seriously challenged, at least domestically, most outlasting the nostalgic dreams and aspirations of counter-revolutionaries.

Revolutions come about as a result of dynamics that are engendered both in the prevailing political structures and the social and cultural makeup of population. That they require weakened political institutions – weak in relation to society – is a given. The causes of that weakness may be indigenous and endemic to the political system or the result of international dynamics – wars, for example – but at any rate they need to occur concurrent with social and cultural developments that make revolutionary mass mobilization feasible and its success probable. Revolutions necessitate the existence and formulation of grievances at the social level, be they based on frustrated political or economic aspirations or unease over the pace and consequences of rapid social change. They cannot, however, be reduced to the efforts of what some psychologists dismiss as "chronic protestors" or other malcontents.[1] Invariably, they are brought about by, and in turn accentuate, popular feelings of nationalism, best represented by the innate message of slogans that gain widespread, though for the most part temporary, popularity during times of revolutionary upheaval. Concurrent with a rise in love for "the motherland" is a rise in the popularity of ideologies that in ordinary times are considered "revolutionary" – Marxism-Leninism is a prime example – or of ideologies that assume an increasingly revolutionary flavor though they may be static in other times – political Islam, for example. Sooner or later, at any rate, an ideology grows to become the dominant theme of the revolution, embodying the main language within which demands for the attainment of a new society are formulated.

Whether revolutions start voluntarily or are the result of largely uncontrollable social and political dynamics depends on the exact nature of the revolution in question. Some begin as carefully planned programs for the overthrow and replacement of the existing state. In these instances, which are often the result of guerrilla warfare, the original objectives and the outcome of the revolution tend to correspond most closely, with successful revolutionaries setting out to implement previously laid-out blueprints for social and political conduct.

Other revolutions, however, involve greater spontaneity, with oppositional activists being propelled into positions of revolutionary leadership as a result of a series of developments with which they originally did not have much to do. In these cases, revolutionary aspirations and demands are formulated as an embryonic oppositional movement snowballs into a full-blown revolution, growing in momentum as situational opportunities facilitate mass mobilization and expedite the collapse of a dying state. At least in their initial stages, these revolutions do not have clear objectives, and neither do they have clear leaders, and revolutionary goals and aspirations are at best summed up and expressed in vague, catch-all slogans. In these circumstances, pre-revolutionary states often hasten their own demise through a series of missteps, in the process deepening the institutional crises that allowed for anti-government protests in the first place. The general population, meanwhile, or at least significant segments of it, participates in revolutions voluntarily, though their negative attitudes toward the old order are already largely shaped by the existence of what they perceive to be exploitative economic and political arrangements.

The success of the revolutionary movements ushers in a new era, one in which even the most mundane facets of life are revolutionized. The state, by nature weak prior to the start of the revolutionary movement, now grows in strength, as well as in intrusive powers and its reliance on and willingness to use coercion. Much of this surge in power comes from the incorporation of previously excluded masses into the political process, coupled with the prevalence of new, zero-sum political values that demand conformity and intolerance of dissent.

As most, but not all, examples from the last few decades have demonstrated, revolutions do not necessarily have to end up in dictatorships. Democratic systems emerged as a result of revolutions in Eastern Europe in the late 1980s and in South Africa in the early 1990s. As in all democracies, of course, the states that emerged out of these revolutions have gone through growing pains, as evident from the many corruption scandals of Jacob Zuma's presidency in South African (in office from 2009 to 2018) or the constraints on political space in Hungary under the populist Prime Minister Viktor Orbán (first elected in 2010 and in office as of this writing). But the ways in which the revolutions of Eastern Europe and South Africa turned out were decisively different from the other planned and spontaneous revolutions discussed in Chapters 2 and 3, as were the nature and conduct of state institutions and the overall patterns of state–society relations examined in Chapters 4 and 5.

Four key factors resulted in these revolutions having their particular outcomes. Broadly, these factors can be divided into institutional dynamics, leadership decisions, the international context, and economic issues. In terms of institutional dynamics, the empowerment of social actors and the weakness of state institutions had not reached a stage in which one could effectively overwhelm the other. Instead, a negative equilibrium of sorts had emerged between state and society in which neither revolution nor a return to the status quo ante was possible. A deliberate decision was made by actors on both sides to sit down and negotiate a way out of the stasis. Agency is important, with institutional arrangements providing the context within which key decisions are made.

In addition to the institutional context, these decisions were heavily influenced by the broader international environment within which they were made. The East European revolutions were occurring in a region in which democracy had by the 1980s become an established and sought-after norm. Regardless of their specific ideologies, post-revolutionary states in France in the 1790s, Russia in the 1920s and 1930s, China in the 1950s, and Iran in the 1980s – as well as many other similar examples – did not evolve in regions where democratic principles and practices had been firmly grounded. By the 1980s, however, most if not all of Europe had had a long and relatively successful marriage with democracy, which the newcomers, who were escaping from the communist antithesis, could not overlook. If for no other reason, the element of a common cultural identity, jealously guarded by most Europeans, was an important determinant of the democratic character of Europe's post-communist regimes.

Related to this is the even more important factor of economic needs. In each of the former communist counties of Europe, moves toward the establishment of democratic institutions were seen as instrumental in attracting economic assistance from abroad, either in terms of direct grants or investments. Whereas the foreign policies of other post-revolutionary states were largely xenophobic, or at least critical of the international status quo, the post-communist states of Europe needed to pursue policies aimed at international economic integration and acceptance by Europe's older – and richer – democracies. These were, after all, states that emerged after having lost the Cold War and were then eager to join the community of the victors.

The contrasting examples of the Arab Spring are instructive. To begin with, there was no institutional negative equilibrium. In most cases, the armed forces abandoned ruling autocrats and popular protests brought the revolutionary movement to a head. Leadership decisions and the international context moved the Tunisian and Egyptian revolutions in two different directions. In Tunisia, the revolutionaries, headed by the Islamically inclined Ennahda Movement, decided to negotiate both with other revolutionary groups and with soft-liners from the former regime. This, in turn, helped ameliorate concerns of foreign powers such as the United States and France that Tunisia was moving in an "Islamist," potentially anti-Western direction. In Egypt, on the other hand, the army initially sought to control the post-Mubarak transition through the institution of the Supreme Council of the Armed Forces, SCAF. But when presidential elections brought to office the Muslim Brotherhood's Mohamed Morsi, the new president showed no appetite for power-sharing, and, despite only a slim electoral victory, set out to implement policies that neither the military nor the United States necessarily approved of. The army, with American approval, overthrew Morsi and began to rule Egypt directly.[2]

Back in 2001, Robin Wright, an astute observer of the Middle East and especially Iran, called the Iranian revolution "the last great revolution" of its kind.[3] So far, it seems, Wright's assertion has withstood the test of time, though the jury on the broader historical consequences of the Arab Spring is still out. There are several reasons for this scarcity of contemporary revolutions, one of the most important of which has to do with the proliferation of what may be called "competitive authoritarian" states. These are hybrid states with important characteristics of both democracy and authoritarianism. They are

> civilian regimes in which formal democratic institutions exist and are widely viewed as the primary means of gaining power, but in which the incumbents' abuse of the state places them at a significant advantage vis-à-vis their opponents. Such regimes are competitive in that opposition parties use democratic institutions to contest seriously for power, but they are not democratic because the playing field is heavily skewed in favor of incumbents. Competition is thus real but unfair.[4]

These competitive authoritarian states are likely to follow one of three trajectories: democratization, unstable authoritarianism, and stable authoritarianism. These different pathways in large measure depend on the densities of ties and linkages with the West in economic, political, diplomatic, and social domains as well as on cross-border flows of capital goods, services, and people. Equally important are the incumbents' organizational power and the scope and cohesion of state structures such as governing parties and elites.[5] In addition to the personal preferences of state leaders – in fact, much more important – it is a combination of opportunities and constraints that determine whether competitive authoritarian states opt for democratization in preference over power maintenance, even if it means resorting to non-authoritarian methods.[6] Whatever their trajectory may be, nonetheless, these types of states are unlikely to succumb to revolutions.

The extent to which competitive authoritarian systems can prevent revolutionary circumstance from boiling over to the surface is context specific. Full-blown revolutions have historically been quite infrequent, and, with ever more effective instruments of state surveillance and control, not to mention hybridity, there will likely to be even fewer revolutions with time. As we have seen, the occurrence of revolutions depends on a coalescence of historical, political, sociocultural, and international developments. So long as these developments do not simultaneously occur and manifest in specific revolutionary circumstances, instances of sporadic violence and instability are the most that nondemocratic states are likely to face. Hope for revolutions, even if aborted, will continue to inspire generations of political activists in those systems that block, or are perceived to block, the political and economic aspirations of their citizens. Only meaningfully functioning democratic systems, with broad legitimacy, can fully safeguard themselves against revolutions. Otherwise, in the many instances where the institutional means of political competition are absent or meaningless, the tendency toward violence and revolutions remains a distinct possibility.

* * *

I will end this book on a personal note. I first came to the academic study of revolutions as a twenty-something graduate student while working on a dissertation on the causes of the Iranian revolution. While my social science training dictated that I remain objective and non-emotional toward the subject of my study, my personal upbringing in Iran, and my distaste for the pre-revolutionary state, filled me with pride at the Shah's overthrow. Like millions of other Iranians, I found myself in broad agreement with the revolution's goals and objectives. Until, that is, a reign of terror set in and the post-revolutionary state resorted to depths of repression that were previously unfathomable. Those conflicting emotions have not subsided in me, reflecting a much broader mixture of triumphs and torments that Iran has experienced since its revolution back in 1978–1979. A more recent account by an activist in Tunisia's 2011 revolution echoes my own sentiments from all those decades ago:

> At first everyone was on a high: the President's flight abroad, the rapid revolutionary changes imposed by an enthusiastic public, the thundering roar of a public who had risen from beneath the ashes of misery and fear like a phoenix. It was pure romance, and I remember it now with much nostalgia and awe. But then things changed. New balances of power, new circles of influence, new political relationships began to take shape, and it seemed to me, and others like me, that the dictator's departure had not resulted in the departure of dictatorship. Corruption still riddled the body politic and the corrupt themselves, the "followers of the former regime," still crept through the veins of state agencies, the media, and the judiciary.[7]

Revolutions, all revolutions, are ultimately about human emotions. And whether they occur or not depends in large measure not only on the structural dynamics to which so much of this book has been devoted, but on the perceptions and lived experiences of those who pour into the streets or hide in the jungle, clench their fists or take up arms, and sacrifice daily routines and jobs and probably much more in order to move the revolution forward. If the repressive outcomes of past revolutions are within living memory, then fewer individuals are likely to be moved to launch yet another revolution. But for those not having been through or closely experiencing a revolution, given the right combination of circumstances, the desire to strive for a better future is just as compelling. As long as there is hope, and as long as there are perceptions of injustice and inequity and a chance of overcoming them, revolutions remain a distinct possibility.

CHRONOLOGY OF REVOLUTIONS

The French Revolution

Date	*Event*
1787	February 22: Assembly of Notables is convened
	August 14: Louis XVI imposes new taxes and exiles Parlement of Paris to Troyes
	Mid-August: Paris demonstrations in support of Parliament
1788	August 8: State announces The Estates General will meet May 1, 1789 the *Ancien Regime* government collapses
	December 5: Louis XVI agrees to double the representation of the Third Estate in the Estates-General
1789	January–March: Urban riots throughout France
	April 27–28: Riots in Paris
	May 5: Opening session of the Estates General
	May 6: Deputies of the Third Estate refuse to meet as a separate chamber
	June 17: Third Estate declares itself a National Assembly
	June 19: First Estate votes to join the National Assembly
	June 20: Tennis Court oath
	June 23: Louis XVI announces rejection of resolutions proposed by the Third Estate
	June 27: Louis XVI releases order to clergy and nobility to join the Third Estate
	July 13: The National Guard is formed

July 14: The storming and fall of the Bastille
July 17: Beginning of municipal revolts and the "Great Fear," featuring peasant revolts against feudalism and alleged "aristocratic conspiracy"
August 5–11: Feudal privileges are abolished, taxes are made equal and offices are sold
August 26: National Assembly announces its approval of "Declaration of the Rights of Man and of the Citizen"
September: Louis XVI refuses to approve decrees abolishing privilege
October 5–6: "October Days," the King is brought to Paris
October 10: Louis XVI given the title "King of the French" instead of "King of France"
November 2: Nationalization of Church property
December 14–16: Legislation calling for the reorganization of the local government

1790 February 13: Religious orders and monastic vows are suppressed
June 19: Constituent Assembly announces abolition of nobility and titles
July 12: Civil Constitution of the Clergy
July 14: Bastille Day celebrated for the first time

1791 June 20: Flight of Varennes as Louis XVI and his family attempt to escape from Paris
June 25: King forcibly returns to Paris
July 17: Massacre on the Champ de Mars in Paris
September 13–14: King officially approves constitution
September 30: Dissolution of Constituent Assembly
October 1: Legislative Assembly inaugural meeting

1792 January–February: Riots in Paris over high prices of sugar and coffee
February–March: Food riots throughout France
April 20: France declares war on Austria
August 10–13: "10 August" Revolution, Tuileries is stormed, King and family imprisoned
September 2–6: "September Massacres" marks mass killings of prisoners in Paris

September 20: First meeting of the National Convention
December 11: Beginning of king's trial
1793 January 21: Execution of Louis XVI
April: Forming of the Committee for Public Safety
September 5: Robespierre declares Terror as "the order of the day"
October 10: National Convention decrees that government will be revolutionary until the return of peace
October 16: Execution of Marie-Antoinette
November 10: Festival of Liberty in Paris; Notre Dame Cathedral declared a Temple of Reason
December 25: Robespierre reports to the National Convention on the principles of revolutionary government
1794 July 27: Reign of Terror ends

The Russian Revolution

Date	*Event*
1890s	Mass urbanization and industrialization leads to socioeconomic stresses for the agricultural sector; starvation and poverty in the rural areas
	November 1: Nicholas II assumes the throne after his father Tsar Alexander III dies due to illness
	December: Lenin exiled to Siberia
1903	Social Democrat Party splits into the Bolshevik and Menshevik factions
1905	January: Bloody Sunday, as 1,000 peaceful demonstrators are gunned down by troops and police; Nicholas II is blamed by the media
	June: Mutiny at sea on the Potemkin battleship, which leads to riots in Odessa; Tsar sends orders for troops to quash the riots
	October: Tsar Nicholas II's October Manifesto is issued, promising civil liberties and the election of a Duma; the monarch's absolute power is somewhat restricted, and a Fundamental Laws of 1906 is subsequently drafted
1907	"June 1907 Coup" by PM Pyotr Stolypin and the Tsar dissolves the Second State Duma and some of its members are arrested; some electoral provisions of the Fundamental Law revised and restricted
1914–1917	WWI leads to sociopolitical stresses; Russia loses territory to Germany; mass mobilization of men causes social dislocation; population levels decline drastically; economy shrinks as trade patterns are disrupted and agricultural farmers revert to subsistence farming
1917	February: Rumors spread in St. Petersburg of disruptions to food stocks, including rations of flour and bread
	February 23: Due to its association with socialism, International Women's Day marches add to the rising tensions within the city
	February 24: 30,000 demonstrators go on strike and join the marches

February 25–26: Crowds of demonstrators increase to 300,000, while police and Cossack forces are reluctant to use force against them

February 27: Men of the Volynskii Regiment shoot their officers; other officers revolt against their garrison commanders

March 1: St. Petersburg Soviet issues Order No. 1, ordering the military to obey the Soviets instead of the Provisional Government

March 1–2: The Duma meets to establish a Provisional Committee for the Restoration of Order; Soviet Executive Committee endorses a Provisional Government, resulting in "Dual Power"; Tsar Nicholas II fails to muster troop support to restore order and tries to escape by train; he is instead ordered by the Duma to abdicate

March 2: Nicholas II abdicates and removes his 12-year-old son, Aleksei, from the succession

March 3: Nicholas II's brother, Mikhail Aleksandrovich, declines the throne; the Russian monarchy ends; Provisional Government takes control

April 16: Lenin arrives back in St. Petersburg from Switzerland, having travelled through Germany

July 3–7: Known as July Days, witnessing widespread, spontaneous demonstrations in St. Petersburg by soldiers, sailors, and industrial workers against the Provisional Government

September 9: The Kornilov Affair – General Kornilov's coup fails after he sends troops to St. Petersburg to combat the Bolsheviks, only leading to a strengthening of Bolshevik power

October 10–16: Lenin sends letters and makes speeches at Bolshevik's Central Committee, advocating for the Bolshevik seizure of power

October 23–24: Bolshevik leader Jaan Anvelt leads the seizure of power at Ravel and other major points across St. Petersburg

October 24: PM A. F. Kerensky attacks the Bolsheviks, ordering the re-arrest of Bolshevik members involved in the July Days; Bolshevik newspapers are shut down in St. Petersburg

October 25: The Bolsheviks and Left Socialist Revolutionaries stage a bloodless coup and seize control of St. Petersburg; Trotsky orders the Military–Revolutionary Committee of the St. Petersburg Soviet to seize control of the city's amenities and arrest government officials gathered at the Winter Palace

October 26–27: Trotsky's forces take control of Moscow

November: Socialist Revolutionaries claim most of the seats at the Constituent Assembly elections; Bolsheviks earn less than a quarter of the vote

December: Armistice signed by Russia and Central powers and fighting ceases

1918 January 18–19: The Constituent Assembly, elected in November 1917, is dissolved by the Bolsheviks

March 3: Brest-Litovsk Treaty – Russia ends its participation in the First World War

March 8: The Bolsheviks change the name of their party to the Russian Communist Party; Russia's capital is moved to Moscow

July 16–17: Tsar Nicholas II and his family are executed by the Bolsheviks in Yekaterinburg

August 30: "Red Terror" – After sustaining serious injury from an attempted assassination, Lenin orders multiple arrests and executions and the Red Terror begins

1921 March: Kronstadt mutiny – failed anti-Bolshevik uprising

March: "War Communism" comes to an end; "New Economic Policy" is introduced

1922 April 3: Joseph Stalin is appointed Secretary General of the Communist Party

December: The Soviet Union is created

1924 January 21: Lenin dies; in the ensuing power struggle within the party, Stalin emerges as party leader, and his rival Trotsky is dismissed and exiled

The Vietnamese Revolution

Date	*Event*
1887	Vietnam is under French rule and part of a colonial system, French Indochina, that consisted of several colonial territories in the region
1919	Ho Chi Minh lives and works in France until 1923
1920	July 19–August 7: The Second Congress of Comintern is held in Moscow
1923	Ho Chi Minh travels to the Soviet Union and joins the Comintern
1924	Ho establishes the Vietnamese Revolutionary Youth Association
1930	February: Ho Chi Minh establishes the Indochinese Communist Party
1940	Ho Chi Minh returns to Vietnam and establishes a revolutionary base in Northern Vietnam
	September: Japanese forces invade Vietnam without French troops
1941	May: Led by Ho Chi Minh and fellow communists, the League for the Independence of Vietnam, the Viet Minh, challenge French and Japanese rule over the country
1945	March 9–10: Japanese forces attack French posts
	March 10: Riots ensue in the north and south; guerrillas led by the feudal lord Hoang Hoa Tham target both the French and Japanese colonist agents
	French surrender to the Japanese forces in Indochina
	March: Liberation Committees, established by communist guerrilla fighters in the north, begin to gather support for a revolution
	April: At the Revolutionary Military Conference of North Vietnam, in Bac Giang, the General Command of the North Vietnam Liberation Army devises a "general insurrection preparatory plan"
	June: Vietminh General Committee declares six provinces in the north of Vietnam, which are "free zones," to be "The New Vietnam" and under the control of communist guerrillas
	July 17–August 2: Plans made for a meeting of the National Congress, to be headed by Ho Chi Minh

August 9: The Soviet Red Army launches attack on Manchuria, China, in order to defeat Japanese occupation forces
August 9–13: Following a general insurrection by the National Congress, Vietnam becomes a Republic
August 14: Japan agrees to Allies surrender terms; WWII ends, revealing a power vacuum in Vietnam
August 16: News of Japan's surrender spreads and meetings are held in numerous provinces in Vietnam; Ho Chi Minh is declared President
August 17–18: General strikes begin, and the Viet Minh call on the revolutionaries to seize power
August 19: Ho Chi Minh's forces seize Hanoi, marking an "August General Uprising"; uprisings against the French spread across the country; King Bao Dai, titular head of Vietnam, abdicates and the Vietnamese Communist Party takes over
August 26: Vietnamese Communist Party orders an insurrection in Southern Vietnam
August 27: First cabinet meeting held by Ho Chi Minh
August 29: Forces of the Liberation Army enter Hanoi
September 2: National Independence Day, and Hanoi is named the capital city

The Chinese Revolution

Date	*Event*
1911	October 10: Soldiers in Hubei break out in the Wuchang Uprising, also known as the "Double Tenth Uprising," in response to the policies of the Qing state; localized revolts in other provinces follow and many declare independence
	November 1: The Qing emperor appoints Yuan Shikai as prime minister and passes the "Nineteen Articles," ending autocratic imperial rule
	December 25: Sun Yat Sen returns to China from exile
1912	January 1: Sun Yat Sen declared as President of the Republic of China; Kuomintang Party (KMT) founded
	February 12: Qing emperor Puyi is forced to abdicate, thus ending the 267 years of Qing dynasty
	February 14: Sun Yat Sen steps down from the presidency
	March 10: Yuan Shikai is hailed as president
	August 25: Various revolutionary and anti-monarchist groups consolidate to form the Kuomintang political party
1913	July: Sun Yat Sen launches a "second revolution" against the presidency of Yuan Shikai in response to the assassination of Kuomintang party leader
	September: Sun Yat Sen's revolution fails and he is forced into exile; Yuan Shikai's troops retake Nanjing
1915	January 18: The Japanese issue the Twenty-One Demands to Yuan Shikai, who accepts them with little resistance
	December 12: Yuan Shikai declares himself Emperor of China
	December 25: Provincial uprisings emerge in response to Yuan Shikai's intention to restore the monarchy
1916	January 1: The imperial rule of Yuan Shikai begins
	June 6: Yuan Shikai dies, further weakening the national government and increasing the power of provincial warlords
1917	July: Former president Sun Yat Sen returns to Guangzhou from Shanghai and invites former members of the National Assembly to form a republican government
	September 1: The Republicans elect Sun Yat Sen as *generalissimo* of the Guangzhou military government

1918 May 21: Warlords gain control of the Guangzhou military government, and force Sun Yat Sen into exile

1919 Sun Yat Sen reorganizes KMT as a Revolutionary Movement to defeat Northern Chinese regime

The May Fourth Movement breaks out over the passing of Chinese land to Japan as stipulated in the Versailles Treaty

July 25: Russia surrenders its colonized territory in China under communist control

1921 July 1: Chinese Communist Party is founded; Sun Yat Sen becomes supreme leader of KMT and announces its ideology of Three Principles of the People – nationalism, people's rights, and people's livelihoods

1923 January 16: Sun Yat Sen's forces regain control of Guangzhou province

January 26: Soviet diplomat Adolph Joffe and Sun Yat Sen sign a cooperation agreement in Shanghai

1924 First alliance between CCP and KMT, named the United Front, with aid from the Comintern

1925 March 12: Sun Yat Sen dies from sudden illness and is replaced by Chaing Kai-shek as leader of KMT

1926 July 1: The National Revolutionary Army mobilizes a campaign to end warlordism and reunify China

1927 March 23: British and American warships open fire on Nanjing, in response to violence, looting, and attacks on foreigners, shelling parts of the city; Chaing Kai-shek blames the Nanjing Incident on the CCP

April: Civil War starts when Chaing Kai-shek orders a purge of communist allies of KMT

1934 February 19: Chaing Kai-shek initiates the New Life Movement, a campaign promoting Confucian and neo-fascist social values

October: CCP soldiers retreat against the KMT in Jiangxi Province to Yan'an, beginning of the Long March

1935 January: Mao is declared as the military commander of CCP

October: Long March ends

1936 Chaing Kai-shek is kidnapped and forced into alliance with Communists in fight against the Japanese

1937 July 7: Full scale invasion by Japanese forces starts the Sino-Japanese War

December–January 1938: The "Rape of Nanking" as Japanese forces inflict systematic violence, rape, and murder of 50,000 soldiers and 300,000 civilians in Nanking

1938 Chiang Kai-shek assumes role of exalted leader of KMT; Mao made Chairman of CCP

1942–1944 Mao Zedong becomes supreme leader of CCP after the "Yan'an Way" Ratification Campaign

1945 April: Mao outlines plan for "New Democracy" at Seventh National Party Conference

August–September: Japan is defeated in Sino-Japanese War; China given sovereignty over Taiwan

KMT and CCP engage in peace talks

1946 May 1: The CCP reforms the Red Army to form the People's Liberation Army

May: CCP issues first land reform directive

August: KMT occupies key areas in China

1947 mid-1947: KMT takes control of Yan'an

July: CCP begins a year and a half encirclement of KMT forces in northeast and central China

1948 late: KMT forces flee to Taiwan after defeat in Chinese Civil War

November 2: Manchuria comes under Communist control

1949 January 10: Battle of Huaihai ends in KMT defeat; Chiang Kai-shek flees to Taiwan

October 1st: Mao Zedong proclaims the establishment of the People's Republic of China in Tiananmen Square, Beijing

December: Remaining KMT forces flee to Taiwan

1951 Mao enacts "Thought Reform," orchestrated by the CCP

May: China claims sovereignty over Tibet, and armed resistance ends

1956 January: Start of the Hundred Flowers Campaign

May: Mao Zedong endorses the campaign

1957 February: Mao advocates for greater openness and critique of the CCP

	February 27: The Hundred Flowers campaign is launched by Mao, encouraging criticism of the CCP; the CCP subsequently cracks down on its critics
	April: CCP calls for non-communist intellectuals to contribute to its Ratification Campaign
	June: Anti-Rightist Campaign begins when *The People's Daily* denounces CCP's opponents
	July: Violence escalates, and Mao orders an end to the Hundred Flowers movement
1958	August: Great Leap Forward finalized at Beidaihe Conference
1960–1962	Period known as the "Three Bitter Years" marked by famine and privation following the Great Leap Forward
1964	April: The CCP publishes its first copy of the Red Book, a compilation of quotations from Mao Zedong
	October 16: China successfully tests an atomic weapon, becoming the world's fifth nuclear power
1966	April 10: CCP issues statement calling for a Great Cultural Revolution
	May 16: Members of the CCP vote to declare war on bourgeoisie members
	August: Eleventh Plenum of the CCP approves resolution to "revolutionize" the Chinese state, marking beginning of Cultural Revolution
	August 19: Start of the "Red August" as Beijing's Red Guards declare war on the Four Olds – Old Customs, Old Culture, Old Habits, and Old Ideas – assumed to be elements of traditional Chinese culture
	December 15: CCP issues statement authorizing ruralization of Cultural Revolution
1968	April 23–July 26: "One Hundred Days of Armed Struggle" is instigated on the Tsinghua University campus, precipitating the CCP's disbanding of the Red Guards
1969	April 1–24: Lin Biao is announced as Mao's successor at Ninth National Congress of the CCP
1970	March 27: CCP starts investigation into supporters of May 16 Counterrevolutionary Clique; 3.5 million people are falsely implicated

1971	September 12: Lin Biao allegedly involved in assassination plot to kill Mao; he dies in plane crash as he attempts to escape from China
1975	April 5: Chiang Kai-shek dies in Taiwan
1976	September 9: Mao dies of a heart attack; the Cultural Revolution ends

The Cuban Revolution

Date	*Event*
1868–1878	First War of Cuban independence
1895	March 19: Hero of Cuban independence, José Martí, is killed in battle
1895–1898	Spain is defeated in the Spanish American War; the United States takes control of Cuba; second war of Cuban independence ensues
1902–1929	Cuba declares independence, but according to the Platt Amendment is still a US protectorate; the US continues to intervene in Cuban politics; Cuba experiences severe economic crisis after 1929
1925	The Cuban Communist Party is established
1929	Stock market crashes; Cuba suffers as the price of sugar, a main export, falls in the crash; economic strife gives rise to revolutionary sentiments
1952	Former President Fulgencio Batista (1940–1945) seizes power, suspends the 1940 constitution, and cancels upcoming presidential elections; the Batista regime is soon recognized by the United States
1953	July 26: Fidel Castro leads a rebel attack against the Moncada Barracks in Santiago de Cuba, most of his forces are killed
	September 21: Castro attributes José Martí with the inception of the rebel attack in a court appearance
	October 6: Castro is convicted for the Moncada attack and is sentenced to 15 years in prison; other survivors of the attacks are also imprisoned
	October 31: The Cuban Communist Party is outlawed
1954	Castro's speech during trial, "History will Absolve Me," spreads as a rebel manifesto across the country
1955	February 25: Fulgencio Batista is elected president again
	May 15: Castro is given amnesty and released from prison, leaving Cuba for Mexico; Ernesto "Che" Guevara joins Castro's group of revolutionaries, calling themselves the M-26-7

1956 November: The disastrous landing of the yacht *Granma* back in Cuba; Castro and a few remaining survivors launch a guerrilla war against the Batista government from the Sierra Maestra mountains

1957 February: Castro is declared dead by the government; rebel forces invite *The New York Times* to interview Castro to counter rumors of his death

March: The Revolutionary Directorate (DR) draws the "urban-based" rebels to join an unsuccessful assault on the National Palace in Havana to kill Batista

Until 1958: Castro's followers fail to attack oil facilities, government buildings, and radio stations

1958 March: Batista's growing unpopularity prompts the Eisenhower administration in the US to stop military shipments to the Cuban government

September–October: Castro ordered two guerrilla units to advance into the lowlands

December: Santiago is surrounded by rebels

December 31: Santiago falls to rebel command

1959 January 1: Rebel forces led by Che Guevara seize control of the capital; Batista flees to the Dominican Republic

January 7: With a military and arms, Castro enters Havana and the US recognizes the new Cuban government; Batista officials and guards are tried and executed; Castro becomes prime minister and launches a drive to nationalize the economy

April: Castro visits the US and expresses desire for friendship and continued trade

June: Che Guevara opens talks with the Soviets during a visit to Egypt designed to deepen the cooperation between Cuba and the USSR

October: Raul Castro becomes Minister of the Armed Forces; the US imposes sanctions and an embargo on Cuba

1960 Ties between the Soviet Union and Cuba are formalized, and Soviet oil and weaponry are supplied to Cuba

October 19: The US imposes partial trade embargo on Cuba

1961	January 3: Washington cuts diplomatic ties with Havana
	April 16: Castro declares Cuba to be a Socialist state
	April 19: The CIA-organized invasion of the Bay of Pigs is defeated
1962	February: The US imposes partial trade embargo on Cuba
	October: The Cuban Missile Crisis
1967	October 9: Che Guevara is captured and killed in Bolivia

The Iranian Revolution

Date	*Event*
1963	Shah Mohammad Reza Pahlavi launches the White Revolution, later known as the Shah and People Revolution, meant to foster social and economic modernization in Iran
	June: Riots break out in Tehran and other cities despite growth in the powers of the secret police, SAVAK
1964	Ayatollah Ruhollah Khomeini denounces the Shah, is exiled to Turkey
1975	The Shah establishes the Rastakhiz Party and proclaims Iran to be at the forefront of the start of a "Great Civilization"
1977	Anti-government protests begin to appear as unemployment rises due to a sudden slowdown in the construction sector
	June 12: The National Front, one of the country's oldest opposition parties, publishes 20,000 copies of an open letter calling on the Shah to introduce democratic reforms
	June 18: The well-known public intellectual Ali Shariati dies, suspected of having been poisoned by SAVAK
	October: Protests spread across the country; cassette recordings of Ayatollah Khomeini's sermons are smuggled into Iran; Khomeini's son dies, causing angst and grievance amongst supporters, demonstrations follow.
1978	January 7: *Ettela'at*, a national newspaper, publishes article personally attacking Khomeini
	May: Mass demonstrations continue
	August–September: Scattered strikes and mass protests continue and often become violent, sparked by an arson attack at a movie theatre in city of Abadan that kills hundreds; the government responds with a combination of overtures to the protesters and harsh military crackdowns on street demonstrations
	September: Martial Law is imposed
1979	January 16: The Shah leaves Iran, asking the military command to obey orders from newly appointed PM Shapour Bakhtiar, long-time member of the National Front; military desertions continue at unprecedented scale
	February 1: Khomeini returns to Iran amid celebrations by millions of Iranians

February 7: Lower ranking Air Force personnel pledge their allegiance to Khomeini; armed street clashes between pro- and anti-Shah forces in Tehran; Imperial Guards remain loyal to the Bakhtiar government

February 10–11: Amid mutiny by Air Force cadets, the armed forces declare their "neutrality in the on-going political conflict" and refuse order from Bakhtiar, who goes into hiding and soon flees the country

March 31: Referendum approves the formal establishment of the Islamic Republic of Iran

The South African Revolution

Date	*Event*
1910	Former British colonies of the Cape and Natal form the Union of South Africa
1912	South African Native National Congress (SANNC) founded
1913	Native Land Act divides South Africa into black and white areas
1918	Secret brotherhood established to advance the Afrikaner cause
1923	SANNC organization renamed the African National Congress
1929	In general elections for the House of Assembly, the National Party wins 52 percent majority after targeted "Black Danger" campaign
1934	South Africa is declared an independent state, removing the final vestiges of British authority over the country
1936	Legislative passage of Representation of Natives Act, Natives Trust Act, and Land Act further restrict black rights
1948	May: National Party wins power and introduces apartheid laws
1950	Prohibition of Mixed Marriages Act
	December: ANC congress adopts a "Programme of Action"; Group Areas Act is passed to enforce segregation of blacks and whites; the Communist Party is banned; Nelson Mandela leads ANC's response with a campaign of civil disobedience
1951	Attempts to remove colored vote is met by civilian groups rallying in support of colored voters
1952	Pass Law enacted, restricting movement of blacks across the country
1953	South African Communist Party (SACP) formed away from state surveillance; the passage of Separate Amenities Act enforces segregated public facilities; Bantu Education Act legalizes inferior education for blacks
1959	April: Pan Africanist Congress (PAC) is formed under the leadership of R. M. Sobukwe
1960	Parliamentary representation for Africans removed

	March 21: Police open fire kills 69 people during anti-apartheid protests in Sharpeville
	March 30–June: State of Emergency is declared
	April 8: ANC and PAC are banned
1961	\March 25–26: Nelson Mandela proposes armed struggle at "All-in conference" in Pietermaritzburg
	May 31: ANC adopts armed struggle
1962	January–June: Mandela tours African and European states to gain support for armed struggle
	August 5: Mandela arrested, later sentenced to life imprisonment in trial taking place between October 9, 1963 and June 12, 1964
	United Nations adopts economic and diplomatic sanctions against South Africa
1964	July: African Resistance Movement orchestrates numerous acts of sabotage and attacks
	Nelson Mandela is sentenced to life imprisonment
1966	Prime Minister Hendrik Verwoerd is assassinated
1967	Passage of landmark Terrorism Act allows for indefinite detention without trial on authority of the police
1968	Representation for colored persons completely abolished
1970	Passing of Bantu Homelands Citizenship Act, over 3 million people forcibly resettled in defined black regions
	Connie Mulder of National Party reported saying "There should be no black South African citizens"
1972	Black People's Convention formed
1976–1977	Continued protests and riots
1977	Black leader Steve Biko dies in police custody; further government clamp-down on activists; United Nations imposes arms embargo on South Africa
1980	Price of gold soars globally, creating an economic boom in South Africa
	January: Start of the "Release Mandela" campaign
	June: Senate is abolished and replaced by a multiracial President's Council, made up of nominated members and meant to establish a new constitution
1983	August: United Democratic Front is established

November: Referendum on the new constitution passes with two-thirds of white voters saying "yes"; the constitution allows for separate houses by race: White, Coloured, and Indians, with a distinction of "general" and "own" affairs

1985 February: Nelson Mandela's daughter reads a statement from him in prison, saying he refuses conditional freedom and that "he will return"

March: Riots and protests erupt, leading to clashes between civil right activists and the police; partial state of emergency announced on July 20

1986 June: National State of Emergency is declared; Mixed Marriages Act, parts of the Immorality Act, and the Prohibition of Political Interference Act are repealed; Pass Laws also abolished

1987 June: State of Emergency is renewed

1988 October: All races in municipalities go to polls in local government elections for the first time

1990 Newly elected President F. W. de Klerk (1989) acknowledges apartheid has failed, frees political prisoners, including Mandela, and legalizes ANC and other banned groups

1991 January: President de Klerk begins process of repealing apartheid laws

July: Mandela is elected president of the ANC

1993 October: United Nations lift all but arms sanctions on South Africa; President De Klerk and Mandela awarded Nobel Peace Prize

1994 April 26–29: First multiracial Presidential elections held

May 9: Nelson Mandela is elected President of South Africa

The Eastern European Revolutions

Date	*Event*
1956	February: Communist Party in power across Eastern Europe, branching away from former Soviet Union Stalinist policies; student-led protests in Hungary quickly spread nationwide and "Hungarian Revolution of 1956," from October 23 to November 10, ends when the Soviet Union invades the country
	October–November: Soviet Union forces suppress uprisings of "Polish October" and anti-Stalinist Hungarian Revolution
1968	August: USSR occupies Czechoslovakia following the "Prague Spring" protests; Soviet leader Leonid Brezhnev encourages other socialist states to intervene to protect socialism
1970	Mass strikes in Poland
1975	Poland experiences economic stagnation and continued increase in foreign debt
1977	"Charter 77" declared by human rights movement in Czechoslovakia
1980	Economic stagnation along with rising nationalist sentiments results in tensions between East European and USSR; in Poland, a worker protest movement turns into the Solidarity Labor Union
1985	Mikhail Gorbachev is appointed as General Secretary of Communist Party of the Soviet Union
1986	Start of Gorbachev's policies of reconstruction (*glasnost*) and openness (*perestroika*)
1988	Mikhail Gorbachev is appointed President of Soviet Union
1989	February–April: Start of roundtable discussions between Communist and opposition leaders in Hungary, Poland, and Czechoslovakia
	March: Demonstrations in Budapest calling for democracy; opposition roundtable is formed in Hungary
	May 2: Hungarian Prime Minister Miklos Nemeth announces the start of open border with Austria
	June–September: Roundtable discussion in Hungary
	June 4: Solidarity Party of Poland triumphs in elections; Poland leaves the Soviet orbit

June 27: Austrian and Hungarian foreign ministers cut through the border fence between the two countries as a symbol for Pan-European unity

July 7–8: The Summit of Warsaw Pact fails to agree on common agenda on reform

August 24: Tadeusz Mazowiecki of Polish Solidarity party is elected as first non-communist prime minister since 1947

September 10–11: Hungary's announcement of open border policy for refugees of East Germany sparks refugee crisis

September–October: Mass vigils and demonstrations in East German cities

October 7: Hungarian Socialist Workers' Party (MSzMP) changes name to Hungarian Socialist Party (MSZP)

October 9: Mass demonstrations in Leipzig to protest Hungary's refusal to repatriate East German refugees

October 18: Erich Honecker, leader of East Germany since 1971, resigns

October 23: The Hungarian People's Republic renamed Hungarian Republic

November 4: Over a million people demonstrate in East Berlin's iconic Alexanderplatz

November 9: The Berlin Wall falls

November 10: Palace Revolution in Bulgaria

November 17: "Velvet Revolution" in Czechoslovakia

December 25: Nicolae Ceauşescu, general secretary of the Romanian Communist Party and the country's leader since 1965 and his wife Elena are tried and executed

1990 February: Soviet leaders agree to hold democratic elections

March–June: Hungary and Czechoslovakia introduce non-communist regimes; post-communist parties remain in Romania and Bulgaria

October: Germany reunifies

1991 Solidarity Party of Poland splits into 5 sections after parliamentary elections

August: In Moscow, hardliners attempt a coup to oust Gorbachev

December: USSR breaks up; Boris Yeltsin becomes President of the Russian Federation

The Arab Spring

Date	*Event*
Tunisia	
2010	December 17: Mohamed Bouazizi's self-immolation triggers the Arab uprisings; protesters take to the streets of Sidi Bouizid
	December 19: Protests spread farther throughout the country
	December 20: Pledge of a $10 million employment program by the Development Minister fails to appease protesters
	December 21: President Ben Ali reshuffles his cabinet and issues warning to protesters of harsh response to continued rioting
	December 22–27: Street protests spread throughout the country, often met by violent response from the police
	December 28: Ben Ali and Muammar Qaddafi talk via telephone; Ben Ali threatens protesters with firm punishment on national television
	December 29: Nessma TV starts live broadcast of the protests
2011	January 2: Cyberactivist group, Anonymous, hacks a number of Tunisian government websites in "Operation Tunisia"
	January 13: Ben Ali declares on national television that he would not be seeking reelection in 2014
	January 14: Ben Ali imposes state of emergency and purges the government of alleged corrupt officials, declaring new legislative elections within six months; declaring itself "neutral in the political conflict," the Tunisian military seizes control of the airport and closes the country's airspace; Ben Ali transfers power over to PM and flees to Jeddah, Saudi Arabia
	January–February: Street protests continue, demanding resignation of the PM and elections for a Constituent Assembly to draft a new constitution
	February: Amid continuing public protests, PM Mohammed Ghannouchi resigns
	May 2: Curfew imposed on fresh street protests
	March 1: An umbrella group called the Authority for the Realization of the Objectives of the Revolution, Political Reform and Democratic Transition is established, formed from the merger of several different political factions

October 23: A 217-member Constituent Assembly is elected and charged with writing a new constitution within a year; the Ennahda Party, the largest party in the Assembly and with an Islamist platform, agrees to power-sharing arrangement with other parties

Clashes continue between Islamist-led government and protesters

2014 October 26: Tunisia's first free parliamentary elections are won by new political bloc, Nidaa Tounes, made up of secularists and led by a former minister, Beji Caid Essebsi

December 22: Essebsi is declared the winner of the Tunisia's first free presidential elections

Egypt

2010 June: "We Are All Khaled Said" Facebook page created by Wael Ghonim

2011 January 25: "Day of rage" marked by mass protests and police clashes in Tahrir Square

January 26: Protests and street clashes spread across Egypt; US President Barack Obama issues statement, expressing support for the protesters

January 27: Mohamed ElBaradei arrives in Egypt to support protesters; Twitter, Facebook, and Blackberry Messenger services are disrupted; Wael Ghonim imprisoned and Facebook page has a resurgence of popularity

January 28–29: President Mubarak dismisses his government and appoints Omar Suleiman as the country's first Vice President since 1981

February 1: Mubarak announces he will remain in office but will not run for reelection; Tahrir Square protests continue to grow

February 4: "Day of Departure" is named after anti-government protestors gathered in Tahrir Square

February 11: Hosni Mubarak resigns from the presidency and hands power over to the Supreme Council of the Armed Forces (SCAF)

February 12: Travel bans are imposed on former government officials

November 28: Islamists, led by Muslim Brotherhood, win nearly 90 percent of votes in parliamentary elections

2012 June 15–16: Military suspends parliament the day before second-round presidential elections MB's Mohamed Morsi narrowly wins presidential elections August; Morsi retires top generals, proceeds to grant himself more powers, and the MB drafts Islamist constitution and restricts freedom of speech and assembly

2013 January: Protests against Morsi government held to mark one-year anniversary of revolution

February–April: Anti-government protests spread across Cairo and other Egyptian cities

June–July: Defense Minister Abdel Fatah el-Sisi repeatedly warns Morsi and issues ultimatum of the military's "duty to put forward a road map for the future instead"

July 3: The military removes Morsi from office

December: SCAF declares Muslim Brotherhood a terrorist organization

2014 January: Parties formed on the basis of religion banned by the new constitution

May: Sisi elected president with 97 percent of the votes cast

Libya

2011 January 25–February 15: State passes emergency measures

February: The National Transition Council (NTC) is formed by main opposition figures to coordinate the rebellion against Qaddafi rule

February 15–16: "The Libyan Long Track" protesters and the army clash in Benghazi

February 17: Street protests erupt throughout Libya, organized with the help of Facebook and Twitter users

February 20: Saif al-Islam, Muammar Qaddafi's son, issues threat of severe punishment of protesters

February 27: The National Transitional Council is formed

February 28: The European Union announce sanctions on Qaddafi and his family

March 17: UN Security Council endorses foreign intervention in Libya under the auspices of "responsibility to protect"

March 19: In "Operation Odyssey Dawn," British, French, and US forces attack Libyan military assets from the air
August 28: Tripoli is captured by rebel forces
October: Qaddafi flees to Sirte
October 23: Qaddafi is captured and killed

2012 January–March: Tensions mount between NTC figures in cities of Benghazi and Tripoli
June: Growth in power of local militias across the country as tensions mount and there is an absence of central government
August: Transitional government hands down power to the General National Congress, which was elected in July

2014 February: Protests erupt when the General National Congress refuses to disband after mandate expires; Libya plunges into civil war

Yemen

2011 January 27: Demonstrators call for resignation of President Ali Abdullah Saleh
February 2: Saleh announces he will not run for reelection in 2013, and he will not hand over power to his son
February 3: "Day of rage" declared, protesters gather in Sanaa's Change Square
March 7: Security forces open fire on detainees in Sanaa prison who had gathered to show support for the protesters
March 18: Saleh declares state of emergency
March 20: Saleh dismisses cabinet; Yemen's UN ambassador resigns in solidarity with the protesters
March 21: Military forces are deployed in Sanaa to protect protesters after top military commanders' defect; defections from the state continue as Yemen's Ambassador to Syria resigns in solidarity with the anti-government movement
November: Amid growing defections and continued protests, Saleh hands power over to his deputy, Abdrabbuh Mansour Hadi

2012 February: Hadi wins the presidency in uncontested elections

	Suicide attack on the presidential palace on the day Hadi is sworn in as president, Al Qaeda claims responsibility for attack
2013	Regional rebellions, led principally by Houthi rebels and by al-Qaeda in the Arabian Peninsula (AQAP), plunge the country into civil war
Bahrain	
2011	February 15–March 14: Protests in Manama's Pearl Roundabout
	February 17: "Bloody Thursday," an organized attack by police at 3 a.m. on Pearl Roundabout
	February 18: Bharani Defence Force troops repeat attack on protesters; ambulances and medical personnel are forbidden from helping the injured at the Pearl Roundabout
	February 22, 25, and March 1: Large scale demonstrations by anti-government protestors
	February 26: The National Coalition (*al-I'tilaf al-Watani*) form Leader of *Haqq* movement, Hasan Mushayma returns from exile
	February 27: National Coalition demands a new social contract
	March 4: Mass demonstrations by supporters of the National Coalition demand democratic reforms
	March 10: High school students join the protests, clashes continue between Sunni and Shia citizens
	March 14: Troops from Saudi Arabia and the UAE enter Bahrain
	March 18: Government forces, backed by Saudi and Emirati troops, reoccupy Pearl Roundabout and proceed to demolish the iconic monument

NOTES

1 Introduction

1 Zoltan Barany, *How Armies Respond to Revolutions and Why* (Princeton, NJ: Princeton University Press, 2016), p. 7. Original emphasis. For an examination of the concept of revolution, also see James Farr, "Historical Concepts in Political Science: The Case of 'Revolution,'" *American Journal of Political Science*, Vol. 26, No. 4 (November 1982), pp. 688–708; and John Dunn, "Revolution," in *Political Innovation and Conceptual Change*, Terence Ball, James Farr, and Russell Hanson, eds. (Cambridge: Cambridge University Press, 1988).

2 John Dunn, *Modern Revolutions: An Introduction to the Analysis of a Political Phenomenon*, 2nd edn (Cambridge: Cambridge University Press, 1989), p. xvi.

3 Mark Irving Lichbach, *The Rebel's Dilemma* (Ann Arbor, MI: University of Michigan Press, 1998), pp. 16–17.

4 Ibid., p. 18. Original emphasis.

5 Ibid., pp. 22–25.

6 George Lawson, "Negotiated Revolutions: The Prospects for Radical Change in Contemporary World Politics," *Review of International Studies*, Vol. 31 (2005), p. 481.

7 Devora Grynspan, "Nicaragua: A New Model for Popular Revolution in Latin America," in *Revolutions of the Late Twentieth Century*, Jack A. Goldstone, Ted Robert Gurr, and Farrokh Moshiri, eds. (Boulder, CO: Westview, 1991), p. 97.

8 Harald Wydra, "Revolution and Democracy: The European Experience," in *Revolution in the Making of the Modern World: Social Identities, Globalization and Modernity*, John Foran, David Lane, and Andreja Zivkovic, eds. (London: Routledge, 2008), p. 43.

9 Asef Bayat, *Revolution without Revolutionaries: Making Sense of the Arab Spring* (Stanford, CA: Stanford University Press, 2017), p. 11.

10 Ibid., p. 17.

11 Ibid., p. 18. As for why this would be the case, Bayat points to the "geopolitical exceptionalism of the Middle East, shaped by oil and Israel" (p. 16).

12 George Lawson, *Negotiated Revolutions: The Czech Republic, South Africa and Chile* (Burlington, VT: Ashgate, 2005), pp. 47–70.

13 Critical junctures may be defined as "relatively short periods of time during which there is a substantially heightened probability that agents' choices will affect the outcome of interest." More specifically, they are "characterized by a situation in which the structural (that is, economic, cultural, ideological, organizational) influences on political action are significantly relaxed for a relatively short period, with two main consequences: The range of plausible choices open to powerful political actors expands substantially and the consequences of their decisions for the outcome of interest are potentially much more momentous. Contingency, in other words, becomes paramount." Giovanni Capoccia and R. Daniel Kelemen, "The Study of Critical Junctures: Theory, Narrative, and Counterfactuals in Historical Institutionalism," *World Politics*, Vol. 59, No. 3 (April 2007), pp. 343, 348.

2 From Rebellion to Revolution

1 Walden Bellow, "Introduction," in *Down with Colonialism!*, Ho Chi Minh, ed. (London: Verso, 2007), p. xxvii.
2 Pierre Brocheux, *Ho Chi Minh: A Biography*, translated by Claire Duiker (Cambridge: Cambridge University Press, 2007), pp. 13–14.
3 Ho Chi Minh, *Down with Colonialism!* (London: Verso, 2007), p. 8.
4 Quoted in, Brocheux, *Ho Chi Minh*, p. 24.
5 Ho, *Down with Colonialism!*, p. 5; Brocheux, *Ho Chi Minh*, p. 26.
6 The book, which presents a wide array of examples of French colonial exploits in Africa, Indochina, and the Levant, can be found in *Ho Chi Minh on Revolution, Selected Writings, 1920–66*, Bernard B. Fall, ed. (New York: Signet, 1967), pp. 73–126.
7 Bellow, "Introduction," p. xv.
8 Ho, *Down with Colonialism!*, p. 133.
9 Brocheux, *Ho Chi Minh*, p. 87.
10 See, for example, Ho, *Down with Colonialism!*, pp. 62–63.
11 Quoted in, Brocheux, *Ho Chi Minh*, p. 83.
12 Ibid., p. 74.
13 When Ho wrote the Vietnamese Declaration of Independence, he deliberately started the document with the same wording used in the American Declaration of Independence: "All men are created equal. They are endowed by their Creator with certain unalienable Rights; among them are Life, Liberty and the pursuit of Happiness." On September 2, 1945, he read the declaration to several tens of thousands of people in Hanoi. Ho, *Down with Colonialism!*, p. 53.
14 Brocheux, *Ho Chi Minh*, p. 102.
15 Frederick C. Teiwes, "Mao and His Followers," in *A Critical Introduction to Mao*, Timothy Cheek, ed. (Cambridge: Cambridge University Press, 2010), p. 132.
16 Edgar Snow, *Red Star over China* (New York: Grove Press, 1968), p. 410.
17 Sebastian Balfour, *Castro*, 3rd edn (Harlow, UK: Pearson Longman, 2009), p. 26.
18 Ibid., p. 10.
19 Nelson Mandela, *Long Walk to Freedom* (New York: Little, Brown and Co., 1994), p. 141.
20 Ibid., p. 600.
21 Seán Sheehan, *Lenin* (London: Haus, 2009), p. 72.
22 Robert Service, *Lenin: A Biography* (Cambridge, MA: Harvard University Press, 2000), p. 145.
23 Sheehan, *Lenin*, p. 71.

24 Ibid., p. 70.
25 Brantly Womack, "From Urban Radical to Rural Revolutionary: Mao from the 1920s to 1937," in *A Critical Introduction to Mao*, Timothy Cheek, ed. (Cambridge: Cambridge University Press, 2010), p. 85.
26 Timothy Cheek, "Mao, Revolution, and Memory," in *A Critical Introduction to Mao*, Timothy Cheek, ed. (Cambridge: Cambridge University Press, 2010), p. 10.
27 Quoted in, Balfour, *Castro*, p. 37.
28 Quoted in, Carlos Franqui, *Diary of the Cuban Revolution* (New York: Viking, 1980), p. 67.
29 Ibid., pp. 67–71.
30 Quoted in, Ibid., p. 90.
31 Che recorded the meeting in his diary: "A political event was that I met Fidel Castro, the Cuban revolutionary. He is a young, intelligent guy, very sure of himself and extraordinarily audacious. I think we hit it off well." Ernesto Che Guevara, *Che: The Diaries of Ernesto Che Guevara* (Melbourne: Ocean Press, 2008), p. 28.
32 Balfour, *Castro*, p. 4.
33 Paul Le Blanc, "Ten Reasons for Not Reading Lenin," in *Revolution, Democracy, Socialism*, V. I. Lenin, ed. (London: Pluto, 2008), pp. 39–40.
34 Ibid., p. 20.
35 Ibid., pp. 7–9.
36 Ibid., p. 14.
37 Quoted in, Sheehan, *Lenin*, p. 102.
38 Ibid., p. 103.
39 Ibid., p. 109.
40 Mao Tse-Tung, *Quotations from Chairman Mao Tse-Tung* (Peking: Foreign Language Press, 1976), p. 4.
41 Snow, *Red Star over China*, p. 219.
42 Delia Davin, *Mao: A Very Short Introduction* (Oxford: Oxford University Press, 2013), p. 38.
43 Snow, *Red Star over China*, p. 99.
44 Mao, *Quotations from Chairman Mao*, p. 24.
45 Ibid., p. 7.
46 Davin, *Mao*, p. 48.
47 The Great Leap Forward, meant to leapfrog China's agrarian economy into industrialization, was characterized by extreme anti-expert and anti-intellectual bias. The campaign caused widespread famine and privation across China. The Cultural Revolution was equally disastrous. When Mao died in 1976, the Communist leadership denounced the Cultural Revolution as the "ten year catastrophe." Davin, *Mao*, p. 80.
48 Brocheux, *Ho Chi Minh*, p. 41.
49 Ibid., p. 46.
50 Ho, *Down with Colonialism!*, p. 41.
51 Ibid., p. 42.
52 Ibid., p. 45.
53 Brocheux, *Ho Chi Minh*, pp. 37–39.
54 Ho, *Down with Colonialism!*, p. 154.
55 Ibid., p. 153.
56 Brocheux, *Ho Chi Minh*, p. 72.
57 Ibid., p. 131.
58 Ibid., p. 96.
59 Ibid., p. 104.

60 Balfour, *Castro*, p. 28.
61 Quoted in, Ibid., p. 34.
62 Balfour, Ibid., pp. 40–41.
63 Franqui, *Diary of the Cuban Revolution*, p. 199.
64 Ibid., p. vi.
65 According to Julia Sweig, the fighters of the July 26 Movement fought desperately to maintain their autonomy and independence from the other revolutionary groups. Julia Sweig, *Inside the Cuban Revolution: Fidel Castro and the Urban Underground* (Cambridge, MA: Harvard University Press, 2002), p. 10.
66 Franqui, *Diary of the Cuban Revolution*, p. x.
67 Balfour, *Castro*, p. 44.
68 Guevara, *Che*, p. 38.
69 Ibid., p. 71.
70 A first-hand account of the attack can be found in, Franqui, *Diary of the Cuban Revolution*, pp. 147–148.
71 Ibid., pp. 314–315.
72 Guevara, *Che*, p. 76.
73 Eric Selbin, "Spaces and Places of (Im)Possibility and Desire: Transversal Revolutionary Imaginaries in the Twentieth Century Americas," *Forum for Inter-American Research*, Vol. 9, No. 1 (May 2016), p. 29.
74 Franqui, *Diary of the Cuban Revolution*, p. 140.
75 Sweig, *Inside the Cuban Revolution*, pp. 110–111.
76 Ibid., p. 9.
77 Franqui, *Diary of the Cuban Revolution*, p. 432–433.
78 Gratuitous violence has prompted some observers to accuse some revolutionary leaders of resorting to violence for the sake of violence. One of Lenin's biographers, for example, writes the following of the leader of the Russian revolution: "He displayed a virtual lust for violence. While he personally had not ambition to kill or maim or even to witness any butchery, he took a cruel delight in recommending such mayhem." Service, *Lenin*, p. 177. Regardless of whether or not Lenin suffered from a pathological lust for violence, planned revolutions have a logic of their own, one in which instrumentalist use of violence can beget more violence, setting into motion a vicious circle.
79 Quoted in Davin, *Mao*, p. 21.
80 Mao, *Quotations from Chairman Mao*, p. 58. Original emphasis.
81 Ibid., p. 61.
82 Quoted in, Henry Russell, *Let Freedom Reign: The Words of Nelson Mandela* (Northampton, MA: Interlink, 2010), p. 35.
83 Ho, *Down with Colonialism!*, p. xxi.
84 Ibid., p. xxi.
85 Ibid., p. 90. Original emphasis. In another one of his declarations to his compatriots, Ho Chi Minh maintained that "to fight we must carry out destruction. If we do not do so, the French will occupy our country once more. If our houses are solid enough to be used as bases, they will use tanks and vessels to attack us, and they will burn or plunder our property" (Ibid., p. 56). This declaration dates from February 1947, when after months of protracted negotiations, Ho and others in the Indochinese Communist Party had come to the realization that the French were not about to leave Vietnam and had settled on a "war of resistance" as their only viable option.
86 Ibid., p. 92.
87 Ibid., p. 65. Original emphasis.
88 Quoted in, Davin, *Mao*, p. 34.

89 Mao, *Quotations from Chairman Mao*, p. 126.
90 Davin, *Mao*, p. 23.
91 Ibid., p. 26.
92 Joseph W. Esherick, "Making Revolution in Twentieth-Century China," in *A Critical Introduction to Mao*, Timothy Cheek, ed. (Cambridge: Cambridge University Press, 2010), p. 55.
93 Mao, *Quotations from Chairman Mao*, p. 90.
94 Davin, *Mao*, pp. 28–29. Only thirty-five women were among the original marchers, mostly wives of Communist leaders, one of whom included Mao's wife He Zizhen, who gave birth to a fourth child. Soon after birth, however, the child had to be abandoned with local peasants.
95 Ibid., p. 30.
96 Mao, *Quotations from Chairman Mao*, p. 60.
97 Ibid., pp. 61, 63.
98 Timothy Wickham-Crowley, "Toward a Comparative Sociology of Latin American Guerrilla Movements," in *Revolutions: Theoretical, Comparative, and Historical Studies*, 3rd edn, Jack Goldstone, ed. (Belmont, CA: Wadsworth/Thompson, 2003), p. 288.
99 James Scott, "Hegemony and the Peasantry," *Politics and Society*, Vol. 7, No. 3 (1977), p. 294.
100 Theda Skocpol, "What Makes Peasants Revolutionary?" *Comparative Politics*, Vol. 14, No. 3 (April 1982), p. 364.
101 Scott, "Hegemony and the Peasantry," p. 295.
102 Gerard Chaliand, *Revolution in the Third World: Myths and Prospects* (New York: Viking Press, 1977), p. 48.
103 Samuel Huntington, *Political Order in Changing Societies* (New Haven, CT: Yale University Press, 1968), p. 290.
104 Jeff Goodwin and Theda Skocpol, "Explaining Revolutions in the Contemporary Third World," *Politics and Society,* Vol. 17, No. 4 (December 1989), p. 496.
105 Chaliand, *Revolution in the Third World,* p. 35.
106 Stuart Schram, *The Political Thought of Mao Tse Tung* (New York: Praeger, 1972), p. 253.
107 Scott, "Hegemony and the Peasantry," p. 289.
108 Eric Wolf, *Peasant Wars of the Twentieth Century* (New York: Harper & Row, 1969), p. 276.
109 Ibid., p. 279. Also see Theda Skocpol, "What Makes Peasants Revolutionary?" *Comparative Politics,* Vol. 14, No. 3 (April 1982), pp. 351–375.
110 T. David Mason, "Indigenous Factors," in *Revolution and Political Change in the Third World*, Barry M. Schutz and Robert O. Slater, eds. (Boulder, CO: Lynne Rienner, 1990), p. 42.
111 Goodwin and Skocpol, "Explaining Revolutions in the Contemporary Third World," p. 493.
112 Service, *Lenin*, p. 145.
113 Vladimir I. Lenin, *Collected Works*, Vol. 10 (Moscow: Progress Publishers, 1965), p. 40.
114 Vladimir I. Lenin, *Collected Works*, Vol. 25 (Moscow: Progress Publishers, 1977), p. 286.
115 Vladimir I. Lenin, *Alliance of the Working Class and the Peasantry* (Moscow: Progress Publishers, 1965), p. 12.
116 Ibid., p. 241. Original emphasis.
117 Brocheux, *Ho Chi Minh*, p. 27.

118 Ho, *Down with Colonialism!*, p. 69. Original emphasis.
119 Mao, *Quotations from Chairman Mao*, p. 88.
120 Ibid.
121 Quoted in, Davin, *Mao*, p. 20.
122 Snow, *Red Star over China*, p. 216.
123 Ibid., pp. 221–223.
124 Ernesto Che Guevara, *Guerrilla Warfare* (Melbourne: Ocean Press, 2006), pp. 55–56.
125 Quoted in, Franqui, *Diary of the Cuban Revolution*, p. 100.
126 Ibid., p. 182.
127 Guevara, *Guerrilla Warfare*, p. 13.
128 Guevara, *Che*, p. 97.
129 Guevara, *Guerrilla Warfare*, p. 17.
130 Ibid., p. 23. Original emphasis.
131 Ibid., p. 15.
132 Ernesto Che Guevara, *The Bolivian Diary* (Melbourne: Ocean Press, 2006), p. 40.
133 Guevara, *Che*, p. 126.
134 Ibid., p. 138.
135 Ibid., p. 141.
136 Ibid., p. 144.
137 Ibid., pp. 147, 151.
138 Guevara, *The Bolivian Diary*, p. 208.
139 For an eyewitness account of Che Guevara's capture, which involved the help of the CIA, see Clare Hargreaves, "'It's over': How I Captured Che Guevara," *Financial Times* (October 6, 2017), www.ft.com/content/63632118-a891-11e7-ab55-27219df83c97.
140 Guevara, *Che*, p. 32.
141 Karl Marx, *The 18th Brumaire of Louis Bonaparte* (India: CreateSpace, 2015), p. 148; Karl Marx and Friedrich Engles, *The Communist Manifesto* (Tustin, CA: Brandywine, 2008), p. 14.

3 From Social Movement to Revolution

1 Jack A. Goldstone, "An Analytical Framework," in *Revolutions of the Late Twentieth Century*, Jack A. Goldstone, Ted Robert Gurr, and Farrokh Moshiri, eds. (Boulder, CO: Westview, 1991), pp. 37–40.
2 The structural analysis adopted here closely follows insights originally offered by Theda Skocpol and Ellen Trimberger, who maintain that structural relationships are key to the strength or weakness of states, especially relationships between the state and elites, between peasants and landlords, and between the pre-revolutionary state and other states. The state is also in a dynamic relationship with the elite. Theda Skocpol and Ellen Kay Trimberger, "Revolutions: A Structural Analysis," in *Revolutions: Theoretical, Comparative, and Historical Studies*, 3rd edn, Jack A. Goldstone, ed. (Belmont, CA: Thomson Wadsworth, 2003), p. 63.
3 T. David Mason, "Indigenous Factors," in *Revolution and Political Change in the Third World*, Barry M. Schutz and Robert O. Slater, eds. (Boulder, CO: Lynne Rienner, 1990), p. 33.
4 See Mehran Kamrava, *Revolution in Iran: Roots of Turmoil* (London: Routledge, 1990), pp. 30–32 and 40–45; and Laszlo Bruszt, "1989: The Negotiated Revolution in Hungary," *Social Research*, Vol. 57, No. 2 (Summer 1990), pp. 381–382.

5 Jeff Goodwin and Theda Skocpol, "Explaining Revolutions in the Contemporary Third World," *Politics and Society*, Vol. 17, No. 4 (December 1989), p. 501.
6 Barry M. Schutz and Robert O. Slater, "Patterns of Legitimacy and Future Revolutions in the Third World," in *Revolution and Political Change in the Third World*, Barry M. Schutz and Robert O. Slater, eds. (Boulder, CO: Lynne Rienner, 1990), p. 248.
7 Goodwin and Skocpol, "Explaining Revolutions in the Contemporary Third World," p. 502.
8 William Foltz, "External Causes," in *Revolution and Political Change in the Third World*, Barry M. Schutz and Robert O. Slater, eds. (Boulder, CO: Lynne Rienner, 1990), pp. 54–59.
9 George Lawson, "Revolutions and the International," *Theory and Society*, Vol. 44, No. 4 (July 2015), p. 308.
10 See Bruce Miroff, *Pragmatic Illusions: The Presidential Politics of John F. Kennedy* (New York: David McKay, 1976), especially pp. 110–166. A discussion of US foreign policy toward Latin America can be found in Thomas Paterson, J. G. Clifford, and Kenneth Hagan, *American Foreign Policy: A History* (Lexington, MA: D. C. Heath & Co., 1991), pp. 588–590 and 627–632.
11 Quoted in Clifford Krauss, "Revolution in Central America?" *Foreign Affairs*, Vol. 65, No. 3 (1987), p. 564.
12 Ibid., pp. 564–565.
13 Paterson, Clifford, and Hagan, *American Foreign Policy,* p. 588.
14 Daniel Ritter, who has studied this democratic–autocratic dynamic in relation to Iran, Tunisia, and Egypt, maintains that "to legitimize close relations with a non-democratic state, it is therefore essential that the authoritarian regime *appears* to be democratic, as the successful execution of this charade helps facilitate the consummation of the democracy–autocracy relationship." Daniel P. Ritter, *The Iron Cage of Liberalism: International Politics and Unarmed Revolutions in the Middle East and North Africa* (Oxford: Oxford University Press, 2015), p. 18. Original emphasis.
15 Mehran Kamrava, "The Arab Spring and the Saudi-Led Counterrevolution," *Orbis,* Vol. 56, No. 1 (Winter 2012), pp. 96–104.
16 Bijan Khajehpour, "Re-Mapping the Corporate Landscape in Iran," in *Inside the Islamic Republic: Social Change in Post-Khomeini Iran*, Mahmood Monshipouri, ed. (New York: Oxford University Press, 2016), pp. 275–277.
17 Sharon Erickson Nepstad, *Nonviolent Revolutions: Civil Resistance in the Late 20th Century* (New York: Oxford University Press, 2011), pp. 133–135.
18 Lucian Pye, "The Legitimacy Crisis," in *Crises and Sequences in Political Development,* Lucian Pye, et al. (Princeton, NJ: Princeton University Press, 1971), p. 153.
19 Chalmers Johnson, *Revolutionary Change* (London: Longman, 1983), p. 65.
20 Pye, "The Legitimacy Crisis," p. 138.
21 Ibid., p. 141.
22 Barry M. Schutz and Robert O. Slater, "A Framework for Analysis," in *Revolution and Political Change in the Third World,* Barry M. Schutz and Robert O. Slater, eds. (Boulder, CO: Lynne Rienner, 1990), p. 5.
23 Goodwin and Skocpol, "Explaining Revolutions in the Contemporary Third World," pp. 498–499.
24 Ibid., p. 500.
25 Barry M. Schutz and Robert O. Slater, "Patterns of Legitimacy and Future Revolutions in the Third World," in *Revolution and Political Change in the Third World,* Barry M. Schutz and Robert O. Slater, eds. (Boulder, CO: Lynne Rienner, 1990), p. 248.

26 Charles Gore, "The Rise and Fall of the Washington Consensus as a Paradigm for Developing Countries," *World Development*, Vol. 28, No. 5 (2000), pp. 791–792.
27 Skocpol, *States and Social Revolutions* (Cambridge: Cambridge University Press, 1979), p. 286.
28 Schutz and Slater, "A Framework for Analysis," p. 5.
29 James Davies, "Toward a Theory of Revolution," *American Sociological Review*, Vol. 27, No. 1 (February 1962), p. 17.
30 Ted Robert Gurr, *Why Men Rebel* (Princeton, NJ: Princeton University Press, 1970), pp. 121–122.
31 Juan J. Linz, *Totalitarian and Authoritarian Regimes* (Boulder, CO: Lynne Rienner, 2000), p. 54.
32 Ibid., p. 159.
33 Ibid., p. 160.
34 Jack A. Goldstone, "Revolutions in Modern Dictatorships," in *Revolutions: Theoretical, Comparative, and Historical Studies*, 3rd edn, Jack A. Goldstone, ed. (Belmont, CA: Thomson Wadsworth, 2003), p. 70.
35 Ibid., p. 76.
36 Linz, *Totalitarian and Authoritarian Regimes*, p. 162.
37 Jason Brownlee, *Authoritarianism in the Age of Democratization* (Cambridge: Cambridge University Press, 2007), p. 26.
38 Jennifer Gandhi, *Political Institutions under Dictatorships* (Cambridge: Cambridge University Press, 2008), p. 78.
39 Brownlee, *Authoritarianism in the Age of Democratization*, pp. 8–9.
40 Milan W. Svolik, *The Politics of Authoritarian Rule* (Cambridge: Cambridge University Press, 2012), pp. 86–87.
41 Goodwin and Skocpol, "Explaining Revolutions in the Contemporary Third World," p. 500.
42 Brownlee, *Authoritarianism in the Age of Democratization*, p. 12.
43 Jack A. Goldstone, "Predicting Revolutions: Why We Could (and Should) Have Foreseen the Revolutions of 1989–1991 in the U.S.S.R. and Eastern Europe," in *Debating Revolutions*, Nikki Keddie, ed. (New York: New York University Press, 1995), p. 49.
44 John Foran, "Revolutionizing Theory/Theorizing Revolutions: State, Culture, and Society in Recent Works on Revolution," in *Debating Revolutions*, Nikki Keddie, ed. (New York: New York University Press, 1995), p. 113.
45 Svolik, *The Politics of Authoritarian Rule*, p. 87.
46 Zoltan Barany, *How Armies Respond to Revolutions and Why* (Princeton, NJ: Princeton University Press, 2016), p. 16.
47 Ibid., p. 40.
48 Joshua Stacher, *Adaptable Autocrats: Regime Power in Egypt and Syria* (Stanford, CA: Stanford University Press, 2012), p. 4.
49 David Mason, "Indigenous Factors," p. 40.
50 R. Ben Jones, *The French Revolution* (London: Hodder and Stoughton, 1985), p. 16.
51 Ibid., p. 37.
52 Ibid., p. 59.
53 Actually, the prison had already been scheduled for demolition and at the time of its fall had only seven prisoners, of whom four had been jailed for forgery, two were lunatics, and one was the son of an aristocrat whose father had him jailed for bad behavior. Sylvia Neely, *A Concise History of the French Revolution* (Lanham, MD: Rowman & Littlefield, 2008), p. 74.
54 Ibid., p. 76.

55 Ibid., pp. 92–94.
56 Ibid., p. 84.
57 Sheila Fitzpatrick, *The Russian Revolution, 1917–1932* (Oxford: Oxford University Press, 1982), p. 10
58 Tim McDaniel, "The Russian Revolution of 1917: Autocracy and Modernization," in *Revolutions: Theoretical, Comparative, and Historical Studies*, 3rd edn, Jack A. Goldstone, ed. (Belmont, CA: Thomson Wadsworth, 2003), p. 186.
59 Fitzpatrick, *The Russian Revolution,* p. 16.
60 Ibid., p. 33.
61 Keddie, "Can Revolutions Be Predicted; Can Their Causes Be Understood?" in *Debating Revolutions*, Nikki Keddie, ed. (New York: New York University Press, 1995), p. 17.
62 This was the title of the Shah's last book before the revolution. See Mohammad Reza Pahlavi, *Be Sooye Tammadon-e Bozorg (Toward the Great Civilization)* (Tehran: Center for Political and Cultural Research and Publications of the Pahlavi Era, 1977).
63 Kamrava, *Revolution in Iran*, p. 47.
64 Stacher, *Adaptable Autocrats*, pp. 6–7.
65 Sidney Tarrow, *Power in Movement: Social Movements and Contentious Politics*, 3rd edn (Cambridge: Cambridge University Press, 2012), pp. 28–29.
66 Chenoweth and Stephan use "civil resistance" to refer to "a type of political activity that deliberately or necessarily circumvents normal political channels and employs noninstitutional (and often illegal) forms of action against an opponent." Erica Chenoweth and Maria J. Stephan, *Why Civil Resistance Works* (New York: Columbia University Press, 2011), p. 12. Kurt Schock prefers *unarmed insurrections*, which he defines as "organized popular challenges to government authority that depend primarily on methods of nonviolent action rather than on armed methods." Kurt Schock, *Unarmed Insurrections: People Power Movements in Nondemocracies* (Minneapolis, MN: University of Minnesota Press, 2005), p. xvi.
67 Timur Kuran, "Why Revolutions Are Better Understood than Predicted: The Essential Role of Preference Falsification," in *Debating Revolutions*, Nikki Keddie, ed. (New York: New York University Press, 1995), p. 32. Even "after the fact," according to Kuran, preference falsification "masks the factors that were working against change."
68 Pedro Perez Sarduy, "Culture and the Cuban Revolution," *The Black Scholar*, Vol. 20, Nos. 5–6 (Winter 1989), p. 18.
69 Kamrava, *Revolution in Iran,* p. 68.
70 Bruszt, "1989: The Negotiated Revolution in Hungary," p. 386.
71 Jones, *The French Revolution,* p. 14.
72 On Rousseau, Jones observed that "the influence of his political writings before the Revolution has been greatly exaggerated." Ibid., p. 13.
73 McDaniel, "The Russian Revolution of 1917," p. 190.
74 Kamrava, *Revolution in Iran,* p. 66.
75 Tarrow, *Power in Movement,* p. 6.
76 Charles Tilly and Lesley J. Wood, *Social Movements 1768–2012* (Boulder, CO: Paradigm Publishers, 2012), p. 13.
77 Ibid., p. 14.
78 Sidney Tarrow, *Strangers at the Gates: Movements and States in Contentious Politics* (Cambridge: Cambridge University Press, 2012), p. 1.
79 Ibid., p. 21.
80 Chenoweth and Stephan, *Why Civil Resistance Works*, p. 10.

81 Ibid., p. 11.
82 Tilly and Wood, *Social Movements*, p. 15; Chenoweth and Stephan, *Why Civil Resistance Works*, pp. 10–11.
83 Nepstad, *Nonviolent Revolutions*, p. 126.
84 Schock, *Unarmed Insurrections*, p. 143.
85 Tarrow, *Power in Movement,* p. 118.
86 Ibid., p. 11.
87 Nepstad, *Nonviolent Revolutions*, p. 135.
88 Tilly and Wood, *Social Movements*, p. 112.
89 Linda Herrera, *Revolution in the Age of Social Media: The Egyptian Popular Insurrection and the Internet* (London: Verso, 2014), p. 5.
90 Ibid., p. 6.
91 Ibid., p. 12.
92 The State Department's stated objective, according to its own press briefing at the time, was to launch "a war of ideas [and to] use the tools of ideological engagement – words, deeds, images – to create an environment hostile to violent extremism. That's our mission. We want to break the linkages between groups like al-Qaeda and their target audience." As Herrera observes, however, "This ideological war depended on recruiting young people, particularly young Muslims, to serve as the proxies of the US." Herrera, *Revolution in the Age of Social Media*, p. 33. As it turns out, the spread of digital media does not necessarily serve as a panacea for extremism and can, in fact, help its spread. See, for example, Max Fisher and Amanda Taub, "How Algorithms Breed Extremism," *The New York Times*, International Edition (April 28–29, 2018), p. 2.
93 Wael Ghonim, *Revolution 2.0: The Power of the People Is Greater than the People in Power: A Memoir* (Boston: Houghton Mifflin Harcourt, 2012), p. 101.
94 Ibid., original emphasis.
95 Foran, "Revolutionizing Theory/Theorizing Revolutions," p. 118.
96 Charles Tripp, *The Power and the People: Paths of Resistance in the Middle East* (Cambridge: Cambridge University Press, 2013), p. 6.
97 Eric Selbin, "Stories of Revolution in the Periphery," in *Revolution in the Making of the Modern World: Social Identities, Globalization and Modernity*, John Foran, David Lane, and Andreja Zivkovic, eds. (London: Routledge, 2008), p. 134.
98 Ibid., pp. 134–135.
99 As Donatella della Porta has observed, the effects of mass uprisings – or "contentious waves," as she calls them – are complex, "never fully meeting the aspirations of those who protest, but rarely leaving things unchanged." Donatella della Porta, *Where Did the Revolution Go? Contentious Politics and the Quality of Democracy* (Cambridge: Cambridge University Press, 2016), p. 3.
100 Goldstone, "An Analytical Framework," p. 45.
101 Foran, "Revolutionizing Theory/Theorizing Revolutions," p. 118.
102 Edward Berenson, "The Social Interpretation of the French Revolution," in *Debating Revolutions*, Nikki Keddie, ed. (New York: New York University Press, 1995), p. 91.
103 Devora Grynspan, "Nicaragua: A New Model for Popular Revolution in Latin America," in *Revolutions of the Late Twentieth Century*, Jack A. Goldstone, Ted Robert Gurr, and Farrokh Moshiri, eds. (Boulder, CO: Westview, 1991), p. 97.
104 John Foran, *Taking Power: On the Origins of Third World Revolutions* (Cambridge: Cambridge University Press, 2005), p. 21.
105 Goldstone, "An Analytical Framework," p. 50.

106 Malek Sghiri, "Greetings to the Dawn: Living through the Bittersweet Revolution (Tunisia)," in *Diaries of an Unfinished Revolution*, Layla Al-Zubaidi and Matthew Cassel, eds. (New York: Penguin, 2013), p. 20. Sidi Bouzid is the small Tunisian city in which anti-regime protests erupted in December 2010 following the self-immolation of the fruit vendor Mohammad Bouazizi in protest over unemployment and state arbitrariness.
107 Ibid., pp. 21–22.
108 Ghonim, *Revolution* 2.0, p. 294. Original emphasis.
109 Sghiri, "Greetings to the Dawn," p. 22.
110 Ibid., p. 27.
111 Foran, "Revolutionizing Theory/Theorizing Revolutions," p. 123.
112 Ghonim, *Revolution* 2.0, pp. 58–59.
113 Lawson, "Revolutions and the International," p. 315.
114 Ghonim, *Revolution* 2.0, p. 133.
115 George Lawson, *Negotiated Revolutions: The Czech Republic, South Africa and Chile* (Burlington, VT: Ashgate, 2005), pp. 229–230.
116 Ibid., p. 229.

4 Revolutionary States

1 George Lawson, *Negotiated Revolutions: The Czech Republic, South Africa and Chile* (Burlington, VT: Ashgate, 2005), pp. 229–234.
2 Left on their own, revolutions are likely to eventually peter out. More often they are fought against, or at least undermined, often by their enemies or by those increasingly marginalized or purged from the revolutionary alliance. Not surprisingly, revolutionary leaders often resort to unrelenting rhetoric while in office. Similarly, they frequently engage in activities or launch initiatives that may appear illogical by conventional norms. Their rhetoric and seemingly unreasonable efforts are all part of the process of institutionalization, designed to maximize their own longevity by prolonging the fervor of the revolution and at the same time redirecting it into politically advantageous energies.
3 Theda Skocpol, *States and Social Revolutions* (Cambridge: Cambridge University Press, 1979), p. 163.
4 Ibid., pp. 163–164.
5 Crane Brinton, *The Anatomy of Revolution* (New York: Prentice Hall, 1952), p. 134.
6 Ibid., p. 226.
7 Ibid., p. 136.
8 Ibid., pp. 158–159.
9 Ibid., p. 163.
10 Ibid., p. 179.
11 Ibid., pp. 163–164.
12 Ibid., p. 224.
13 Ibid., p. 229.
14 Skocpol, *States and Social Revolutions*, p. 171.
15 Ibid.
16 Ibid., p. 280.
17 Ibid., p. 284.
18 S. N. Eisenstadt, *Revolution and the Transformation of Societies* (New York: Free Press, 1978), p. 251. Eisenstadt also draws attention to the "major institutional

derivatives of the symbolic orientations and their institutional derivatives such as, of human activities or the ground rules of social interaction, the structure of centers, center–periphery relations, the structure of markets, and so on. (Also important are,) among the principle actors in the revolutionary processes, the major carriers of such orientations; that is, the institutional entrepreneurs and elites that shape the institutional contours through which seemingly similar institutional interests are modeled in different ways." Ibid., p. 222.

19 Theda Skocpol, "Rentier State and Shi'a Islam in the Iranian Revolution," *Theory and Society*, Vol. 11, No. 3 (May 1982), p. 277. Original emphasis. The reference to modernity in this passage has to do with the author's discussion of the social background of the Iranian revolution, prior to which extensive social and economic changes occurred.

20 Ibid., pp. 275–276.

21 Brinton, *Anatomy of Revolution.*

22 For critical examinations of Skocpol's analysis, see the articles by Nikki Keddie, Eqbal Ahmad, and Walter Goldfrank in *Theory and Society*, Vol. 11, No. 3, pp. 285–303; and Jerome Himmelstein and Michael Kimmel, "Review Essay: States and Social Revolutions: The Implications and Limits of Skocpol's Structural Model," *American Journal of Sociology*, Vol. 86, No. 5 (1981), pp. 1145–1154.

23 See Eisenstadt, *Revolutions and the Transformation of Societies*, pp. 223–251.

24 See Brinton, *The Anatomy of Revolution*, chaps. 4 and 5, and Eisenstadt, *Revolution and the Transformation of Societies*, pp. 222–223.

25 Skocpol, *States and Social Revolutions*, p. 165.

26 Ibid., p. 165. Emphasis original.

27 Skocpol, "Rentier State and Shi'a Islam in the Iranian Revolution," p. 277.

28 R. Ben Jones, *The French Revolution* (London: Hodder & Stoughton, 1967), pp. 99–100. The *sans-culottes* were a group that fell "midway between what could be called working class and the petty bourgeoisie ... They were distinguished by their dress: trousers were worn by the workers, not the knee-breeches (*culottes*) of their richer lawyers ... It was a symbol of their egalitarian outlook, for they were resentful of 'rank-pulling.' They were distinguished by a social antagonism, too, for they regarded themselves as virtuous poor and the wealthy as likely to be corrupt and 'aristocratic' (a word which for them came to represent anyone against the revolution)." Ibid., pp. 27–28.

29 Ibid., p. 105.

30 Ibid., p. 121.

31 John Dunn, *Modern Revolutions: Introduction to a Political Phenomenon* (Cambridge: Cambridge University Press, 1972), p. 40.

32 Ibid., pp. 42–43.

33 See Shaul Bakhash, *The Reign of the Ayatollahs: Iran and the Islamic Revolution* (London: I. B. Tauris, 1985), pp. 56–64.

34 Ibid., p. 31.

35 James DeFronzo, *Revolutions and Revolutionary Movements*, 5th edn (Boulder, CO: Westview, 2015), p. 220. FSLN stands for *Frente Sandanista de Liberacion Nacional.*

36 Brinton, *The Anatomy of Revolution*, p. 135.

37 These issues were the preoccupation, for example, of French *philosophes* and the *physiocrats* prior to 1789, as discussed in Chapter 2.

38 Ernest Gellner, *Plough, Sword and Book: The Structure of Human History* (Chicago: University of Chicago Press, 1988), p. 147.

39 Seán Sheehan, *Lenin* (London: Haus, 2009), p. 116.

40 Brinton, *The Anatomy of Revolution*, p. 136.
41 Eisenstadt, *Revolutions and the Transformation of Society*, p. 217.
42 Peter Calvert, *Politics, Power and Revolution: An Introduction to Comparative Politics* (London: Wheatsheaf, 1983), p. 165.
43 Max Weber, *On Charisma and Institution Building*, S. N. Eisenstadt, ed. (Chicago, IL: University of Chicago Press, 1968), p. 54.
44 Barry M. Schutz and Robert O. Slater, "A Framework for Analysis," in *Revolution and Political Change in the Third World*, Barry M. Schutz and Robert O. Slater, eds. (Boulder, CO: Lynne Rienner, 1990), p. 9.
45 Barry Rubin, *Modern Dictators: Third World Coup Makers, Strongmen, and Populist Tyrants* (New York: McGraw Hill, 1987), p. 283.
46 Forrest Colburn, *Post-Revolutionary Nicaragua: State, Class, and the Dilemmas of Agrarian Policy* (Berkeley, CA: University of California Press, 1986), p. 22.
47 Theda Skocpol, "Social Revolutions and Mass Military Mobilization," *World Politics*, Vol. 40, No. 2 (January 1988), p. 149.
48 Jan Leighley, "Participation as a Stimulus for Political Conceptualization," *The Journal of Politics*, Vol. 53, No. 1 (February 1991), p. 198.
49 E. B. Portis, "Charismatic Leadership and Cultural Democracy," *Review of Politics*, Vol. 41, No. 2 (February1987), pp. 237–238.
50 Skocpol, "Social Revolutions and Mass Military Mobilization," p. 160.
51 Ibid., p. 164.
52 Ibid., pp. 167–168.
53 B. E. Aguirre, "The Conventionalization of Collective Behavior in Cuba," *American Journal of Sociology*, Vol. 90, No. 3 (1984), p. 589.
54 Skocpol, "Social Revolutions and Mass Military Mobilization," p. 164.
55 Dunn, *Modern Revolutions*, p. 256.
56 Ted Robert Gurr, "War, Revolution, and the Growth of the Coercive State," *Comparative Political Studies*, Vol. 21, No. 1 (April 1988), p. 49.
57 Ibid., p. 53.
58 DeFronzo, *Revolutions and Revolutionary Movements*, p. 101.
59 Eisenstadt, *Revolution and the Transformation of Societies*, p. 218.
60 Clement Moore, "The Single Party as a Source of Legitimacy," in *Authoritarian Politics in Modern Society*, Samuel Huntington and Clement Moore, eds. (London: Basic Books, 1970), p. 50.
61 Ibid., p. 51.
62 Vicky Randall, "Introduction," in *Political Parties in the Third World*, Vicky Randall, ed. (London: Sage, 1988), pp. 2–3.
63 Rubin, *Modern Dictators*, p. 312.
64 For more on the Islamic Republican Party and reasons for its dissolution, see Maziar Behrooz, "Factionalism in Iran under Khomeini," *Middle Eastern Studies*, Vol. 27, No. 4 (October 1991), pp. 597–614.
65 For a detailed and insightful discussion of patrimonial political arrangements, see James A. Bill and Robert Springborg, *Politics in the Middle East*, 5th edn (New York: Longman, 1999), pp. 112–113.
66 For a discussion of tendencies within the post-revolutionary Russian government to export the revolution, see DeFronzo, *Revolutions and Revolutionary Movements*, pp. 48–51; in the case of China, see Frederick Teiwes, *Politics at Mao's Court: Gao Gang and Party Factionalism in the Early 1950s* (Armonk, NY: M. E. Sharp, 1990).
67 Manus Midlarsky, "Scarcity and Inequality: Prologue to the Onset of Mass Revolution," *Journal of Conflict Resolution*, Vol. 26, No. 1 (March 1982), p. 22.
68 Eisenstadt, *Revolution and the Transformation of Societies*, p. 279.

69 For a discussion of post-revolutionary economic decline in Nicaragua, for example, see Colburn, *Post-Revolutionary Nicaragua*, pp. 13–18.
70 Quoted in, Dunn, *Modern Revolutions*, p. 62.
71 See Ibid., pp. 52–66.

5 Revolutionary Polities

1 S. N. Eisenstadt, *Revolution and the Transformation of Societies* (New York: Free Press, 1978), p. 217.
2 John Dunn, *Modern Revolutions: Introduction to the Analysis of a Political Phenomenon*, 2nd edn (Cambridge: Cambridge University Press, 1988), p. 239.
3 Eisenstadt, *Revolution and Transformation of Societies*, p. 218.
4 Crane Brinton, *The Anatomy of Revolution* (New York: Prentice Hall, 1952), p. 200.
5 In its attempts to reorganize society and collectivize farming, the campaign was a disaster and brought famine, hunger, death, and untold misery to millions of Chinese. For a concise analysis of the Great Leap Forward, see Hans J. Van de Ven, "War, Cosmopolitanism, and Authority: Mao from 1937 to 1956," in *A Critical Introduction to Mao*, Timothy Cheek, ed. (Cambridge: Cambridge University Press, 2010), pp. 81–109.
6 Fredrerick C. Teiwes, "Mao and His Followers," in *A Critical Introduction to Mao*, Timothy Cheek, ed. (Cambridge: Cambridge University Press, 2010), p. 146.
7 For a brief examination of Stalin's Cultural Revolution, see Sheila Fitzpatrick, *The Russian Revolution, 1917–1932* (Oxford: Oxford University Press, 1982), pp. 129–134; for the Chinese Cultural Revolution, see Immanuel Hsu, *The Rise of Modern China*, 4th edn (Oxford: Oxford University Press, 1990), pp. 658–660; for Iran, see Mehran Kamrava, *The Political History of Modern Iran: From Tribalism to Theocracy* (Westport, CT: Praeger, 1992), chap. 4.
8 Arshin Adib-Moghaddam, *On the Arab Revolts and the Iranian Revolution: Power and Resistance Today* (London: Bloomsbury, 2013), p. 3.
9 Frederick C. Teiwes, "Mao and His Followers," in *A Critical Introduction to Mao*, Timothy Cheek, ed. (Cambridge: Cambridge University Press, 2010), p. 153.
10 Ervand Abrahamian, *Tortured Confessions: Prison and Modern Recantations in Modern Iran* (Berkeley, CA: University of California Press, 1999), p. 209.
11 For a discussion of women's roles and issues in post-revolutionary Iran, see Farah Azari, "The Post-Revolutionary Women's Movement in Iran," in *Women of Iran: The Conflict with Fundamentalist Islam*, Farah Azari, ed. (London: Ithaca Press, 1983), pp. 190–225.
12 Haleh Esfandiari, *Reconstructed Lives: Women and Iran's Islamic Revolution* (Baltimore, MD: The Johns Hopkins University Press, 1997), p. 49.
13 Jerrold Green, "Counter Mobilization as a Revolutionary Form," *Comparative Politics*, Vol. 16, No. 2 (January 1984), p. 157.
14 Yasmine El Rashidi, "Cairo, City in Waiting (Egypt)," in *Diaries of an Unfinished Revolution*, Layla Al-Zubaidi and Matthew Cassel, eds. (New York: Penguin, 2013), p. 64.
15 Jan Leighley, "Participation as a Stimulus for Political Conceptualization," *The Journal of Politics*, Vol. 53, No. 1 (February 1991), p. 207.
16 Dunn, *Modern Revolutions*, p. 53.
17 Nathan J. Brown, *Arguing Islam After the Revival of Arab Politics* (New York: Oxford University Press, 2017), p. 12. Original emphasis.

18 William Gamson, "Commitment and Agency in Social Movement," *Sociological Forum*, Vol. 6, No. 1 (1991), p. 42.
19 Ibid., p. 45.
20 Ibid., p. 46.
21 Ibid., p. 47.
22 James Davies, "Maslow and Theory of Political Development: Getting to Fundamentals," *Political Psychology*, Vol. 12, No. 3 (1991), p. 400.
23 Pierre Brocheux, *Ho Chi Minh: A Biography*, translated by Claire Duiker (Cambridge: Cambridge University Press, 2007), p. 143.
24 The concept of "ethics of struggle" is elaborated on, though in a different context, in Tom Denyer, "The Ethics of Struggle," *Political Theory*, Vol. 17, No. 4 (November 1989), pp. 535–549. Relevant to this discussion, however, is Denyer's assertion that "as a practical matter, an ethics of struggle can be produced and evaluated in the course of the struggle itself." p. 536.
25 B. E. Aguirre, "The Conventionalization of Collective Behavior in Cuba," *American Journal of Sociology*, Vol. 90, No. 3 (1984), p. 560.
26 Roy Medvedev, *Let History Judge: The Origins and Consequences of Stalinism* (New York: Alfred Knopf, 1971), p. 518–519.
27 Wars, as discussed in Chapter 4, are common occurrences following revolutions, not only because revolutions tend to upset the immediate regional balance of power but also because post-revolutionary states have immense power to mobilize citizens for wars.
28 See Stephen Chilton, "Defining Political Culture," *Western Political Quarterly*, Vol. 41, No. 3 (September 1988), pp. 419–445.
29 Gabriel Almond and Sidney Verba, *The Civic Culture: Political Attitudes and Democracy in Five Nations* (London: Sage, 1989), p. 13.
30 Ibid., p. 32.
31 Ibid., p. 25.
32 Samuel Huntington, *Political Order in Changing Societies* (New Haven, CT: Yale University Press, 1968), p. 310.
33 Rafael Hernandez and Harolda Dilla, "Political Culture and Popular Participation in Cuba," *Latin American Perspectives*, Vol. 18, No. 2 (Spring 1991), p. 53.
34 Lucian Pye, "Tiananmen and Chinese Political Culture," *Asian Survey*, Vol. 30, No. 4 (April 1990), pp. 331–332.
35 Lowell Dittmer, "Mao and the Politics of Revolutionary Morality," *Asian Survey*, Vol. 27, No. 3 (March 1987), p. 335.
36 Eisenstadt, *Revolution and the Transformation of Societies,* p. 243.
37 Ernest Gellner, *Plough, Sword, and Book: The Structure of Human History* (Chicago: University of Chicago Press, 1988), p. 147.
38 It can be argued that the post-revolutionary Chinese did not achieve a complete victory in the ensuing civil war since they were unable to suppress the Nationalist control of Taiwan.
39 Sheila Fitzpatrick, *The Russian Revolution, 1917–1932,* pp. 67–69.
40 Ted Gurr, "War, Revolution, and the Growth of the Coercive State," *Comparative Political Studies*, Vol. 21, No. 1 (April 1988), p. 53.
41 R. Ben Jones, *The French Revolution* (London: Hodder & Stoughton, 1967), pp. 75–78; for Iranian *emigres,* see Mehdi Bozorgmehr and Georges Sabagh, "High Status Immigrants: A Statistical Profile of Iranians in the United States," *Iranian Studies*, Vol. 21, Nos. 3–4 (1988), pp. 5–35.
42 See for example, Bozorgmehr and Sabagh, "High Status Immigrants."
43 Eric Scheye, "Psychological Notes on Central Europe: 1989 and Beyond," *Political Psychology*, Vol. 12, No. 2 (1991), p. 334.
44 Ibid., p. 337.

6 Conclusion

1 William Blanchard, *Revolutionary Morality: A Psychosexual Analysis of Twelve Revolutionists* (Oxford: ABC-Clio, 1984), p. xv.
2 I have discussed these and other Arab Spring cases in some detail in *Inside the Arab State* (New York: Oxford University Press, 2018).
3 Robin Wright, *The Last Great Revolution: Turmoil and Transformation in Iran* (New York: Vintage, 2001).
4 Steven Levitsky and Lucian A. Way, *Competitive Authoritarianism: Hybrid Regimes after the Cold War* (Cambridge: Cambridge University Press, 2010), p. 5.
5 Ibid., p. 23.
6 Ibid., p. 82.
7 Malek Sghiri, "Greetings to the Dawn: Living through the Bittersweet Revolution (Tunisia)," in *Diaries of an Unfinished Revolution*, Layla Al-Zubaidi and Matthew Cassel, eds. (New York: Penguin, 2013), p. 43.

BIBLIOGRAPHY

Abrahamian, Ervand. *Tortured Confessions: Prison and Modern Recantations in Modern Iran*. Berkeley, CA: University of California Press, 1999.

Adib-Moghaddam, Arshin. *On the Arab Revolts and the Iranian Revolution: Power and Resistance Today*. London: Bloomsbury, 2013.

Aguirre, Benigno E. "The Conventionalization of Collective Behavior in Cuba," *American Journal of Sociology*, Vol. 90, No. 3 (1984), pp. 541–566.

Almond, Gabriel A., and Sidney Verba. *The Civic Culture: Political Attitudes and Democracy in Five Nations*. London: Sage, 1989.

Azari, Farah. "The Post-Revolutionary Women's Movement in Iran" in *Women of Iran: The Conflict with Fundamentalist Islam*, Farah Azari, ed. London: Ithaca Press, 1983, pp. 3–26.

Bakhash, Shaul. *The Reign of the Ayatollahs: Iran and the Islamic Revolution*. London: I. B. Tauris, 1985.

Balfour, Sebastian. *Castro*, 3rd edn. Harlow, UK: Pearson Longman, 2009.

Barany, Zoltan. *How Armies Respond to Revolutions and Why*. Princeton, NJ: Princeton University Press, 2016.

Bayat, Asef. *Revolution without Revolutionaries: Making Sense of the Arab Spring*. Stanford, CA: Stanford University Press, 2017.

Behrooz, Maziar. "Factionalism in Iran under Khomeini," *Middle Eastern Studies*, Vol. 27, No. 4 (October 1991), pp. 597–614.

Bello, Walden. "Introduction," in *Down with Colonialism!* London: Verso, 2007, pp. ix–xxxix.

Berenson, Edward. "The Social Interpretation of the French Revolution," in *Debating Revolutions*, Nikki Keddie, ed. New York: New York University Press, 1995, pp. 85–111.

Bill, James A., and Robert Springborg. *Politics in the Middle East*, 5th edn. New York: Longman, 1999.

Blanchard, William. *Revolutionary Morality: A Psychosexual Analysis of Twelve Revolutionists*. Santa Barbara, CA: ABC-Clio, 1984.

Bozorgmehr, Mehdi, and Georges Sabagh. "High Status Immigrants: A Statistical Profile of Iranians in the United States," *Iranian Studies*, Vol. 21, Nos. 3–4 (1988), pp. 5–35.

Brinton, Crane. *The Anatomy of Revolution*. New York: Prentice Hall, 1952.

Brocheux, Pierre. *Ho Chi Minh: A Biography*, translated by Claire Duiker. Cambridge: Cambridge University Press, 2007.

Brown, Nathan J. *Arguing Islam after the Revival of Arab Politics*. New York: Oxford University Press, 2017.

Brownlee, Jason. *Authoritarianism in the Age of Democratization*. Cambridge: Cambridge University Press, 2007.

Bruszt, Laszlo. "1989: The Negotiated Revolution in Hungary," *Social Research*, Vol. 57, No. 2 (Summer 1990), pp. 365–387.

Calvert, Peter. *Politics, Power, and Revolution: An Introduction to Comparative Politics*. London: Wheatsheaf, 1983.

Capoccia, Giovanni, and R. Daniel Kelemen. "The Study of Critical Junctures: Theory, Narrative, and Counterfactuals in Historical Institutionalism," *World Politics*, Vol. 59, No. 3 (April 2007), pp. 341–369.

Chaliand, Gerard. *Revolution in the Third World: Myths and Prospects*. New York: Viking Press, 1977.

Cheek, Timothy. "Mao, Revolution, and Memory," in *A Critical Introduction to Mao*, Timothy Cheek, ed. Cambridge: Cambridge University Press, 2010, pp. 3–30.

Chenoweth, Erica, and Maria J. Stephan. *Why Civil Resistance Works*. New York: Columbia University Press, 2011.

Chilton, Stephen. "Defining Political Culture," *Western Political Quarterly*, Vol. 41, No. 3 (September 1988), pp. 419–445.

Colburn, Forrest. *Post-Revolutionary Nicaragua: State, Class, and the Dilemmas of Agrarian Policy*. Berkeley, CA: University of California Press, 1986.

Davies, James. "Maslow and the Theory of Political Development: Getting to Fundamentals," *Political Psychology*, Vol. 12, No. 3 (1991), pp. 389–420.

Davies, James. "Toward a Theory of Revolution," *American Sociological Review*, Vol. 27, No. 1 (February 1962), pp. 7–19.

Davin, Delia. *Mao: A Very Short Introduction*. Oxford: Oxford University Press, 2013.

DeFronzo, James. *Revolutions and Revolutionary Movements*, 5th edn. Boulder, CO: Westview Press, 2015.

della Porta, Donatella. *Where Did the Revolution Go? Contentious Politics and the Quality of Democracy*. Cambridge: Cambridge University Press, 2016.

Denyer, Tom. "The Ethics of Struggle," *Political Theory*, Vol. 17, No. 4 (November 1989), pp. 535–549.

Dittmer, Lowell. "Mao and the Politics of Revolutionary Morality," *Asian Survey*, Vol. 27, No. 3 (March 1987), pp. 316–339.

Dunn, John. *Modern Revolutions: An Introduction to the Analysis of a Political Phenomenon*, 2nd edn. Cambridge: Cambridge University Press, 1988.

Dunn, John. "Revolution," in *Political Innovation and Conceptual Change*, Terence Ball, James Farr, and Russel Hanson, eds. Cambridge: Cambridge University Press, 1988, pp. 333–356.

Dunn, John. *Modern Revolutions: Introduction to a Political Phenomenon*. Cambridge: Cambridge University Press, 1972.

Eisenstadt, S. N. *Revolution and the Transformation of Societies*. New York: Free Press, 1978.

El Rashidi, Yasmine. "Cairo, City in Waiting (Egypt)," in *Diaries of an Unfinished Revolution*, Layla Al-Zubaidi and Matthew Cassel, eds. New York: Penguin 2013, pp. 48–65.

Esfandiari, Haleh. *Reconstructed Lives: Women and Iran's Islamic Revolution*. Baltimore, MD: The Johns Hopkins University Press, 1997.

Esherick, Joseph W. "Making Revolution in Twentieth-Century China," in *A Critical Introduction to Mao*, Timothy Cheek, ed. Cambridge: Cambridge University Press, 2010, pp. 31–60.

Fall, Bernard B., ed. *Ho Chi Minh On Revolution, Selected Writings, 1920–66*, New York: Signet, 1967.

Farr, James. "Historical Concepts in Political Science: The Case of 'Revolution,'" *American Journal of Political Science*, Vol. 26, No. 4 (November 1982), pp. 688–708.

Fitzpatrick, Sheila. *The Russian Revolution, 1917–1932*. Oxford: Oxford University Press, 1982.

Foltz, William. "External Causes," in *Revolution and Political Change in the Third World*, Barry M. Schutz and Robert O. Slater, eds. Boulder, CO: Lynne Rienner, 1990, pp. 54–68.

Foran, John. *Taking Power: On the Origins of Third World Revolutions*. Cambridge: Cambridge University Press, 2005.

Foran, John. "Revolutionizing Theory/Theorizing Revolutions: State, Culture, and Society in Recent Works on Revolution," in *Debating Revolutions*, Nikki Keddie, ed. New York: New York University Press, 1995, pp. 112–135.

Franqui, Carlos. *Diary of the Cuban Revolution*. New York: Viking, 1980.

Gamson, William. "Commitment and Agency in Social Movement," *Sociological Forum*, Vol. 6, No. 1 (1991), pp. 27–50.

Gandhi, Jennifer. *Political Institutions under Dictatorships*. Cambridge: Cambridge University Press, 2008.

Gellner, Ernest. *Plough, Sword and Book: The Structure of Human History*. Chicago: University of Chicago Press, 1988.

Ghonim, Wael. *Revolution 2.0: The Power of the People Is Greater than the People in Power: A Memoir*. Boston: Houghton Mifflin Harcourt, 2012.

Goldstone, Jack A. "Revolutions in Modern Dictatorships," in *Revolutions: Theoretical, Comparative, and Historical Studies*, 3rd edn., Jack A. Goldstone, ed. Belmont, CA: Thomson Wadsworth, 2003, pp. 69–76.

Goldstone, Jack A. "Predicting Revolutions: Why We Could (and Should) Have Foreseen the Revolutions of 1989–1991 in the U.S.S.R. and Eastern Europe," in *Debating Revolutions*, Nikki Keddie, ed. New York: New York University Press, 1995, pp. 39–64.

Goldstone, Jack A. "An Analytical Framework," in *Revolutions of the Late Twentieth Century*, Jack A. Goldstone, Ted Robert Gurr, and Farrokh Moshiri, eds. Boulder, CO: Westview, 1991, pp. 37–51.

Goodwin, Jeff, and Theda Skocpol. "Explaining Revolutions in the Contemporary World," *Politics and Society*, Vol. 17, No. 4 (December 1989), pp. 489–509.

Gore, Charles. "The Rise and Fall of the Washington Consensus as a Paradigm for Developing Countries," *World Development*, Vol. 28, No. 5 (2000), pp. 789–804.

Green, Jerrold. "Counter Mobilization as a Revolutionary Form," *Comparative Politics*, Vol. 16, No. 2 (January 1984), pp. 153–169.

Grynspan, Devora. "Nicaragua: A New Model for Popular Revolution in Latin America," in *Revolutions of the Late Twentieth Century*, Jack A. Goldstone, Ted Robert Gurr, and Farrokh Moshiri, eds. Boulder, CO: Westview, 1991, pp. 88–115.

Guevara, Ernesto Che. *Che: The Diaries of Ernesto Che Guevara*. Melbourne: Ocean Press, 2008.

Guevara, Ernesto Che. *Guerrilla Warfare*. Melbourne: Ocean Press, 2006.

Guevara, Ernesto Che. *The Bolivian Diary*. Melbourne: Ocean Press, 2006.

Gurr, Ted Robert. "War, Revolution, and the Growth of the Coercive State," *Comparative Political Studies*, Vol. 21, No. 1 (April 1988), pp. 45–65.

Gurr, Ted Robert. *Why Men Rebel*. Princeton, NJ: Princeton University Press, 1970.

Hernandez, Rafael, and Harolda Dilla. "Political Culture and Popular Participation in Cuba," *Latin American Perspectives*, Vol. 18, No. 2 (Spring 1991), pp. 38–54.

Herrera, Linda. *Revolution in the Age of Social Media: The Egyptian Popular Insurrection and the Internet*. London: Verso, 2014.

Himmelstein, Jerome, and Michael Kimmel. "Review Essay: The Implications and Limits of Skopol's Structure Model," *American Journal of Sociology*, Vol. 86, No. 5 (March 1981), pp. 1145–1154.

Hsu, Immanuel. *The Rise of Modern China*, 4th edn. Oxford: Oxford University Press, 1991.

Huntington, Samuel. *Political Order in Changing Societies*. New Haven, CT: Yale University Press, 1968.

Johnson, Chalmers. *Revolutionary Change*. London: Longman, 1983.

Jones, R. Ben. *The French Revolution*. London: Hodder & Stoughton, 1967.

Kamrava, Mehran. *Inside the Arab State*, New York: Oxford University Press, 2018.

Kamrava, Mehran. "The Arab Spring and the Saudi-Led Counterrevolution," *Orbis*, Vol. 56, No. 1 (Winter 2012), pp. 96–104.

Kamrava, Mehran. *The Political History of Modern Iran: From Tribalism to Theocracy*. Westport, CT: Praeger, 1992.

Kamrava, Mehran. *Revolution in Iran: Roots of Turmoil*. London: Routledge, 1990.

Keddie, Nikki R. "Can Revolutions Be Predicted; Can Their Causes Be Understood?" in *Debating Revolutions*, Nikki Keddie, ed. New York: New York University Press, 1995, pp. 3–26.

Khajehpour, Bijan. "Re-Mapping the Corporate Landscape in Iran," in *Inside the Islamic Republic: Social Change in Post-Khomeini Iran*, Mahmood Monshipouri, ed. New York: Oxford University Press, 2016, pp. 263–286.

Krauss, Clifford. "Revolution in Central America?" *Foreign Affairs*, Vol. 65, No. 3 (1987), pp. 564–581.

Kuran, Timur. "Why Revolutions are Better Understood than Predicted: The Essential Role of Preference Falsification," in *Debating Revolutions*, Nikki Keddie, ed. New York: New York University Press, 1995, pp. 27–35.

Lawson, George. "Revolutions and the International," *Theory and Society*, Vol. 44, No. 4 (July 2015), pp. 299–319.

Lawson, George. *Negotiated Revolutions: The Czech Republic, South Africa and Chile*. Burlington, VT: Ashgate, 2005.

Lawson, George. "Negotiated Revolutions: The Prospects for Radical Change in Contemporary World Politics," *Review of International Studies*, Vol. 31 (2005), pp. 473–493.

Le Blanc, Paul. "Ten Reasons for Not Reading Lenin," in *V. I. Lenin, Revolution, Democracy, Socialism: Selected Writings*, Paul Le Blanc, ed. London: Pluto, 2008, pp. 3–80.

Leighley, Jan. "Participation as a Stimulus for Political Conceptualization," *The Journal of Politics*, Vol. 53, No. 1 (February 1991), pp. 198–212.

Lenin, V. I. *Lenin: Collected Works*, Vol. 25, translated and edited by Stepan Apresyan and Jim Riordan. Moscow: Progress Publishers, 1977.

Lenin, V. I. *Alliance of the Working Class and the Peasantry*. Moscow: Progress Publishers, 1965.

Lenin, V. I. *Lenin: Collected Works*, Vol. 10, translated and edited by Andrew Rothstein. Moscow: Progress Publishers, 1965.

Levitsky, Steven, and Lucian A. Way. *Competitive Authoritarianism: Hybrid Regimes after the Cold War*. Cambridge: Cambridge University Press, 2010.

Lichbach, Mark Irving. *The Rebel's Dilemma*. Ann Arbor, MI: University of Michigan Press, 1998.

Linz, Juan J. *Totalitarian and Authoritarian Regimes*. Boulder, CO: Lynne Rienner, 2000.

Mandela, Nelson. *Long Walk to Freedom*. New York: Little, Brown and Co., 1994.

Marx, Karl. *The 18th Brumaire of Louis Bonaparte*. India: CreateSpace, 2015.

Marx, Karl, and Friedrich Engles. *The Communist Manifesto*. Tustin, CA: Brandywine, 2008.

Mason, T. David. "Indigenous Factors," in *Revolution and Political Change in the Third World*, Barry M. Schutz and Robert O. Slater, eds. Boulder, CO: Lynne Rienner, 1990, pp. 30–53.

McDaniel, Tim. "The Russian Revolution of 1917: Autocracy and Modernization," in *Revolutions: Theoretical, Comparative, and Historical Studies*, 3rd edn., Jack A. Goldstone, ed. Belmont, CA: Thomson Wadsworth, 2003, pp. 183–190.

Medvedev, Roy. *Let History Judge: The Origins and Consequences of Stalinism*. New York: Alfred Knopf, 1971.

Midlarsky, Manus. "Scarcity and Inequality: Prologue to the Onset of Mass Revolution," *Journal of Conflict Resolution*, Vol. 26, No. 1 (March 1982), pp. 3–38.

Minh, Ho Chi. *Down with Colonialism!* London: Verso, 2007.

Miroff, Bruce. *Pragmatic Illusions: The Presidential Politics of John F. Kennedy*. New York: David McKay, 1976.

Moore, Clement. "The Single Party as Source of Legitimacy," in *Authoritarian Politics in Modern Society*, Samuel Huntington and Clement Moore, ed. London: Basic Books, 1970, pp. 48–72.

Neely, Sylvia. *A Concise History of the French Revolution*. Lanham, MD: Roman & Littlefield, 2008.

Nepstad, Sharon Erickson. *Nonviolent Revolutions: Civil Resistance in the Late 20th Century*. New York: Oxford University Press, 2011.

Pahlavi, Mohammad Reza. *Be Sooye Tammadon-e Bozorg (Toward the Great Civilization)*. Tehran: Center for Political and Cultural Research and Publications of the Pahlavi Era, 1977.

Paterson, Thomas, J. Garry Clifford, and Kenneth J. Hagan. *American Foreign Policy: A History*. Lexington, MA: D. C. Heath & Co, 1991.

Portis, E. B. "Charismatic Leadership and Cultural Democracy," *Review of Politics*, Vol. 41, No. 2 (February 1987), pp. 231–250.

Pye, Lucian. "Tiananmen and Chinese Political Culture," *Asian Survey*, Vol. 30, No. 4 (April 1990), pp. 331–347.

Pye, Lucian. "The Legitimacy Crisis," in *Crises and Sequences in Political Development*, Leonard Binder and Joseph La Palombara, eds. Princeton, NJ: Princeton University Press, 1971, pp. 135–158.

Randall, Vicky, ed. "Introduction," in *Political Parties in the Third World*, London: Sage, 1988, pp. 1–6.

Reich, Walter, ed. *Origins of Terrorism: Psychologies, Ideologies, Theologies, States of Mind*. Cambridge: Cambridge University Press, 1990.

Ritter, Daniel P. *The Iron Cage of Liberalism: International Politics and Unarmed Revolutions in the Middle East and North Africa*. Oxford: Oxford University Press, 2015.

Rubin, Barry. *Modern Dictators: Third World Coup Makers, Strongmen, and Populist Tyrants*. New York: McGraw Hill, 1987.

Russell, Henry. *Let Freedom Reign: The Words of Nelson Mandela*. Northampton, MA: Interlink, 2010.

Sarduy, Pedro Perez. "Culture and the Cuban Revolution," *The Black Scholar*, Vol. 20, Nos. 5–6 (Winter 1989), pp. 17–23.

Scheye, Eric. "Psychological Notes on Central Europe: 1989 and beyond," *Political Psychology*, Vol. 12, No. 2 (1991), pp. 331–334.

Schock, Kurt. *Unarmed Insurrections: People Power Movements in Nondemocracies*. Minneapolis, MN: University of Minnesota Press, 2005.

Schram, Stuart. *The Political Thought of Mao Tse Tung*. New York: Praeger, 1972.

Schutz, Barry M., and Robert O. Slater. "A Framework for Analysis," in *Revolution and Political Change in the Third World*, Barry M. Schutz and Robert O. Slater, eds. Boulder, CO: Lynne Rienner, 1990, pp. 3–18.

Schutz, Barry M., and Robert O. Slater. "Patterns of Legitimacy and Future Revolutions in the Third World," in *Revolution and Political Change in the Third World*, Barry M. Schutz and Robert O. Slater, eds. Boulder, CO: Lynne Rienner, 1990, pp. 247–250.

Scott, James. "Hegemony and the Peasantry," *Politics and Society*, Vol. 7, No. 3 (1977), pp. 267–296.

Scott, James. *Domination and the Art of Resistance: Hidden Transcripts*. New Haven, CT: Yale University Press, 1990.

Selbin, Eric. "Spaces and Places of (Im)Possibility and Desire: Transversal Revolutionary Imaginaries in the Twentieth Century Americas," *Forum for Inter-American Research*, Vol. 9, No. 1 (May 2016), pp. 19–40.

Selbin, Eric. "Stories of Revolution in the Periphery," in *Revolution in the Making of the Modern World: Social Identities, Globalization and Modernity*, John Foran, David Lane, and Andreja Zivkovic, eds. London: Routledge, 2008, pp. 130–147.

Service, Robert. *Lenin: A Biography*. Cambridge, MA: Harvard University Press, 2000.

Sghiri, Malek. "Greetings to the Dawn: Living through the Bittersweet Revolution (Tunisia)," translated by Robin Moger. In *Diaries of an Unfinished Revolution: Voices from Tunis to Damascus*, Layla Al-Zubaidi and Matthew Cassel, eds. New York: Penguin, 2013, pp. 9–47.

Sheehan, Seán. *Lenin*. London: Haus, 2009.

Skocpol, Theda. "Social Revolutions and Mass Military Mobilization," *World Politics*, Vol. 40, No. 2 (January 1988), pp. 147–168.

Skocpol, Theda. "Rentier State and Shi'a Islam in the Iranian Revolution," *Theory and Society*, Vol. 11, No. 3 (May 1982), pp. 265–283.

Skocpol, Theda. "What Makes Peasants Revolutionary?" *Comparative Politics*, Vol. 14, No. 3 (April 1982), pp. 351–375.

Skocpol, Theda. *States and Social Revolutions*. Cambridge: Cambridge University Press, 1979.

Skocpol, Theda, and Ellen Kay Trimberger. "Revolutions: A Structural Analysis," in *Revolutions: Theoretical, Comparative, and Historical Studies*, 3rd edn., Jack A. Goldstone, ed. Belmont, CA: Thomson Wadsworth, 2003, pp. 63–69.

Snow, Edgar. *Red Star over China: The Classic Account of the Birth of Chinese Communism*. New York: Grove Press, 1968.

Stacher, Joshua. *Adaptable Autocrats: Regime Power in Egypt and Syria*. Stanford, CA: Stanford University Press, 2012.

Svolik, Milan W. *The Politics of Authoritarian Rule*. Cambridge: Cambridge University Press, 2012.

Sweig, Julia E. *Inside the Cuban Revolution: Fidel Castro and the Urban Underground*. Cambridge, MA: Harvard University Press, 2002.

Tarrow, Sidney. *Power in Movement: Social Movements and Contentious Politics*. Cambridge: Cambridge University Press, 2012.

Tarrow, Sidney. *Strangers at the Gates: Movements and States in Contentious Politics*. Cambridge: Cambridge University Press, 2012.

Teiwes, Frederick C. "Mao and His Followers," in *A Critical Introduction to Mao*, Timothy Cheek, ed. Cambridge: Cambridge University Press, 2010, pp. 129–157.

Teiwes, Frederick C. *Politics at Mao's Court: Gao Gang and Party Factionalism in the Early 1950s*. Armonk, NY: M. E. Sharp, 1990.

Tilly, Charles, and Lesley J. Wood. *Social Movements, 1768–2012*, 3rd edn. Boulder, CO: Paradigm Publishers, 2013.

Tripp, Charles. *The Power and the People: Paths of Resistance in the Middle East*. Cambridge: Cambridge University Press, 2013.

Tse-Tung, Mao. *Quotations from Chairman Mao Tse-Tung*. Peking: Foreign Language Press, 1976.

Van de Ven, Hans J. "War, Cosmopolitanism, and Authority: Mao from 1937 to 1956," in *A Critical Introduction to Mao*, Timothy Cheek, ed. Cambridge: Cambridge University Press, 2010, pp. 87–109.

Weber, Max. *On Charisma and Institution Building*, S. N. Eisenstadt, ed. Chicago, IL: University of Chicago Press, 1968.

Wickham-Crowley, Timothy P. "Toward a Comparative Sociology of Latin American Guerrilla Movements," in *Revolutions: Theoretical, Comparative, and Historical*

Studies, 3rd edn., Jack A. Goldstone, ed. Belmont, CA: Wadsworth/Thompson, 2003, pp. 285–294.

Womack, Brantly. "From Urban Radical to Rural Revolutionary: Mao from the 1920s to 1937," in *A Critical Introduction to Mao*, Timothy Cheek, ed. Cambridge: Cambridge University Press, 2010, pp. 61–86.

Wolf, Eric R. *Peasant Wars of the Twentieth Century*. New York: Harper & Row, 1969.

Wright, Robin. *The Last Great Revolution: Turmoil and Transformation in Iran*. New York: Vintage, 2001.

Wydra, Harald. "Revolution and Democracy: The European Experience," in *Revolution in the Making of the Modern World: Social Identities, Globalization and Modernity*, John Foran, David Lane, and Andreja Zivkovic, eds. London: Routledge, 2008, pp. 27–44.

INDEX

Adib-Moghaddam, Arshin, 108
African National Congress (ANC), 6
Alliance of Youth Movement (YAM), 66
Almond, Gabriel, 114–115
ANC. *See* African National Congress
anti-democratic trends, in post-revolutionary societies, 118
anti-revolutionary revolutions, 6
Arab Spring
  post-revolutionary society after, 111
  as "refolution," 7–8
  social media as influence on, 65–66
  timeline of, 155–158
  in Tunisia, 69–70
  Western involvement in, 128–129
  YAM and, 66
armed violence, in political revolution
  Ho Chi Minh on, 28
  Lenin on, 163
  Mandela on, 27–28
  in planned revolutions, 27–30
    in China, 27–30
    in Vietnam, 28
Assad, Bashar, 56
authoritarian states
  spontaneous revolutions in, 50
    nationalism in, 72
  trajectories of, 129–131
autocratic systems
  international influences on, 47
  in weak states, 53–56

Barany, Zoltan, 1
Batista, Fulgencio, 24
Bayat, Asef, 7–8, 160
Ben Ali, Zein el Abidin, 71
Bolivia, Guevara in, 39–40
Bolsheviks. *See* communism; Russia
Bonaparte, Napoleon, 79
Bouazizi, Mohammad, 170
bourgeois revolution, 23
Bouzid, Sidi, 69–70
Brezhnev Doctrine, 46
Brinton, Crane, 8, 78, 107
Brown, Nathan, 111
Buazizi, Mohammed, 71

Castro, Fidel, 9
  as charismatic authority, 88
  Guevara and, 18, 25–26, 162
  July 26 Movement, 24–26
  leadership of, 17–18
  literary influences on, 18
  on peasants' role in revolution, 37–40
Castro, Raul, 25–26
CCP. *See* Chinese Communist Party

Central Europe, negotiated revolutions in, 4
Cervantes, Miguel de, 18
charismatic authority, 88
China. *See also* Mao Zedong
CCP in, 15
Ho Chi Minh influenced by, 22–23
peasant organization by, 29–30
Cultural Revolution in, 22, 108, 162
Great Leap Forward, 22, 108, 162
KMT in, 15, 29–30
Long March and, 30
planned revolution in, 140–145
armed struggle as part of, 27–30
leadership issues in, 17
nationalism and, 15
Sun Yat Sen and, 21–22
vanguard parties in, 21–22. *See also* Chinese Communist Party
women in, 164
post-revolutionary society in, 108, 116–117
Taiwan and, 174
Chinese Communist Party (CCP), 15
Ho Chi Minh influenced by, 22–23
peasant organization by, 29–30
Sun Yat Sen and, 21–22
civil resistance, 168
collective identity, in post-revolutionary societies, 112
communism
CCP, 15
Ho Chi Minh on, 14
nationalism and, 14
counter-revolutionaries, 89–90
in post-revolutionary societies, 108–109
propaganda by, 123
Cromwell, Oliver, 79
Cuba
Batista in, 24
nationalism in, 15–16
planned revolutions in, 145–148. *See also* Castro, Fidel; Guevara, Ernesto "Che"
July 26 Movement, 24–26
leadership in, 17–18
Martí as influence on, 15–16
nationalism and, 15–16
vanguard parties in, 24–27
Cultural Revolution, in China, 22, 108, 162

Declaration of Independence (Vietnam), 15, 161
della Porta, Donatella, 169
democracies
in post-revolutionary states, 127
street, in post-revolutionary societies, 115–116
dictators, during revolutions, 2–3
dictatorships, institutional composition of, 54–55
dissent, in post-revolutionary societies, 118–121
dissynchronization, 49
Dostoevsky, Fyodor, 18

Eastern Europe, negotiated revolutions in, 4, 6, 153–155
Egypt
January 25th Revolution, 7
military regimes in, 61
Muslim Brotherhood in, 7
power centralization in, 56
spontaneous revolutions in, 3–4, 7–8
Eisenstadt, S. N., 81, 170–171
ElBaradei, Mohamed, 71
emigre communities, 122–123
European Union (EU). *See* Central Europe; Eastern Europe

factionalism, 97
foot soldiers. *See also* peasants
in planned revolutions, 31–40
Foran, John, 69–70

France
  royal authority in, collapse of, 57–59
  social movements in, 63
  spontaneous revolutions in, 3–4
Franqui, Carlo, 24–26
French Colonialism on Trial (Ho Chi Minh), 14
French Revolution
  causes of, 57–59
  Louis XVI and, 58–59
  royal authority and, collapse of, 57–59
  sans-culottes in, 171
  timeline of, 132–135
FSLN. *See* Sandinista National Liberation Front

Gamson, William, 111
Gellner, Ernest, 86
Ghonim, Wael, 67, 70
Goldstone, Jack, 8, 43–44
Gorky, Maxim, 18
Great Leap Forward, 22, 108, 162
Guevara, Ernesto "Che," 6
  Castro, Fidel, and, 18, 25–26, 162
  Marx as influence on, 41
  on peasants' role in revolution, 37–40
    in Bolivia, 39–40
    fundamental lessons for, 38
    romanticization of, 39
  on planned revolutions, 40–41

He Zizhen, 164
Herrera, Linda, 66
Ho Chi Minh, 9, 14, 16, 22–24, 108, 163
  on armed violence, 28
  CCP as influence on, 22–23
  Declaration of Independence written by, 15, 161
  February Revolution, 14
  Indochinese Communist Party, 23
  Marx as influence on, 41
  Marxist-Leninism for, 23
  nationalism for, 13–15
    communism and, 14
  October Revolution, 14
  on peasants' role in revolution, 36–37
  on revolution, types of, 23
Hugo, Victor, 18

identity. *See* collective identity; national identities
institutionalization. *See* state institutions
insurrections. *See* revolutions; unarmed insurrections
intellectual movements, 63
internationalism, 13
Iran
  monarchy in, collapse of, 60–61
  post-revolutionary society in, 108, 117
  spontaneous revolutions in, 3–4, 84, 148–150
Ivan the Terrible, 113

January 25th Revolution, 7
July 26 Movement, in Cuba, 24–26
  peasants' role during, 37–38

Khan, Genghis, 113
Khomeini, Ruhollah (Ayatollah), 7, 9, 71
Kuomintang (KMT), 15, 29–30
  Long March and, 30
Kuran, Timur, 62

land reform, in post-revolutionary states, 99
lawlessness, in post-revolutionary societies, 105–106
Lawson, George, 8, 45–46, 74
leadership
  middle-class, of peasants, 32
  in planned revolutions, 11–12, 16–18
    in China, 17. *See also* Mao Zedong
    in Cuba, 17–18. *See also* Castro, Fidel
    violence and, use of, 86
  in post-revolutionary states, 77–87
    composition of, 77–78
    new generations of leaders in, 75–76
    after spontaneous revolutions, 78
legitimacy. *See* political legitimacy

legitimacy crises, in weak states, 49–52
  nationalism and, 50–51
Lenin, Vladimir, 9, 17. *See also* Marxist-Leninism
  on armed violence, in political revolution, 163
  democratic centralism, 19–20
  on intellectualism, 17
  on internationalism, 13
  Marxist ideology for, 19–21
  on peasants' role in revolution, 35–36
    working class coalitions and, 35–36
Lichbach, Mark, 3
Long March, 30
Louis XVI (King), 58–59

Mandela, Nelson, 6, 16, 108
  on armed violence for political revolution, 27–28
Mao Zedong, 9, 16
  on armed violence as political tool, 27–30
  Cultural Revolution under, 22, 108, 162
  Great Leap Forward, 22, 108, 162
  leadership of, 17
  Marx as influence on, 41
  Marxist-Leninism for, 21
  nationalism and, 15
  organization of revolution under, 21–22
  on peasants' role in revolution, 37
  on revolution as "people's war," 29
Martí, José, 15–16, 113
Marx, Karl, 18, 41
  as revolutionary influence, 41
Marxist-Leninism, 21, 23, 126
Mexico, post-revolutionary government in, 103
middle-class leadership, of peasants, 32
military regimes
  in Egypt, collapse of, 61
  institutional composition of, 55–56
  in Tunisia, collapse of, 61
monarchies, collapse of
  in France, 57–59. *See also* French Revolution
  in Iran, 60–61
  in Russia, 59–60
Moore, Barrington, 8
Morsi, Mohamed, 129
the "motherland," 113, 126
Mubarak, Hosni, 56
Muslim Brotherhood, 7, 129

Napoleon Bonaparte. *See* Bonaparte, Napoleon
national identities, in post-revolutionary states
  political legitimacy and, 93
  reconstruction of, 92–93
national revolution, 23
nationalism
  in authoritarian states, 72
  for Ho Chi Minh, 13–15
    communism and, 14
  legitimacy crises and, 50–51
  planned revolutions and, 13–16
    Castro, Fidel, on, 15–16
    Ho Chi Minh on, 13–15
    Lenin on, 13–14
    Mao Zedong on, 15
  in post-revolutionary societies, 113–114, 124
    the "Motherland," 113
  spontaneous revolutions and, 72
  in weak states, 50–51
negotiated revolutions, 1, 4, 6. *See also* post-revolutionary societies; post-revolutionary states; *specific countries*; *specific revolutions*
  elections after, 74
  non-ideological character of, 73
  from state weakness, 74
neopatrimonial states, 53–56. *See also* monarchies
Nepstad, Sharon Erickson, 47
newspapers, in post-revolutionary states, 96

Nicaragua
FLSN in, 6
planned revolution in, 6
spontaneous revolution in, 84–85

one-party systems, in post-revolutionary states, 94–96
Orbán, Viktor, 127
Ortega, Daniel, 97–98

patron states, 45–46
peasants, in revolutions
Castro, Fidel, on, 37–40
exploitation of, 34
as foot soldiers, 31–35
Guevara on, 37–40
in Bolivia, 39–40
fundamental lessons for, 38
romanticization of peasants, 39
Ho Chi Minh on, 36–37
ideological purity of, 33
in July 26 Movement, 37–38
Lenin on, 35–36
on working class coalitions, 35–36
Mao Zedong on, 37
middle-class leadership of, 32
mobilization of, 31–32
by political activists, 32–33
through provision of goods and services, 34–35
"people's war," 29
personalist systems, 52–53
planned revolutions, 1, 5–6. *See also* post-revolutionary societies; post-revolutionary states; *specific countries*; *specific revolutions*
armed struggle and violence as part of, 27–30
in China, 27–30
in Vietnam, 28
in China. *See also* Mao Zedong
armed struggle as part of, 27–30
leadership issues in, 17
nationalism and, 15
vanguard parties in, 21–22. *See also* Chinese Communist Party
in Cuba. *See also* Castro, Fidel; Guevara, Ernesto "Che"
July 26 Movement, 24–26
leadership in, 17–18
nationalism and, 15–16
vanguard parties in, 24–27
foot soldiers in, 31–40. *See also* peasants
leadership issues in, 11–12, 16–18
in China, 17. *See also* Mao Zedong
in Cuba, 17–18. *See also* Castro, Fidel
mobilization in, 102
nationalism and, 13–16
Castro, Fidel, on, 15–16
Ho Chi Minh on, 13–15
Lenin on, 13–14
Mao Zedong on, 15
political party issues and, 11–12
in Russia. *See also* Lenin, Vladimir
April Thesis, 20
Bolshevik political parties in, 19–21
nationalism and, 13–14
vanguard parties in, 19–21
state institutions after, 87–98, 102
state weakness in, 5
vanguard parties in, 18–27
CCP, 21–22
in Cuba, 24–27
objectives of, 19
in Russia, 19–21
in Vietnam, 22–24
in Vietnam. *See also* Ho Chi Minh
armed violence in, 28
nationalism and, 13–15
vanguard parties in, 22–24
political culture, in post-revolutionary societies, 114–118, 124
anti-democratic trends in, 118
dogmatic nature of, 117
street democracy in, 115–116
political culture of opposition, 69

political legitimacy, in post-revolutionary states, 90–91
national identity through, 93
through public participation in political processes, 91
populism, in post-revolutionary states, 89–92
post-revolutionary societies, 105–114
after Arab Spring, 111
in China, 108, 116–117
collective identity in, 112
counter-revolutionaries in, 108–109
propaganda by, 123
dissent in, 118–121
elite in, treatment of, 122–123
emigre communities in, 122–123
in Iran, 108, 117
lawlessness in, 105–106
nationalism in, 113–114, 124
the "Motherland," 113
political conflict within, 107
polarization as result of, 109–112
political culture in, 114–118, 124
anti-democratic trends in, 118
dogmatic nature of, 117
street democracy in, 115–116
political opposition in, 118–121
through anti-state sentiments, 119
social polarization in, 109–112
state institutions in, 106
post-revolutionary states, outcomes in. *See also* Cuba; Egypt; Russia; Vietnam
access to resources, 84
analytical approaches to, 81–83
Castro, Fidel, and, 75
charismatic authority in, 88
Castro, Fidel, as, 88
counter-revolutionaries in, 89–90
democracies in, 127
economy in, 98–101
contextual examination of, 101
land reform, 99
redistributive agendas in, 99–100
Eisenstadt on, 81
factionalism in, 97
leadership in, 77–87
composition of, 77–78
new generations of leaders in, 75–76
after spontaneous revolutions, 78
violence and, use of, 86
national identities in
political legitimacy and, 93
reconstruction of, 92–93
political legitimacy in, 90–91
national identity through, 93
through public participation in political processes, 91
political power in, 76–77
consolidation of, 78–79
populism in, 89–92
Skocpol on, 79–81
after spontaneous revolutions
leadership in, 78
state institutions in, 102
state institutions in
elimination of political non-conformists through, 94
newspapers controlled by, 96
in one-party systems, 94–96
after planned revolutions, 102
proliferation of, 87–98
after spontaneous revolutions, 102
power centralization
in Egypt, 56
in Syria, 56
propaganda, by counter-revolutionaries, 123
Pye, Lucian, 116–117

redistributive economic agendas, in post-revolutionary states, 99–100
"refolution," Arab Spring as, 7–8
Reign of Terror, 84
Revolution of 1917 (Russia), 3–6
The Revolutionary Path (Ho Chi Minh), 23

revolutions. *See also* peasants, in revolutions; post-revolutionary states; *specific countries*
  anti-revolutionary, 6
  dictators during, 2–3
  Ho Chi Minh on, 23
  ideal types of. *See* negotiated revolutions; planned revolutions; spontaneous revolutions
  methodological approach to, 8–9
  participation levels for, 3
  as "people's war," 29
  political abuse of term, 2
  as rare occurrence, 2–3
  scope of, 1–2
  strategic objectives of, 12–13
  wars after, 174
Ritter, Daniel, 166
Rolland, Romain, 18
Rousseau, Jean-Jacques, 63
Russia. *See also* Lenin, Vladimir
  planned revolutions in, 135–138. *See also* Lenin, Vladimir
    April Thesis, 20
    Bolshevik political parties in, 19–21
    nationalism and, 13–14
    vanguard parties in, 19–21
  Reign of Terror in, 84
  Russo-Japanese War, 5, 59
  social movements in, 61–63
  spontaneous revolutions in, 3–6, 135–138
    causes of, 59–60
Russo-Japanese War, 5, 59

Said, Khaled Mohamed, 71
Sandinista National Liberation Front (FSLN), 6
sans-culottes, in French Revolution, 171
Schock, Kurt, 168
Selbin, Eric, 67–68
el-Sisi Abdel Fatah, 7, 61
Skocpol, Theda, 8, 51, 76, 165
  on post-revolutionary outcomes, 79–81
Snow, Edgar, 37
Social Contract (Rousseau), 63
social media
  Arab Spring influenced by, 65–66
  social movements influenced by, 65–66
social movements, 61–71
  access to leadership through, 65
  in France, 63
  intellectual movements as, 63
  social media as influence on, 65–66
  in Tsarist Russia, 63
    as people power, 61–62
social revolution, 23
society. *See* post-revolutionary societies
South Africa. *See also* Mandela, Nelson
  African National Congress in, 6
  negotiated revolutions in, 4, 150–153
  planned revolutions in, 6, 150–153
spontaneous revolutions, 1, 3–4. *See also* post-revolutionary societies; post-revolutionary states; weak states; *specific countries*; *specific revolutions*
  in authoritarian states, 50
    nationalism in, 72
  catalytic events as foundation of, 71
  development patterns of, 42–43
    ruling elites in, incapacitation of, 48
  ideologies of, 68–69
  organization of opposition in, 5
  from political culture of opposition, 69
  post-revolutionary states after
    leadership in, 78
    state institutions in, 102
  social movements as influence on, 61–71
    access to leadership through, 65
    in France, 63
    intellectual movements as, 63
    social media as influence on, 65–66
    in Tsarist Russia, 61–63
  state institutions after, proliferation of, 87–98
  state weakness in, 5, 43–61
  success of, 6–8

Stacker, Joshua, 56
Stalin, Josef, 79
state institutions
after planned revolutions, 87–98, 102
in post-revolutionary societies, 106
in post-revolutionary states, 87–98
elimination of political non-conformists through, 94
newspapers controlled by, 96
in one-party systems, 94–96
after planned revolutions, 102
after spontaneous revolutions, 102
state weakness. *See* weak states
street democracy, in post-revolutionary societies, 115–116
Sun Yat Sen, 21–22
Sweig, Julia, 26, 163
Syria
power centralization in, 56
spontaneous revolutions in, 7–8

Taiwan, 174
Tarrow, Sidney, 63
Trimberger, Ellen, 165
Tunisia
Arab Spring in, 69–70
military regimes in, collapse of, 61
spontaneous revolutions in, 3–4, 7–8, 131

unarmed insurrections, 168

vanguard political parties and movements, 18–27
CCP, 21–22
in Cuba, 24–27
objectives of, 19
in Russia, 19–21
in Vietnam, 22–24
Verba, Sidney, 114–115
Vietnam. *See also* Ho Chi Minh
Declaration of Independence for, 15, 161
February Revolution, 14
October Revolution, 14
planned revolutions in, 138–140. *See also* Ho Chi Minh
armed violence during, 28
nationalism and, 13–15
vanguard parties in, 22–24
violence. *See* armed violence

Walesa, Lech, 71
wars, after revolutions, 174
weak states. *See also* monarchies, collapse of
dissynchronization in, 49
domestic institutions in, 44–45, 47–48
institutional composition of, 52–56
autocratic systems, 53–56
dictatorships, 54–55
military regimes, 55–56
neopatrimonial states, 53–56
personalist systems, 52–53
international influences on, 44–47
autocracies and, 47
dependence on foreign powers, 44–45
patron states, 45–46
legitimacy crises in, 49–52
nationalism and, 50–51
planned revolutions in, 5
spontaneous revolutions in, 5, 43–61
Wells, H. G., 18
women, in Chinese revolution, 164
Wright, Robin, 129

YAM. *See* Alliance of Youth Movement
Yemen, spontaneous revolutions in, 7–8

Zapata, Emiliano, 103
Zuma, Jacob, 127